SOCIAL POLICY SIMPLIFIED

SOCIAL POLICY SIMPLIFIED

CONNECTING THEORY WITH PEOPLE'S LIVES

CLIVE SEALEY

 palgrave

First published 2015 by
PALGRAVE

Palgrave in the UK is an imprint of Macmillan Publishers Limited,
registered in England, company number 785998, of 4 Crinan Street,
London, N1 9XW.

Palgrave in the US is a division of St Martin's Press LLC,
175 Fifth Avenue, New York, NY 10010.

Palgrave is a global imprint of the above companies
and is represented throughout the world.

Palgrave® and Macmillan® are registered trademarks in the United States,
the United Kingdom, Europe and other countries.

ISBN 978–1–137–36295–7

This book is printed on paper suitable for recycling and made from fully
managed and sustained forest sources. Logging, pulping and manufacturing
processes are expected to conform to the environmental regulations of the
country of origin.

A catalogue record for this book is available from the British Library.

Library of Congress Cataloging-in-Publication Data
Sealey, Clive.
Social policy simplified : connecting theory with people's lives / by Clive Sealey.
pages cm
ISBN 978–1–137–36295–7
1. Social policy.   I. Title.
HN18.3.S43   2015
303.3—dc23   2015019823

Typeset by MPS Limited, Chennai, India.

Printed in China

This book is dedicated to my beautiful daughter Jacintha,
who I love bigger than the universe
and whose welfare makes the cause necessary

CONTENTS

LIST OF ILLUSTRATIONS

Figures

Tables

Graphs

Real Life Boxes

ACKNOWLEDGEMENTS

I need to thank so many people for assisting me in writing this book. Firstly to the University of Worcester, who gave me study leave to complete the main legwork of the book. Thanks to all the team in the old Unit of Applied Social Sciences, who took me in and looked after me when I first started. Thanks to John Leah, Peter Unwin, Mark Farmer, Olu Hyde and Maddie Burton for comments on draft chapters. Particular thanks to Miriam Isaac for believing in me from day one.

I also need to thank all my students, from whose energy and enthusiasm this book has been written. In particular, the class of 2014, without whose challenge this book would be very different. Special mention to those students who read and commented on drafts, making the book more relevant as a consequence: Nouveau Radford, Rachael Bennett, Victoria Organ, Emily-Rae Maxwell, Emily Brice, Annie Thomas.

Thanks also to all those outside work who took the time to read drafts and guide me with their comments: Daniel Robinson, Louise Overton, Julia Smith, Nana Amoah, Aktar Uddin and Bob Matthews. A special thanks to David Hirst, who first piqued my interest in Social Policy as an undergraduate at the University of Bangor nearly 20 years ago and who took the time out to comment on draft chapters.

Thanks to Simon Heng for agreeing to write Chapter 11, making a much better job of the topic than I could ever have hoped, and being patient when I made demand after demand for change.

I also need to thank my family for being so patient. Thank you Mimi and Jacintha. Finally, my one wish for this book is that those who read it are able to see that our existence is grounded in an everyday reliance on social policy, in ways that we might not have even thought of. If this occurs, we may be able to see that social policy is about more than the current emphasis on it being something for others, or even something for nothing. This will hopefully lead us to reclaim social policy's true worth as something which is relevant to all of us and which we should be prepared to fight for and to defend not only for our own welfare, but the welfare of your family, friends and the community in which we live.

1

WHAT IS SOCIAL POLICY AND WHY IS IT RELEVANT TO YOU?

The aims of this chapter are to:

1. **Outline the everyday relevance of social policy to you**

2. **Discuss what the study of social policy involves**

3. **Detail the areas and issues which will be covered in this book**

The normal way to begin a book about social policy is to try to define precisely what social policy is. However, experience has taught me that this would take a very long time simply because there are so many different things to consider. Rather, I think a much better way of conveying the essence of social policy is to consider a more personal question, which is:

Why is social policy relevant to me?

This makes the topic of social policy more interesting, because the likelihood is that at present, you are:

➤ receiving some type of social policy

AND/OR

➤ paying for social policy provision

Actually, it is very likely that you are both receiving and paying for social policy at present, even though you might not be aware of it. This should become clearer from the specific examples below.

Which social policies do I receive?

Look at the list below of some social policies, and tick the boxes for any of those which you or your family have ever received or done, in the past or the present.

Real Life Box 1.1 **Which social policies do you receive?**

Have you or a member of your family ever...

...visited a GP for health treatment? ☐

...received Child Benefit? ☐

...received Council Tax Reduction for being a student? ☐

...had Junior or Primary local authority, academy or free school schooling? ☐

...placed a child in a nursery? ☐

...been to hospital A&E? ☐

...received Free School meals? ☐

...received free or paid for NHS prescriptions? ☐

...had a vaccination from your GP? ☐

...had free NHS Dentistry? ☐

...used a SureStart centre? ☐

...been referred by your GP to a private hospital for treatment? ☐

...seen a specialist or been an outpatient at an NHS hospital? ☐

...been to a Sixth Form or College? ☐

...received Education Maintenance Allowance? ☐

...been paid the National Minimum Wage? ☐

...paid tuition fees to study at university? ☐

...had Higher Education Student Grants? ☐

...taken out a student loan? ☐

...received Jobseeker's Allowance (JSA)? ☐

...received Income Support (IS)? ☐

...received Statutory Maternity Pay? ☐

...been employed to provide care for someone who is old or has a disability? ☐

▶

◀ ...received Statutory Sick Pay?   ☐

...lived in council or housing association housing?   ☐

...had a CRB or DBS check for employment, study or voluntary work?   ☐

...received Working and/or Child Tax Credits?   ☐

...received Housing Benefit?   ☐

...brought a home under the Right to Buy scheme?   ☐

It is certain that you have ticked at least some of the boxes, especially those related to education (such as 'had Junior or Primary local authority, academy or free school schooling?') or health (such as 'visited a GP?'). You probably have also ticked some related to your level of income, such as receiving JSA, Income Support, or Statutory Sick Pay. As a student, you have possibly also ticked 'received Council Tax Reduction for being a student' and 'paid tuition fees to study at university'. If you have had children, you have probably ticked 'received Child Benefit'. For those who are mature students, 'lived in council housing or housing association housing' might be relevant. And there might be others that you have ticked as having received.

All of these are examples of social policies, some of which you have either received in the past, or you are receiving now. Actually, it is more likely that both of these circumstances apply, and both past and present receipt of social policy applies to you. It also means that unless you or a member of your family have never used the NHS, have never received any benefits such as Child Benefit, Housing Benefit, Jobseeker's Allowance or Tax Credits, have never been to university or have never been paid the National Minimum Wage (NMW), then social policy has relevance to you.

The list of social policies shown above is by no means complete, as there are many other types of social policies that exist and which you may have received, as will become evident throughout this book. However, the limited list above allows us to make five key observations about social policy.

1. Social policy affects all aspects of your life

The first observation relates to the extent that social policy affects you. When you think of social policy, you perhaps think only of specific cash benefits that people receive, such as Jobseeker's Allowance and Income Support. While these are a part of social policy, they are not the only ways that social policies impact on your life. Rather, as the list of social policies on Page 2 shows, there are a variety of different types of social policies, as shown in Table 1.1.

Table 1.1 Different types of social policies

Type of social policy	Example
Providing a basic level of income	Jobseeker's Allowance, Income Support, National Minimum Wage
Providing a basic level of health and health care	NHS, NHS Prescriptions
Providing access to education	Student Tuition Fees for Higher Education
Ensuring a minimum standard for services we use	OFSTED
Regulation of things you are allowed to do	Minimum drinking and smoking age, the minimum age of consent
Ensuring the safety of service users	CRB/DBS requirement
Regulation of things you have to do	Compulsory schooling from 5–16

Table 1.1 shows that social policy is not just about providing cash benefits such as Jobseeker's Allowance, but also about providing a range of
other benefits and services. It is highly likely that you have received or
have benefited from one of these different types of social policy shown in
Table 1.1, and this reinforces the point that social policy is highly relevant
to you.

2. Social policy is wide in scope and nature

The second observation relates to the wide extent of social policy. This
shows that social policy covers a broad range of responsibilities in many
different areas, with a primary focus on meeting the needs of individuals
and families. We can divide the social policies above into five main areas.
These are:

> **health** e.g. been to hospital A&E

> **education** e.g. had junior or primary local authority, academy or free
schooling

> **income maintenance** e.g. received Jobseeker's Allowance

> **housing** e.g. lived in council or housing association housing

> **personal social services** e.g. been employed to provide care for
someone who is old or has a disability

Moreover, the list above should not be seen as covering the entire scope of all social policies, as there are many other related circumstances that could be included, such as employment policy, public health, youth work, human rights and criminal justice which should also be seen as key to understanding social policy. There are also others, such as the environment and transport, which while not necessarily key areas of social policy, are nevertheless essential to its functioning.

3. Social policy is concerned with meeting your basic human welfare needs

If we consider the five main areas of social policy to be health, education, housing, income maintenance and personal social care, we can identify these areas as essential to human existence, as they in some way meet basic human welfare needs. The basic human welfare needs that such provisions meet relate to:

> ➤ having the means to access food and nutrition (income maintenance), shelter and accommodation (housing)

> ➤ good health (health)

> ➤ learning and knowledge (education), and

> ➤ support and care when unable to care for self (social care).

To reinforce this point, we only have to consider what our life would be like without access to the health, education, housing, income maintenance and social care that social policy provides. This significance of social policy to meeting basic human welfare needs goes a long way to explaining why the term 'The Welfare State' is often used as a way to describe social policy.

4. Social policy is provided with ongoing unconditional or conditional entitlement

The type of social policies in the list also highlights another key feature of social policy. Looking at the list again, we can see that entitlement to some provision is available on an unconditional continuous basis regardless of circumstances, such as NHS provision. Entitlement in other areas, however, is conditional and dependent on an individual's circumstance at a specific point in time, such as age (e.g. entitlement to free NHS prescription, child benefit, primary and secondary schooling), or a specific activity such as being a student (e.g. higher education grants/loans, council tax rebate), level of income (e.g. receipt of free school meals, receipt of working tax credits), employment status (e.g. JSA/IS) and health status (e.g. sick pay, statutory maternity pay).

However, a key point here is that although access to social policies can be limited by specific criteria, there is still an *ongoing entitlement* to such provision, once the relevant criteria have been met. This means that although you may not, as you read this, be receiving some of the social policies in the list (for example JSA), the principle of ongoing entitlement means that access is a continuous and prevailing possibility when the criteria are met (i.e. unemployment and actively seeking work).

5. Social policy provides entitlement throughout your lifetime

Finally, and linked to the previous point, the list shows that entitlement to social policy provision starts from an early age, through for example child benefit, continues through childhood with free prescriptions, through to adolescence with access to education, through to adult life with JSA. Some of the provision is available from birth, and continue until a person dies, such as health provision.

There is also some social provision that extends beyond your childhood and working life and into your old age. To emphasize, look at the list below and tick the boxes which you think will be relevant to:

Real Life Box 1.2 **Which social policies will you receive?**

Will you ever...

...receive a private pension?   ☐

...receive the State Pension?   ☐

...need social care due to old age?   ☐

The likelihood is that you answered yes to at least the first question related to receiving a pension, and maybe even the second, but this might be more difficult to comprehend now. If we combine this response with the list of provision on Page 2, we can see that entitlement to social policy provision occurs throughout your life, from birth to old age. We can define this as 'Cradle to Grave' social policy entitlement, which means that you have entitlement to provision from the moment you are born until you die. This is shown in Table 1.2.

Table 1.2 Social policy entitlement – from cradle to grave

Birth	Child Benefit
Early Childhood	Child Tax Credit
Infanthood	Primary School
Early Teenager	Secondary School
Late Teenager	College, National Minimum Wage
Working Adult	JSA, Income Support
Retirement	State Pension

So we can see from Table 1.2 that entitlement to social policy occurs across your lifetime, from cradle to grave. However, if we look in more detail, we see that your entitlement is actually even more extensive than that, starting from before birth and continuing after death, as shown in Table 1.3.

Table 1.3 Social policy entitlement – 'from pre-birth to beyond the grave'

Pre-Birth	Statutory Maternity Pay/Health Start Vouchers/Free Prescription to Expectant Mothers
Birth	Child Benefit
Early Childhood	Child Tax Credit
Infanthood	Primary School
Early Teenager	Secondary School
Late Teenager	College, NMW
Working Adult	JSA, Income Support
Retirement	State Pension
After-Death	Widows Benefit, Funeral Payment

Table 1.3 shows that social policy covers your total lifetime, not just from cradle to grave, but even before and after these events. It also reinforces the point that social policy is something that we have all received at some point in our lives, even though we may not be aware of it, for example the free prescription to expectant mothers for their unborn child.

Working from this small and incomplete list of social policy provision has enabled us to identify five key points about social policy itself. These are:

1. Social policy affects all aspect of your life, as there are so many different types of social policies, not just cash benefits like Jobseeker's Allowance.

2. Social policy provision provides for a broad range of needs, and has health, education, housing, income maintenance and personal social services as its main focus.

3. Meeting basic human needs is at the core of social policy provision, as such provision enables us to meet our welfare in areas that are essential to human well-being and existence.

4. Some social policy provision is available on a continuous basis, while other provision is limited by individual circumstances, but they all provide ongoing entitlement, meaning receipt is available as and when criteria are met.

5. Social policy provision covers the total possible spectrum of ages, from cradle to grave, and even before and after such events.

This highlights social policy as something which we all rely on at points in our lives, and so makes it immediately relevant to you. There is also a second aspect of social policy that highlights its immediate relevance to you, and this is the fact that you pay for social policy.

How do I pay for social policy?

As we saw above, social policy is wide in scope and nature, and entitlement is typically ongoing. This has to be paid for, and the cost implications of this are shown in Graph 1.1, which shows total government spending for the year 2014–15.

The first thing that should strike you from the graph is the amount of money that is spent. If we total up all of these figures, the total comes to £732 billion. That's £732 + 9 zeros (000,000,000), which is a lot of money by anyone's account!

Real Life Box 1.3 **The difference between millions and billions**

The difference between a million and a billion is huge, but sometimes this huge difference is not clear or easy to grasp. But we can get a picture of the difference if we compare them in relation to time, and how long it would take you to count them non-stop in seconds.

To count 1 *million* in seconds, it would take you *11.5 days.*

To count 1 *billion* in seconds, it would take you *31.6 years.*

▶

◀ Comparing them like this, we can see that the difference between a billion and a million is huge, and this needs to be borne in mind when considering the different figures used in this book.

As can be seen from Graph 1.1, the area of government spending which is highest is 'Income Maintenance' at £222 billion (which includes benefits like pensions, disability benefits, tax credits, and unemployment benefits like Jobseeker's Allowance and Income Support), followed by Health at £140 billion, then Education at £98 billion. Expenditure on housing is also evident from the graph, as 'Housing and Environment' accounts for £25 billion of spending, and 'Personal Social Services', which includes social care costs like social work and nursing home care, also accounted for £31 billion. Altogether, these five essential areas of social policy accounted for £516 billion of expenditure, which is 70% of the total government spending, a huge amount of money.

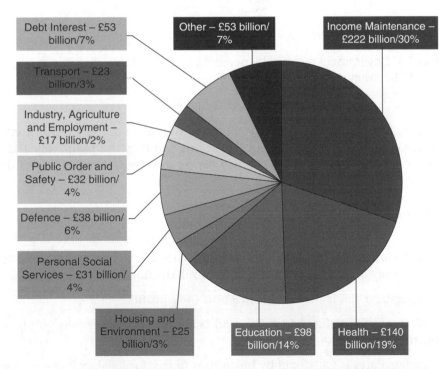

Graph 1.1 Government spending by amount and percentage, 2014–2015
Source: HM Treasury, 2014

So, we can see that the government spends a lot of money on social policy provision. This expenditure has to be paid for somehow, so how is this done? To answer this question, look at the Graph 1.2, which shows 'Government receipts' for the year 2014–15; that is how much money the government collects from its individuals and businesses (you, me and others) to pay for the social policies we receive.

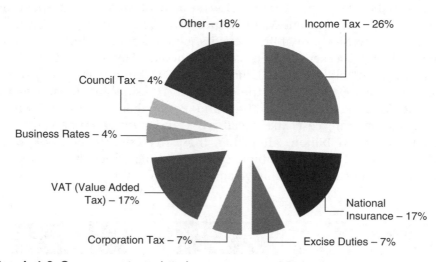

Graph 1.2 Government receipts by percentage, 2014–2015
Source: HM Treasury, 2014

The total amount collected by the government in 2014–15 was £648 billion. Graph 1.2 shows that tax in various forms is the main way that the government collects money to pay for its services. The major types of taxes as shown in the graph are:

➤ Income Tax and National Insurance are both taxes paid mainly from what you earn in employment.

➤ Excise duties are taxes paid on some items after they are made but before they are sold (such as cigarettes and alcohol).

➤ Corporation Tax is paid by business on their profits.

➤ VAT stands for Value Added Tax and is a sales tax, paid when you buy most things.

➤ Business Rates is a tax paid by businesses to pay for local services.

➤ Council Tax is paid by individuals to pay for local services.

> Other can include other taxes, such as the BBC licence fee, or charges for services, such as prescription charges.

So unless you do not work, do not buy anything at all, do not smoke, drink or drive, you will be making some contribution to government receipts, and therefore the payment of social policy highlighted above. This also highlights that like receiving social policy, paying for social policy is ongoing, in the sense that once you meet the relevant criteria, you pay for provision through taxation.

To summarize this chapter so far, in trying to answer the question of why studying social policy is important to you, I have highlighted two significant ways in which social policy is relevant to you. Firstly, you receive social policy through entitlement to a variety of social policies, and secondly you pay for social policy, primarily through taxation of various types. This means that social policy is a very relevant subject of study as it affects all individuals in their everyday life. This now enables us to consider what the study of social policy involves.

What does the study of social policy involve?

In the previous section I began to outline the essence of social policy itself, and why studying it is important to you. As a consequence, it should have started to become apparent that social policies have the potential to impact on your needs and the needs of your family, friends and the community you live in a variety of ways over time, which makes it not only fascinating to study, but also of relevance to your understanding of society in general.

I would hope that by highlighting this evident immediate relevancy, I have also set off a deeper interest about the nature of social policy itself. If I have, then this book aims to kindle that interest by providing introductory discussions of some of the key questions you are likely to have. These key questions form the basis of the chapters that follow.

Chapter 2 – Which benefits do you receive from social policy, and who receives the most benefits?

In Chapter 2, we explore the highly relevant questions of which social policy benefits you receive, and who receives the most benefits from social policy. The chapter analyses the *different types of benefits* that different groups receive, to provide a true picture of who gets the most benefits. It will show that the answer is not as straightforward as we are often led to believe, if we consider the total amount of benefits that social policy provides. By the end of this chapter, you will have a detailed awareness of the range of social policy benefits that exist and that you receive, and which groups receive the most benefits from social policy.

Chapter 3 – How and why has social policy developed cradle to grave entitlement to benefits for you?

In Chapter 3, we will explore why cradle to grave social policy exists as it does today. This will be done through a simplified account of the *historical development of social policy* from the mid-19th century, particularly focussing on why the need for social policy became evident, as a key way to understand the present nature of social policy. By the end of this chapter, you should have an understanding of key lessons which the past of social policy can teach the present, and be able to articulate why social policy exists as it does today.

Chapter 4 – Do you pay too much tax for the social policy benefits you receive?

In Chapter 4, we will look in more detail at the centrality of *taxation* in terms of paying for social policy. The focus of the chapter is on showing how much taxation you pay and what taxation is used for, and this chapter provides a simplified account of the amounts and process of paying taxes and the use of taxation in social policy. This will then enable important principles related to taxation funded social policy to be discussed. By the end of this chapter you should have an understanding of what taxation pays for, the amount of taxation that you pay and how much this contributes to the cost of the social policy provision that you use, how much taxation funded social policy costs in comparison to you paying to meet your own welfare needs, and important principles that underpin taxation funded social policy provision.

Chapter 5 – Can social policy solve the problem of poverty?

In Chapter 5, we will focus on the extent of *poverty* in the UK, and the main issues that social policy faces when dealing with poverty in the UK. The chapter analyses the current official definition of poverty, and what it means in terms of actual numbers of people in poverty. In particular, it will analyse whether current social policy benefit levels contribute to the number of people in poverty. By the end of this chapter, you will have an understanding of the extent of poverty in the UK, the risk that certain groups have of falling into poverty, and the main causes of poverty.

Chapter 6 – Should entitlement to social policy benefits be just for some people or for everyone?

In Chapter 6, we analyse the significance differences between *universal* and *selective* entitlement to social policy. The chapter explores in detail the specific advantages and disadvantages of each type of entitlement. Housing will be the particular focus of this chapter, as it is the social policy area that has undergone a significant shift from universalism to selectivism over the last 30 years. This chapter will also highlight a general and important contemporary shift in policy away from universalism towards selectivism for all groups (children, young people, families and older people), and its implications for social policy. By the end of this chapter, you will have an understanding of differences between universal and selective entitlement to social policy, and how social policy has drifted towards greater selectivism.

Chapter 7 – Which welfare needs should social policy be responsible for meeting?

In Chapter 7, we define and analyse the two main types of *welfare needs* that exist. The Chapter analyses the implications of adopting either of these different types of needs in social policies. There is also a focus on the differing ways that the different social policy areas meet needs, and how current social policy is focussed on meeting welfare needs. The chapter uses health needs as a way to exemplify the consequence of social policy meeting needs in a narrow rather than in a broad way. By the end of this chapter, you should have an understanding of different types of welfare needs, how welfare needs differ from welfare wants, and what the differing implications are of social policy meeting need in a narrow or broad way.

Chapter 8 – Who should provide social policies?

In Chapter 8, we consider whether the state, private companies, voluntary/ community organizations or individuals are the best *provider of social policies*. The chapter uses education policy to discuss the limitations of each, and whether these limitations can be overcome by providing social policies in combination in a mixed economy of welfare. By the end of this chapter, you will be able to discuss the advantages and limitations of different types of social policy providers, and be able to articulate the significance of the mixed economy of welfare to how current social policies are provided.

Chapter 9 – What does the future hold for social policy?

In Chapter 9, we outline some of the key demographic, social, economic and financial changes occurring in UK society, and their actual and potential impact on social policy. The chapter will discuss how these changes are not only impacting on social policy now, but also have the potential to have important effects on *social policy in the future*, both positive and negative. By the end of this chapter, you will have an understanding of key social and economic changes occurring in society, and the impact that these changes could have on social policy in the future. You will also be able to identify some key social policies that have been put in place to deal with the changes in these areas, and what these policies indicate about the future direction of social policy.

Chapter 10 – How can your ideological beliefs make and change social policy?

In Chapter 10, we introduce the concept of *ideology* to discuss how and why individuals and governments differ in their beliefs and approaches to social policy. In particular, there will be a focus on locating and understanding your own key social policy ideological beliefs as a way to understanding the importance of ideology to the development of social policies. By the end of this chapter, you should understand the notion of ideology and the importance of ideology to the development of social policies. You should also be able to articulate and explain how your own ideological beliefs can make and change social policy.

Chapter 11 – Is relying on social policy benefits over a long time an easy life?

Chapter 11 aims to bring together the main themes and issues explored in the previous chapters to provide *a real life experience* of what it is like to be reliant on social policy. It outlines the experiences of a long-term recipient of social policy provision to highlight both the good and bad of such provision. In particular, there will be a focus on contrasting some of the harsh realities of social welfare provision with some of its beneficial outcomes, in terms of considering a prevalent view that living on social policy provision is an easy option. By the end of this chapter, you will understand in detail the lived reality of living on social policy provision, and be able to articulate whether having to rely on social policy benefits means having an easy life and is an easy option.

Chapter 12 – Why is studying social policy relevant to you?

The focus of this concluding chapter is a summary of why studying social policy is both exciting and important to a better understanding of you as an individual and the society you live in. Specifically, this chapter recaps the relevance of social policy from the previous chapters by outlining ten reasons why studying social policy matters to you. By the end of this chapter you will be able to answer the questions of what is social policy, and how it impacts specifically on the needs of you, your family, your friends and the community you live in.

Summary

By the end of this book, you should have become aware of both the real life and academic relevance that studying social policy gives you. In terms of its real life significance, studying social policy provides a deeper and more significant understanding of social policies that directly affect you everyday, meaning that social policy has an ongoing relevance to you as an individual and to society in general. And at the academic level, studying social policy is concerned with the critical exploration of the theories and concepts which underpin such policies. This focuses on the analysis of the effectiveness of policies, and the theories and concepts which underpin such policies. This aspect is concerned with the making of policies which improve individuals and society's well-being. Together, this double relevance makes studying social policy both exciting and important to a better understanding of you as an individual and society you live in.

Key Point

Social policy is relevant to you because you receive and pay for a range of cradle to grave social policies which have the potential to impact on your welfare and the welfare of your family, friends and the community you live in a variety of ways.

2

WHICH BENEFITS DO YOU RECEIVE FROM SOCIAL POLICY, AND WHO RECEIVES THE MOST BENEFITS?

The aims of this chapter are to:

1. Outline the different types of benefits that social policy provides

2. Consider which benefits you receive from social policy

3. Analyse which groups receive the most benefits from social policy

In Chapter 1, we saw that total government spending for the year 2014–2015 was £732 billion. More significantly, government expenditure on the five social policy areas of income maintenance, health, education, housing and personal social services accounted for £516 billion of government expenditure, which is 70% of the total, a huge amount of money. This huge amount of expenditure makes the question of who receives the most benefits from social policy a relevant one.

This chapter explores how this money is spent and who it is spent on. It will show that the answer is not as straightforward as we are often led to believe, if we consider the total amount of benefits that social policy is spent on, and not just certain high profile benefits such as Jobseeker's Allowance and Income Support. It analyses the different types of benefits that different groups receive and which groups receive the most benefit, in order to provide a true picture of who gets the most benefits from social policy.

By the end of this chapter, you will have a detailed awareness of which groups receive the most benefits from social policy, and the many different types of benefits that exist within social policy.

Real Life Box 2.1 **Which social policy benefits are you receiving?**

Make a list of all the social policy benefits that you are receiving or have received in the past.

Which is the most expensive social policy benefit?

As Graph 1.1 in Chapter 1 shows, the area of social policy with the highest expenditure is 'Income Maintenance'. This cost £222 billion in 2014–2015, which is 30% of all government expenditure. This mainly involves benefits such as Jobseeker's Allowance, Income Support and the State Pension. Income maintenance benefits are paid mainly to ensure that individuals have an adequate income. Graph 2.1 below shows how much is spent on each income maintenance benefit, as a percentage of the total amount spent on income maintenance benefits.

Question

Before looking at Graph 2.1, rank the income maintenance benefits listed below from highest to lowest expenditure.

➢ Housing Benefit

➢ Tax Credits

➢ Jobseeker's Allowance

➢ State Pension

➢ Income Support

➢ Child Benefit

➢ Disability Living Allowance

Before discussing Graph 2.1, here is an explanation of some of the benefits it shows which you may not be aware of:

➢ *Disability Living Allowance* is a benefit paid to those under 65 years with a mental or physical disability which means that they have personal care and/or mobility needs, such as needing personal carers or transport. It is being phased out between 2013 and 2016 for adults only, and is being replaced by *Personal Independence Payment*.

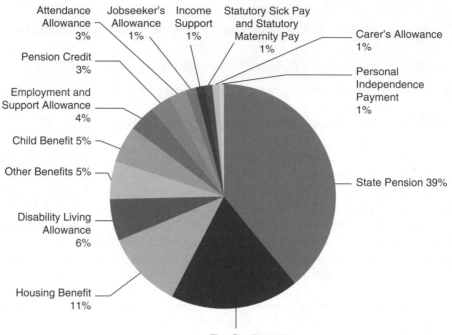

Graph 2.1 Income maintenance benefits expenditure by percentage, 2014–15 forecast
Source: DWP, 2014; DWP, 2014a

> *Other Benefits* includes benefits such as Industrial Injuries Benefit, Free TV Licence for the Over 65s, Maternity Allowance, Bereavement Benefit and Social Fund expenditure.
> *Employment and Support Allowance* is a benefit paid to those who can't work because of sickness or disability, and are not receiving Statutory Sick Pay.
> *Pension Credit* is a benefit paid to pensioners whose income is below a certain amount to bring it up to this amount.
> *Attendance Allowance* is a benefit paid to those aged 65 or over who are physically or mentally disabled to help with personal care costs, such as help or supervision throughout the day or night.
> *Statutory Maternity Pay* is a benefit paid to those who take time off to have and care for a new baby.
> *Carer's Allowance* is a benefit for those aged 16 or over who spend at least 35 hours a week caring for someone with substantial caring needs.
> *Personal Independence Payment* is the replacement for *Disability Living Allowance*. It is a benefit paid to those aged 16–64 to help with some of the extra costs caused by long-term ill health or a disability.

We can immediately see from Graph 2.1 that the most expensive income maintenance benefit is the State Pension. It accounts for nearly 40% of all income maintenance expenditure. The next most expensive income maintenance benefit is Tax Credits, which accounts for nearly 20% of all income maintenance expenditure. The third most expensive income maintenance benefit is Housing Benefit, which accounts for 11% of all income maintenance expenditure.

Together, these three benefits dominate expenditure on income maintenance, and take up nearly 70% of all income maintenance expenditure, which is a huge amount. Expenditure on other benefits is small in comparison to this. For example, expenditure on Jobseeker's Allowance only accounts for 1% of all income maintenance expenditure.

Questions

1. Does the low amount of expenditure on Jobseeker's Allowance surprise you?

2. If expenditure on Jobseeker's Allowance is so low, why do you think there is so much focus on cutting it from politicians and the media?

A key point to note is that the wide variety of income maintenance benefits shown above means that approximately 30 million people in the UK – about half the total population – are receiving at least one income maintenance benefit at any given time (Browne and Hood, 2012). This means that as you read this, there are more families receiving at least one of the income maintenance benefits from social policy shown above than families not receiving anything from social policy (The Observer, 2013).

Which groups get the most benefits?

We can also analyse which groups get the most benefits as a way to answer the question of who get the most benefits.

For the purposes of simplicity we can divide people who receive benefits into two groups, depending on their age or status.

Age

In terms of age, we can distinguish between benefits that are paid to older people (above the retirement age) and benefits that are paid to younger people (below the retirement age).

As Graph 2.1 shows, the State Pension has the largest income mainte‐ nance expenditure, but it is not the only benefit which is aimed at older people. Pension Credit, Attendance Allowance and Free TV Licence for the Over 65s are all benefits which are specifically aimed at older people. In addition, older people can also receive benefits such as Housing Benefit and Carer's Allowance.

The other benefits in Graph 2.1 are for younger people, such as children (Child Benefit) and working people (Jobseeker's Allowance). Graph 2.2 shows the percentage of benefits paid to older people and the percentage of benefits paid to younger people.

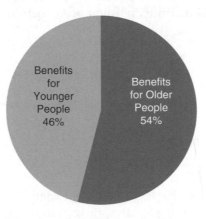

Graph 2.2 Income maintenance benefits received by age
Source: McInnes and Rutherford, 2013

As Graph 2.2 shows, older people receive the majority of benefits. The main reason for this is because of the large amount spent on the State Pension and the other benefits that they get.

Status

In terms of status, we can distinguish between benefits paid to those who are unemployed; those who are sick or disabled; those who are retired; and those on a low income but not unemployed.

➤ The main unemployment benefit is Jobseeker's Allowance.

➤ The main sickness and disability benefits are Employment and Support Allowance, Statutory Sick Pay, Disability Allowance/Personal Indepen‐ dence Payment and Attendance Allowance.

➤ The main retirement benefits are the State Pension and Pension Credit.

➢ The main two benefits for those on a low income but not unemployed are Working Tax Credits for those who are working but on low pay, and Income Support for those who are not working but not registered as unemployed, such as single mothers

There are some benefits which are paid to more than one of these groups, such as Housing Benefit, Child Benefit, Child Tax Credits and Statutory Sick Pay and Statutory Maternity Pay. Graph 2.3 shows the percentage of benefits paid to each of these groups.

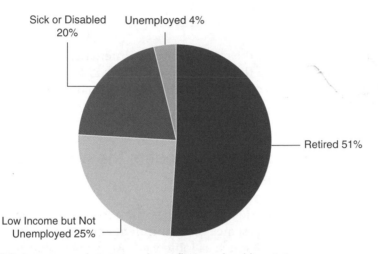

Graph 2.3 Income maintenance benefits received by status
Source: HM Treasury, 2014a: Table 5.2; DWP, 2014a: Table 3a

Graph 2.3 reaffirms what was shown in Graph 2.2 that older people receive the greatest proportion of income maintenance benefits, over half of all benefits spent. In contrast, benefits for those who are unemployed account for a tiny percentage of the total income maintenance benefits spent, the lowest percentage of benefits of all groups.

Why do older people get more income maintenance benefits than other groups?

So far we have seen that older people get the most income maintenance benefits out of all groups. There are two main reasons for this:

i) Older people have a greater need for income maintenance than other groups. This is because they may be unable to work like other groups, and so need to be provided with an income to enable them to live.

This is an example of *redistribution*, where a resource is taken from one group and given to another group to enable them to live adequately. Redistribution is an essential function of social policy.

ii) The majority of older people have paid taxes for income maintenance throughout their working life, and so have built up entitlement to the benefits that they receive when they retire. For example, they would have paid Income Tax from working, and also National Insurance, and this entitles them to draw on the entitlement that they have built up. This is an example of *social insurance*, where individuals pay into the income maintenance fund to enable them to be entitled to benefits at times of need. This is also an essential function of social policy.

So older people receiving the most income maintenance benefits compared to other groups is due to the functions of *redistribution* and *social insurance* within social policy. Both of these functions are explained in more detail in Chapter 4.

Are income maintenance benefits the only type of social policy benefits?

So far we have only considered who gets the most income maintenance benefits, as this is the largest area of government and social policy expenditure. This includes benefits such as Jobseeker's Allowance, Housing Benefit, Child Benefit, Tax Credits and the State Pension. For most people, when they consider the question of who receives the most benefits from social policy, these are the only benefits that they are referring to. This is because these are the most obvious and most talked about social policy benefits.

However, as you should have become aware by now, income maintenance is only one area of social policy, and there are four other main areas of social policy, which are health, education, housing and personal social services. This means that if we only considered income maintenance expenditure benefits, we would be ignoring the majority of social policy expenditure, as while in 2014–2015 income maintenance expenditure was £222 billion, expenditure on health, education, housing and personal social services combined was more than this at £294 billion, as shown in Graph 1.1. This means that to answer the question as fully as possible, we also have to consider how the money is spent in these four other social policy areas. And to do this we need to reconsider what we mean by 'benefits' when talking about social policy.

Income maintenance benefits like Jobseeker's Allowance and the State Pension effectively involve giving cash to individuals. We can define these types of benefits as *cash benefits*, because they effectively involve cash being given by the state to individuals.

However, not all social policy is given as cash. Some social policy is provided as a service. This can be either as a service which is at a subsidized price that is lower than the actual price, or as a service that is totally free at the time of use. A good example of social policy which is provided at a subsidized price that is lower than the actual price is higher education, as the tuition fees that students pay to universities covers part but not the whole cost of their degree course. A good example of social policy which is provided as a service that is free at the time of use is the NHS and associated health services. These types of social policies are known as *in-kind benefits*, because they provide individuals with a benefit which is not money but a service or a good.

Question

Look at the following list of social policy benefits. Which are cash benefits and which are in-kind benefits?

- Free School Meals
- Free 15 Hours Childcare
- Council Housing
- Council Tax Benefit
- Income Support
- Over 75s Television Licence
- Free Prescriptions
- Right To Buy
- Student Maintenance Loan
- Student Maintenance Grants
- Sure Start Centres
- Statutory Sick Pay

So we can divide the social policy that we receive into two types of benefits, *cash benefits* and *in-kind benefits*. This distinction helps us to answer more fully the question of who receives the most benefits from social policy, as it enables us to analyse all the different types of social policy benefits that we receive, not just the income maintenance cash benefits we looked at above.

How does including in-kind benefits affect who gets the most benefits?

Table 2.1 provides a brief list of some of the main examples of in-kind benefits for the five main social policy areas.

There are a number of observations that can be made from Table 2.1. The first is that the variety of in-kind benefits is vast and varied. Some social policy areas provide in-kind benefits that are almost exclusively free

Table 2.1 Social policy in-kind benefits

	Examples of in-kind benefits	
	Free	**Subsidized**
Income maintenance	➢ National Minimum Wage regulation ➢ Health and Safety regulation ➢ Pension Regulator ➢ Bus Passes to over 65s	➢ Child Maintenance Service (previously Child Support Agency)
Education	➢ 15 hours free childcare ➢ Sure Start centres ➢ Primary and secondary schooling ➢ Free school meals ➢ 16–18 education ➢ OFSTED	➢ Higher Education Student Tuition Fees ➢ Higher Education Student Maintenance Loans
Housing	➢ Right to Buy Discounts ➢ Tenancy Deposit Protection regulation ➢ Council Tax Benefit ➢ Housing Ombudsman	➢ Council Housing ➢ Housing Association housing ➢ Help to Buy Loans
Health	➢ Most NHS GP services ➢ NHS A & E services ➢ Some NHS outpatient services, e.g. MRI scans, blood tests ➢ NHS Optical and Dental services for some people ➢ NHS Prescriptions for some people	➢ NHS Prescriptions for some people
Personal Social Services	➢ Social services, e.g. children, mental health, disability and older people social work ➢ Care homes for some older people ➢ Care Quality Commission inspections ➢ Fostering and Adoption services	➢ Care homes for some older people

at the time of use, such as health. Others provide in-kind benefits that are more mixed between free and subsidized, such as housing.

There are also different types of free in-kind benefits. There are free in-kind benefits which involve the transfer of cash but which the individual does not see happening, such as Council Tax Benefit and 15 hours free childcare. There are free in-kind benefits which individuals use directly as a service, such as the NHS, schooling, social services and also Sure Start centres. There are free in-kind benefits which are concerned with monitoring of a service, to ensure that individuals receive a certain quality of service, such as OFSTED. And there are also free in-kind benefits which regulate certain types of services, to ensure that individuals' rights and entitlements are met, such as in relation to the National Minimum Wage, Health and Safety, the Pension Regulator and the Tenant Deposit Protection regulation.

Real Life Box 2.2 **Tenancy Deposit Protection regulation**

Since 2007, the Tenancy Deposit Protection regulation has required landlords and letting agents to protect the deposits that their tenants pay. This is for most tenants who have an assured tenancy, which is most tenants overall, the most obvious exceptions being students living in university run halls of residence, those sharing a home with their landlord and those who rent from their council. So if you live in private rented accommodation including privately run halls of residence, the regulation applies to you.

The regulation means that your landlord cannot hold your deposit, but has to place it with an independent organization. Your landlord also cannot hold onto to your deposit unfairly when you leave, and you get the appropriate amount of deposit back, when you are entitled to it, unless there is a dispute between you and your landlord. So at the end of the tenancy, if there are no disputes over the amount of deposit to be refunded, you will receive the deposit back. If there is a dispute, the disputed amount will be held until the dispute is settled

At the start of your tenancy, your landlord has 30 days to give you details about how your deposit is being protected, including who is holding your deposit and how to apply for the release of the deposit. Failure to do this means you can take legal action against your landlord to get your deposit back.

The Tenancy Deposit Protection regulation is the responsibility of the Department for Communities and Local Government. This means that it provides a licence for companies that hold tenants' deposits, and monitors the scheme for changes that need to be made.

Questions

1. Looking at Table 2.1 above, which of the in-kind benefits have you received in the past, and which do you receive now?

2. Can you think of any other in-kind benefits that you might be receiving?

By outlining the vast range of in-kind benefits that social policy provides, we get a more complete picture of the benefits that individuals receive. This is because it highlights that we all receive benefits from social policy, to greater or lesser extents, even where these benefits are not in the form of cash, and where we might least expect it. So for example, someone at work may be receiving in-kind benefits in the form Health and Safety regulation, National Minimum Work regulation and NHS care. Someone living in private rented accommodation may be benefiting from Council Tax Benefit, the Tenants Deposit Protection regulation, and the NHS.

This shows that if we include in-kind benefits, the range of benefits that individuals receive also increases dramatically, to include things that you may not have considered as benefits but which as part of social policy are essentially benefits, such as healthcare and education. This highlights the importance of in-kind benefits to individuals, as they affect more people than cash benefits. This means that the range of people who receive benefits increases dramatically, to include almost anyone, and shows that the notion of the cradle to grave welfare state applies to almost everyone, to some degree.

Who receives the most total benefits?

The question of who receives the most total benefits is not an easy question to answer as there are so many different types of in-kind benefits. To consider this question, we have to consider both the amount of cash and in-kind benefits that individuals receive.

We saw in Graph 2.3 that retired people receive the most income maintenance cash benefits. Those on a low income but not unemployed are the group to receive the next highest amount of income maintenance cash benefits.

There are some in-kind benefits that are targeted at specific groups. For example, council housing is targeted mainly at vulnerable and low income groups. Similarly, personal social services in-kind benefits are also mainly available to vulnerable and low income groups, such as child protection services for children and families, and social care for older people.

However, not all in-kind benefits are targeted at vulnerable and low income groups. Actually, a lot of in-kind benefits are for all individuals, not just specific individuals or groups. Health through the NHS is a good example of in-kind benefits that are for everyone and not just some groups.

Education is an example of an in-kind benefit that is targeted at a specific group, mainly children and young adults, but not specifically at vulnerable and low income children and young people. This means that all children and young people can access education freely from the ages of 5 to 18. After this age, higher education is subsidized through Higher Education Student Tuition Fees and Higher Education Student Maintenance Loans. This involves significant amounts of money. For example, while the amount of expenditure on Jobseeker's Allowance and Income Support is approximately £6 billion, expenditure on Student Maintenance Loans to students studying at university in England is almost double this amount, at £11.3 billion (HM Treasury, 2014a: Table 1.1).

Real Life Box 2.3 **Student benefits**

As a university student you may be receiving a variety of cash and in-kind benefits from social policy. The main cash benefit that you may be receiving is a Higher Education Maintenance Grant of up to £3,387 a year. Those with dependents such as children may also be receiving a Childcare Grant to pay for childcare while studying, and the Parent's Learning Allowance to enable them to pay for books, study materials and travel.

You may also be receiving a number of in-kind benefits, most notably Higher Education Maintenance Loan and Student Tuition Fee Loan. Other in-kind benefits might include Council Tax Benefit, National Minimum Wage regulation, Health and Safety regulation, the Tenant Deposit Protection regulation, Higher Education Student Tuition Fees, and of course the NHS.

Even students living and studying in Scotland who do not pay tuition fees do receive grants and are entitled to receive a Higher Education Maintenance Loan.

Additionally, some in-kind benefits are also targeted at those who are on a mid to high income. Good examples of this are the *Right to Buy* discount for those wishing to buy their council house, and the *Help to Buy* loan given to first time house buyers.

Real Life Box 2.4 **Right to Buy and Help to Buy in-kind benefits**

Right to Buy and Help to Buy are in-kind benefits which are designed to enable individuals to buy a house.

Right to Buy gives councils tenants a discount on the cost of buying the house if they have lived in it for more than five years. The discount starts at 35% of the value of the house, and goes up to 70% of the value of the house. This means that the price that an individual pays for the house is between 35% and 70% the real price of the house. This is equivalent to a discount of up to £77,000 per house outside London, and £102,000 in London. This is equivalent to someone over 25 years old receiving Jobseeker's Allowance for between 20 and 27 years.

Help to Buy is a loan scheme where the government provides a loan for up to 20% of the cost of a house. This means that the amount of deposit that you need is lower than it would be without the discount. The maximum amount of Help to Buy loan that the government provides is £120,000, which is equivalent to someone over 25 years old receiving Jobseeker's Allowance for 31 years.

The average amount paid for Right to Buy housing in 2014 was £74,000 (DCLOG, 2014), which was approximately three times average income of £25,547 (ONS, 2013a). Similarly, the average amount paid for a house bought with Help to Buy in 2014 was £208,000 (DCLOG, 2014a), which was over eight times the average income of £25,547 (ONS, 2013a).

This shows that Right to Buy and Help to Buy are in-kind benefits that those on a low income would not be able to afford, but are only available to those on a middle to higher income.

It also highlights again that all groups benefit from social policy benefits, not just low income groups. Actually, the majority of households (52%) receive more in benefits (including in-kind benefits such as education) than they pay in all taxes. This means that most people receive more in benefits than they pay in taxes (ONS, 2014). And if we consider the implications of *inverse care law* below, there is a good chance that it is higher to middle income groups that receive the most benefit, rather than lower income groups as most people tend to think.

The inverse care law describes a contradictory relationship between the need for health care and its actual use. This means that on the one hand those who most need health care are least likely to receive it and/or use it least effectively. On the other hand, those with least need of health care tend to use health services more and/or use them more effectively (Tudor Hart, 1971).

As an example, we can consider two people with similar health needs, but with a difference that one is poor and lives in a poor area, and one is rich and lives in a rich area. The person who is poor may not be able to identify adequately what their health needs are, and even if they do, the health services that they access might be poor. In contrast, the person who is rich may be able to access a range of resources to identify what their health needs are, and the health services they have access to may be of a very good quality. Additionally, the person who is rich will have a longer life expectancy than the person who is poor, and so use health services for a longer period. The consequence of this is while the health needs of the two individuals may be the same, the person who is poor may only be able to access health care that is of lower quality than the person who is rich, and for a shorter period of time. This means that they in effect are receiving less health benefits as they use less health resources.

Real Life Box 2.5 **The inverse care law in education**

Health is not the only social policy area that the inverse care law applies to. It applies in all other social policy areas. For example, in education, richer families are able to move to richer areas with the better schools, and are also three times more likely to go to university than poorer students (Independent Commission on Fees, 2014), meaning that it is richer people who use and gain the most from education benefits.

How have recent social policy changes affected who gets the most benefits?

The last 30 years or so has seen some distinct changes to the amount of social policy benefits that certain groups receive. This has meant that some groups have seen their total social policy benefits reduce, while others have seen their total social policy benefits increase.

One group that has seen their total social policy benefits increase has been pensioners. As shown in Graphs 2.1–2.3, it is older people who receive the most benefits from social policy, and the main pensioner benefit, the State Pension, is the cash benefit that has the highest expenditure of all income maintenance benefits. Additionally, recent new benefits for older people include Pension Credit, Winter Fuel Allowance, and Free Bus passes.

In contrast, unemployed people are one group who have seen a constant reduction in the amount of benefits that they receive. This means that Jobseeker's Allowance is now worth much less than it was 30 years ago. Graph 2.4 shows how much the amount spent on Jobseeker's Allowance is as a percentage of total social policy expenditure.

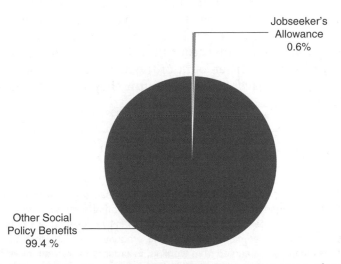

Jobseeker's
Allowance
0.6%

Other Social
Policy Benefits
99.4 %

Graph 2.4 Jobseeker's Allowance expenditure as a percentage of total social policy expenditure

As Graph 2.4 shows, the amount spent on Jobseeker's Allowance represents less than 1% of total expenditure on social policy. This is perhaps surprising when you consider the amount of debate and controversy that surrounds Jobseeker's Allowance in comparison to other benefits.

Real Life Box 2.6 **Changes to young peoples' benefits**

Young people are one group who over the last 30 years have seen reductions in the amount of benefits that they receive, for both cash benefits and in-kind benefits.

For example, there are limits on cash benefits that young people can claim such as Jobseeker's Allowance. While people over 25 are entitled to £72.40 per week, those under 25 are entitled to less, £57.35 per week. Housing Benefit entitlement is also restricted, meaning that single, under-35 people can only get Housing Benefit for bedsit accommodation or a single room in shared accommodation.

There have also been reductions of in-kind benefits. For example, entitlement to higher education in most of the UK has changed from being free to young people, to young people having to pay. This means that young people in higher education now very likely leave higher education with a debt whereas 30 years ago this was not the case. Young people in higher education also had entitlement to Housing Benefit and Jobseeker's Allowance; this is no longer the case and young people are expected to meet these needs themselves.

The election of the 2010 Coalition government has seen these trends in benefits for older people and unemployed people continue. For example, while expenditure on the State Pension has increased every year since 2010, in contrast expenditure on Jobseeker's Allowance has been targeted for continual reductions. This means that while pensioners have seen relatively large increases in the amount of the State Pension that they receive, unemployed people have seen the amount they receive from Jobseeker's Allowance frozen or increased very little.

Real Life Box 2.7 **The benefit cap**

The 2010 Coalition government introduced a benefit cap on the amount of benefits that most people aged 16–64 can claim. This means that the total amount of all the benefits that can be received by any individual or family is capped at £26,000 a year. The main rationale for the cap is to make the amount of benefits that an individual receives less than can be earned from working, in order to make work more attractive than living on benefits. This means that the amount of the benefit cap is less than the average national wage.

There are different capped amounts depending on your circumstances. The amounts are:

➤ £500 a week for couples (with or without children living with them);

➤ £500 a week for single parents whose children live with them;

➢ £350 a week for single adults who don't have children, or whose children don't live with them.

The cap includes benefits such as Jobseeker's Allowance, Housing Benefit, Income Support, Employment and Support Allowance, Child Benefit and Tax Credits, Carer's Allowance and Maternity Benefits.

The cap does not apply to those receiving Working Tax Credits, and some disability benefits.

Question

Look again at the list you made earlier of the social policy benefits that you are receiving or have received in the past. Is there anything from the list that is missing?

Summary

The question of who receives the most benefits from social policy is a relevant one when we consider how much is spent on social policy. This chapter has shown that the answer is not as straightforward as we are often led to believe, if we consider the total amount of benefits that social policy is spent on, and not just certain high profile benefits.

For example, income maintenance cash benefits such as Jobseeker's Allowance and Income Support are what most people think of when they talk about benefits, and they do represent a significant amount of money spent on social policy. However, the cash benefit with the largest expenditure by a long way is the State Pension, and older people in general receive the most income maintenance cash benefits in comparison to other groups. There are specific reasons for this linked to the social policy functions of redistribution and social insurance. In comparison, expenditure on Jobseeker's Allowance and Income Support is very small.

However, to get a truer picture of who gets the most benefits we also need to consider the expenditure on other social policy areas, such as health, housing, education and personal social services, as together these account for more expenditure than income maintenance benefits. When we consider in-kind benefits that are provided in these social policy areas, we see that the range of benefits that individuals receive increases dramatically, to include things that you may not have considered as benefits, but which as a part of social policy is essentially a benefit, such as healthcare and education. Moreover, it shows that benefits are not received by lower income groups only, but by all groups, and there are some in-kind benefits which middle and higher income groups receive the most from, especially if we consider the inverse care law.

This highlights the importance of considering all cash and in-kind benefits that individuals receive, as this shows that the range of people who receive benefits includes almost everyone, meaning that the notion of the cradle to grave welfare state applies to almost everyone, to some degree. It is also important in the context of the 2010 Coalition government's continual reduction in cash benefits for some groups such as the unemployed, which as this chapter has shown is based on the dubious premise that it is such groups which receive the most benefits.

Key Point

Social policy benefits are not just for the poor, and we all receive more social policy benefits that we think we do, especially when we also take into account the *in-kind benefits* that we receive.

3

HOW AND WHY HAS SOCIAL POLICY DEVELOPED CRADLE TO GRAVE ENTITLEMENT TO BENEFITS FOR YOU?

The aims of this chapter are to:

1. **Provide a simplified historical account of why your entitlement to 'cradle to grave' social policy exists at all**

2. **Outline important historical lessons from social policy past for social policy today**

So far this book has outlined some of the key features relevant to the study of social policy. It has highlighted social policy as particularly having a practical relevance to you from cradle to grave, which makes studying social policy both exciting to you as an individual and the society in which you, your family, your friends and your community members live in. It has also highlighted that social policy benefits are not just for the poor, as a consequence of the fact that you very likely receive more social policy benefits than you might have thought.

This chapter will explore why such extensive cradle to grave social policy exists as it does today. It provides a simplified account of the historical development of social policy from the mid-19th century, particularly focussing on why the need for social policy became evident, as a key way to understand the present nature of the benefits you receive. What should become evident from this chapter is that the past of social policy is very much relevant to its present. This is evident from the quote below:

> ...the past remains a central feature of the way in which we understand and make sense of the present, not least in welfare and social policy. Present day ideological and political debates about rights and responsibilities,

organisational and administrative arrangements and demarcations between service sectors, as well as the language and terminology of welfare, all resonate with echoes of the past ... Those who are ignorant of history, as Santayana observed, are doomed to repeat it (Gladstone, 2003: 26).

A good starting point for a discussion of why cradle to grave social policy exists as it does today is to consider why the need for social policy became evident in the first place.

Why did the need for social policy become evident?

The most relevant starting point for a discussion of why the need for social policy became evident is the year 1834, as it was in this year that a significant development in social policy occurred. This was the enactment of the 1834 Poor Law Amendment Act, which is often called the 1834 New Poor Law. As suggested in the title, the 1834 Act was actually an amendment of existing legislation, in fact of several pieces of legislation, often termed the Elizabethan Poor Laws or the Old Poor Laws. The focus of the Old Poor Laws was exclusively on dealing with the problems of poverty and unemployment that existed then, as exemplified by the three main forms of welfare benefits it provided:

1. For those in work, there was the Speenhamland wage system which provided an income subsidy for wages that paid *below subsistence level*, that is wages below what was needed to live on.

2. For those seen as the 'impotent poor', meaning that they were unable to work, such as the sick, disabled or old, there was what was termed *'outdoor relief'*, which was very limited benefits in the form of food or clothes.

3. For those seen as the 'able-bodied poor', meaning those seen as able to work but not willing to do so, there was what was termed *'indoor relief'*. This was where individuals were expected to work in very harsh conditions for any form of benefits in either a House of Correction, House of Industry or Prison.

Adapted from Fraser (2009)

Question

If the House of Correction, House of Industry, or Prison was the main form of welfare benefit for those who were seen as able to work but not willing to do so, what does that say about the way such people were viewed at the time?

As the main forms of state involvement in social policy, these welfare benefits are different from social policy as we know it today, both in terms of the level and type of benefits available, especially if you were viewed as an 'able-bodied' poor, meaning healthy and able to work. Beyond this, individuals were expected and left to meet their own welfare needs, with an emphasis on limited and minimalist state involvement and provision.

This emphasis on limited state involvement was also exemplified by the fact that the welfare benefits outlined above were not administered nationally, but locally, through what were then termed parishes, and this led to variations not only between regions, but also between the large numbers of parishes that existed. So for example, what one person received as outdoor relief in one parish could be very much different from what another person received in another parish. This caused a number of problems in terms of administering welfare from one parish to the next, not least of which was a concern from its administrators with what we would now term 'benefit tourism' on the part of those in poverty, due to the different levels and amounts of provision paid and received (Fraser, 2009).

Questions

1. Can you think of what the implications would be of administering justice and policing on a local rather than a national basis? How can this be applied to the similar administration of social policy during this period?

2. One of the main arguments against the administration of social policy in this way was that it led individuals to move to parishes with more generous welfare provisions than other parishes. How does this relate to contemporary debates about the existence of 'benefit tourism' to the UK?

This minimalist system of social policy focussing almost exclusively on poverty and unemployment had been in place for around 150 years prior to 1834, with minor changes here and there over time. It was supplemented by some limited voluntary provision, for which individuals would have to apply and go through a form of means testing, in effect to consider whether they were 'deserving' or 'undeserving' of provision. The main reason for this limited and strict form of welfare benefits was actually to put people off applying in the first place, or so that they only applied if in desperate need. This was because there was a predominant view that if you made welfare benefits too generous, too many people would apply, hence the need for very low levels of welfare benefits which disincentivized people from applying in the first place. At the time there was a prevailing economic and social view that poverty principally occurred from the personal moral failings of the individual, therefore action needed to be concerned with correcting the moral failing of individuals, not wider economic or social concerns. Other present social policy areas, such as health, housing and social care had even lower levels of state involvement and provision.

The period under discussion also has to be contextualized. The early 1800s was the middle period of what we now term the Industrial Revolution. This was a very important period in the economic and historical development of Britain, as it saw important developments in manufacturing, agriculture, transportation and energy. A significant consequence of these changes was a sustained period of large increases in the population, and unplanned urbanization, which is where there is population movement away from rural to urban areas.

As an example of the enormity of this period of change, in 1801 the population of England and Wales was approximately ten million people, and just over 30% lived in urban areas. By 1901, the population had increased to just over 35 million and 80% of these were living in urban areas (Hamlin and Sheard, 1998).

These huge increases in both population and urbanization led to mounting social problems of poverty, unemployment and disease. It quickly became apparent that the minimalist system in place at the time was unable to deal with these mounting social problems, particularly those relating to the lack of work, whether due to unemployment or under-employment – that is periods of infrequent employment. Even for those employed, as the conditions of Industrialization developed, this in itself caused problems, such as unsafe working conditions, job insecurity and very low pay. Very few people were exempt from the need of Industrialization to have an endless source of cheap labour to feed its growth.

Real Life Box 3.1 **The employment of children**

A good example of the effect of Industrialization is in relation to the employment of children, who were expected to work at a very early age. Indeed, had you lived as a child during this period, unless you were the child of a well-off family, you were more likely to be working formally for a living than to be in education, even from the age of four. Some of this work was very hard and laborious, and children were specifically employed in some circumstances, such as in coal mines where their smaller size meant that they were better able to reach inaccessible places.

The website below provides some interesting accounts of the employment of children during this period.

http://www.historylearningsite.co.uk/children_industrial_revolution.htm

Perhaps not surprisingly in the context of these conditions of Industrialization, particularly of large population growth, expenditure on Old Poor Law social policy benefits increased, causing considerable political controversy. Dominant economic and social theorists and theories of the time outlined the Old Poor Law as being the primary cause of the increased expenditure in several ways.

Real Life Box 3.2 **Dominant social and economic social theories at the time of Industrialization**

Adam Smith's *'An Inquiry into the Cause of the Wealth of Nations'* (often shortened to *'The Wealth of Nations'*), published in 1776, argued individuals pursuing their own self interest was the best way to ensure that their welfare needs were met. This meant that while there was a need for some minimal state intervention to ensure some basic conditions were being met, there was no need for extensive state involvement in meeting welfare, as this would disrupt the far more efficient 'invisible hand' of the market.

T.R. Malthus's *'Essays on the Principle of Population'*, published in 1791, argued that the Old Poor Laws was causing population growth by encouraging or enabling people who could not afford children to have them. The resulting increased population was then the cause of the increased poverty that had occurred.

David Ricardo's *Principles of Political Economy*, published in 1817, argued that there was only a finite amount of money in the economy that could be paid out in wages. He defined the Old Poor Law provisions as a part of this finite amount of money. This meant the money paid out from it was reducing the amount that could be paid out in wages, leading to low wages and increased poverty, especially for those in work.

These theories all blamed the Old Poor Laws' increased expenditure on the overgenerous nature of its benefits. More recent evidence has suggested that the increases in expenditure that occurred were caused by the problems of Industrialization, such as underemployment, where individuals were not able to be employed as often as they needed to be to sustain a living, and there is also an argument that it led to severe reductions in living standards (Woodward, 1981). However, the general concern of increased expenditure was one of the main reasons why a Royal Commission on the Old Poor Laws was set up in 1832. In its report published in 1834, there was a majority view from the Commission, notably Edwin Chadwick, that indeed, the generosity of the scheme's benefits was a major problem. More specifically, the Report argued that the Old Poor Law was causing specific problems, such as:

➢ allowing people to act in certain negative ways, against self help, as a consequence of being too generous;

➢ enabling population growth;

➢ restricting the amount of money available to pay wages;

➢ affecting the free market by depressing wages and setting a ceiling above which wages could not rise.

What social policies were put in place in the New Poor Law to meet these identified problems?

It was on the basis of this Report that the New Poor Law was enacted in 1834, to deal with these problems identified with the Old Poor Laws. The Report made many recommendations for changes. According to Englander (1998), there is still a lot of debate about the guiding principles behind these changes, but there is an influential argument that there were three central principles at the heart of the 1834 New Poor Law:

1. *The Workhouse* – the main New Poor Law principle, with a focus on the punishment in a workhouse for 'paupers', that is those who were seen as able to work but not willing to do so, to discourage their moral deficiencies and weakness;

2. *Less eligibility* – for those in 'poverty', that is unable to work and so in need of some welfare, the principle that welfare relief should be below the wage of the lowest paid labourer;

3. *Administrative centralization and uniformity* – the principle that the New Poor Law system should be administered through a single, central board.

In effect, these first and second New Poor Law principles meant that welfare benefits were made even more limited and minimalist than with the Old Poor Law. There was an even greater emphasis on punishing those who were seen as 'paupers', meaning that their poverty was outlined as occurring from some personal failing, with action aimed at correcting their moral failing as individuals, not wider economic or social concerns. For this reason, such paupers' only form of welfare benefits was through a workhouse, and this was specifically aimed at making the recipients of public welfare contribute to their own keep, to correct their 'laziness' and 'reform' their character.

Real Life Box 3.3 **The New Poor Law in literature**

The novels of Charles Dickens provide a very good account of the lives of the poor and the strict and limited provision available to them during this period, especially the description of 'indoor relief' punishment as experienced in the workhouse in *Oliver Twist*, published in 1838.

A key change of the New Poor Law, however, was the move away from parishes as the main unit of administration, towards a central and uniform system of administration. This responsibility was given to a new Poor Law Commission, and this was the first time that social policy was provided essentially the same across the country, as we tend to know it today.

It was hoped that these changes would solve the problems identified with the Old Poor Law system, especially in terms of reducing its expenditure, but it very quickly became apparent that these particular problems were actually occurring as a consequence of the Industrial Revolution itself. In particular, there were linked problems which the Industrial Revolution was causing, relating to the growing population. For instance, as Industrialization progressed, so the population increased, which in turn led to more urbanization, and unemployment and underemployment, and so more people requiring assistance as a consequence of living in poverty. Additionally, the limitations of the New Poor Law also became apparent, as a consequence of the harsh workhouse diet, which was implicated in high numbers of workhouse deaths, leading to the New Poor Law being called 'the starvation Act' (Hamlin, 1995). However, while most people were aware of these circumstances, the prevailing thinking at the time remained was these problems were being caused by the negative individual behaviour of individuals themselves, through for example the wasteful spending of their money.

How were the social policies of the New Poor Law shown to be inadequate by social scientists?

The prevailing thinking discussed above started to be challenged by the research of Edwin Chadwick, who as a member of Royal Commission on the Old Poor Law had argued in the Commission's Reports that the main problem with the Old Poor Law was 'pauperism', that is healthy people being able to work but being disincentivized from doing so due to the availability of high welfare benefits (see page 37). However, in 1842 Chadwick wrote another report titled *General report on the sanitary condition of the labouring population of Great Britain*. In this Report, Chadwick argued that most recipients of poor relief were actually the dependents of healthy breadwinners suddenly struck down by lethal disease, as a consequence of the appalling conditions in which they lived, thereby leaving their families dependent on New Poor Law welfare benefits. Cholera was one such lethal disease of the time, and Chadwick observed that its spread was facilitated by aspects of the poor urban environment in which poorer individuals were living, such as dirty streets, raw sewage, unsafe drinking water, accumulated rubbish and lack of sanitation, that is toilets. Chadwick argued that these fatal conditions were actually being caused by the rapid and uncontrolled nature of the process of Industrialization, including:

> rapid population growth leading to unemployment and underemployment, particularity in rural areas as machinery took over some of the work of that would normally have been done by farm labourers;

> rapid urbanization from population growth leading to overcrowding in specific urban areas;

> rapid overcrowding meaning a lack of basic facilities such as toilets, causing insanitary conditions which led to the growth of deadly diseases such as typhoid and cholera;

> rapid increase in pollution from the growth in industry and factories, leading to ill health and early death.

These observations convinced Chadwick that, rather than individuals' poverty being the cause of the fatal physical environment in which they lived, it was the fatal physical environment which was the cause of the poverty that individuals were experiencing. This led him to argue that the New Poor Law, which he had been instrumental in setting up, was wrong in merely providing a level of relief which did not enable individuals to overcome their fatal physical environment.

Moreover, Chadwick argued that there was a financial case for more extensive preventative measures to deal with these underlying physical and environmental causes of poverty, disease and death. These preventative measures would result in fewer people falling ill, so fewer people dying, so fewer people dependent on New Poor Law relief. In effect, Chadwick was outlining the need to move away from the *minimalist* conception of poor relief set out in both the Old and New Poor Laws, and towards a more proactive and extensive responsibility for the state than previously envisaged (Hamlin and Sheard, 1998). This Report directly led to the 1848 Public Health Act, in which public health became the responsibility of local areas, which were required to deal with insanitary problems of urbanization. But, perhaps more significantly, at the same time a need for greater central government involvement recognized, not just in health and housing but also in other areas (ibid.).

Real Life Box 3.4 **Sanitation: the greatest medical advance since 1840**

In 2007, readers of the British Medical Journal, which is one of the world's most prominent medical publications, voted 'the sanitary revolution', as pioneered by Edwin

▶

◄ Chadwick in his Report, as the most important medical milestone since 1840. This was ahead of more medicalized advances, such as the discovery of antibiotics, the intro- duction of vaccines and the discovery of the structure of DNA (Ferriman, 2007).

In subsequent years, there were also some important developments in the area of education, such as the 1870 Elementary Education Act which made full-time education compulsory for all children for a minimum of five years, and the 1880 Education Act, which made education compulsory for children aged between 5 and 10. The 1891 Fee Grant Act also established free elementary education. These were the first times that the principles of free and compulsory schooling were established in education, which was also a significant change in terms of increased state social policy provision. However, these developments in education and public health were the exception rather than the rule, as the minimalist system of social policy benefits in all other areas from the New Poor Law stayed in place up to the beginning of the 20th century. Chadwick's Report, however, was important in terms of signifying that the existing minimalist system was inadequate in terms of its focus on punishing those who were in poverty, from the belief that poverty was being caused by the individual. His Report's contradiction of current thinking was reinforced by two other important pieces of social research published as the 20th century approached.

The first of these was Charles Booth's *'Life and Labour of the People'*, published in 1889. Booth carried out research on poverty in the east end of London because he was angered by claims that 25% of people living there were living in dire poverty – rather he was convinced that the incidence of poverty was much lower. Booth carried out research over 17 years to estab- lish what the true figure was. He produced detailed maps showing the levels of poverty and wealth in all areas of London. The significant finding from Booth's work was that he was right that the poverty level in London was not 25%, but he was wrong about it being lower. Actually, Booth's research showed that the level of dire poverty was 35%, or more than one in three people. For Booth, this was pretty sobering and led to a reassessment of his views about the nature of poverty, very similar to what had happened to Edwin Chadwick previously. A definitive outcome was that it led Booth to argue that the state should assume some responsibility for those living in poverty, particularly through some form of Old Age Pension.

Not long after Booth carried out his research in east London, Seebohm Rowntree also carried out a similar survey in York. Rowntree is someone you might have heard of, if you have ever eaten Rowntree's confectionary, such as Rowntree's Fruit Pastilles®, or other confectionary made by Rowntree's.

Rowntree was inspired by his father Joseph Rowntree, who had carried out two major surveys of poverty in York in the 1860s. Seebohm carried out his own survey of York titled *Poverty: A Study of Town Life*, published in 1901. There were two significant aspects of Seebohm Rowntree's study. The first was that he defined poverty by distinguishing between two types poverty:

> *primary poverty* – poverty due to earnings below subsistence;

> *secondary poverty* – poverty due to earnings above subsistence but wasteful spending.

As has been stated above, the predominant thinking at the time was that poverty was mainly caused by what Rowntree termed as *secondary* poverty, that is individual failings such as wasteful expenditure on things such as drinking alcohol. However, Rowntree identified that actually, most poverty was caused by earnings being below the amount that people needed to buy basic essentials, what he termed *primary poverty*. Put simply, most people in poverty were in work, but what they earned did not enable them to stay out of poverty. Again, this was significant because it showed that rather than the individual as the main cause of poverty, it was the nature of the work itself in terms of low pay that was causing poverty. In this sense, it illustrated again the failings of the New Poor Law's emphasis on poverty as stemming from some personal failing so provision was aimed at correcting the moral failing of individuals, not wider economic or social concerns.

Question

Do you think that this distinction Rowntree made between primary and secondary poverty is still relevant today?

Rowntree's observation on the failings of the New Poor Law system was reinforced by his Report's second significant finding, which was that there were certain stages of an individual's life when they were more likely to be living below the poverty line than at other stages of their lives. This became known as the 'lifecycle of poverty', as shown in the Figure 3.1.

In Figure 3.1, the dotted line represents the poverty line, so if you are above the dotted line, you are out of poverty, but if you are below the dotted line you are in poverty. What Rowntree showed was that over an individual's lifetime, people moved above and below the poverty line, but they were more likely to be below the poverty line at specific points in their

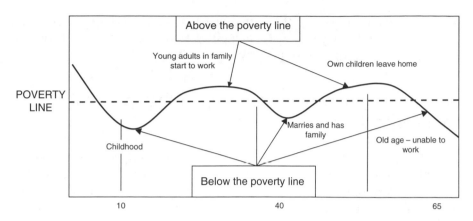

Figure 3.1 Rowntree's lifecycle of poverty
Modified from Rowntree, 1901

lives, such as when very young, when they had children, and when they were old. On the other hand, there were points when they were less likely to be above the poverty line, such as in early adulthood when young adults in the family were able to work, and after their own children in the family had left the home. This highlighted the fact that times in poverty were predictable, depending on family and work circumstances, and these times were explicitly linked to the wages that individuals earned during these circumstances. The possibility of such a prediction based on an individual's life stage again suggested that rather than those in poverty being responsible for their poverty, there were significant factors outside of their control which contributed to their poverty. This in turn led to arguments that new measures were needed to overcome the problems identified by Rowntree's lifecycle of poverty, such as low wages, old age and ill health.

Question

Looking at the figure of the lifecycle of poverty (Figure 3.1), do you think that the periods Rowntree identified as important to being in and out of poverty are still relevant today?

Together, Chadwick's, Booth's, Rowntree's and other reports led to a growing dissatisfaction with the limitations of the New Poor Law's minimalist approach to dealing with the problems of Industrialization, and its effect on poverty. In particular, there was a growing awareness of the extent and nature of working class poverty, and the actual causes of poverty as exemplified by the difference between primary poverty and secondary poverty. These causes suggested that a different approach to dealing with the problems of poverty was necessary.

How did social policies develop in the light of the findings of the social scientists?

A good example of this dissatisfaction was the setting up by government of a Royal Commission into the 'Operation of the New Poor Law' in 1905. The Commission published in two reports in 1909, but in the meantime there were some significant changes to legislation which limited the employment of children under the age of 12 and outlined some new educational responsibilities for local authorities towards children. However, it was the election of the Liberal government in 1906 which saw some wide-ranging and extensive changes to the current system of state policy. Between 1906 and 1914, the Liberal government passed social policy legislation in all areas as we know it today, the most significant of which are shown in Table 3.1.

Table 3.1 The main Liberal government reforms 1906–1911

Year	Social policy	Provision
1906	Provision of School Meals Act	Gave local councils the power to provide free school meals for the poorest families
1908	Children Act	Children became protected persons, meaning that there was the possibility of prosecution for their ill-treatment or neglect; children also banned from working in dangerous trades like scrap metal
1908	Old Age Pensions Act	Non-contributory, means-tested state provided Pension for 'the very poor, the very respectable and the very old' – people over the age of 70, earning less than £31 per year and having lived in Britain for 20 years; criminals and anyone who was felt to be idle did not qualify
1909	Trade Boards Act	Establishment of a minimum wage
1909	Housing and Town Planning Act	Homes required to be built to a certain standard, such as in relation to sanitation, back-to-back housing outlawed, and a planned approach to urban growth
1909	Finance Act	'The People's budget', introduced a more redistributive tax system to pay for reforms
1911	National Insurance Act	Part 1 – general health insurance scheme financed by tripartite social insurance Part 2 – unemployment insurance scheme finance by tripartite social insurance

The social policies of the Liberal government in this period introduced some important principles into the British welfare state. These include:

> - the notion of free provision (free school meals), given as a right without a means test;

> - the notion of protected persons, such as children;

> - a pension in old age, to deal with the conditions of old age;

> - the notion on contributory provision (for health and unemployment insurance), meaning provision given only as a consequence of some form of contribution;

> - the notion of non-contributory provision (for old age pension), meaning provision given as a right without a means test, rather than as a consequence of some form of contribution;

> - the minimum wage;

> - a planned approach to urban development (Housing and Town Planning Act);

> - a redistributive tax system meaning where taxes are paid according to the level of income and/or wealth;

> - and tripartite social insurance (health and unemployment insurance), tripartite meaning an insurance scheme funded by workers, employers and the state, and social insurance meaning a scheme from which you only got out something if you paid something in.

This also increased the scope of state social policies to include areas not previously considered the concern of government welfare, such as housing, health, social services, and extended the scope of others which were previously only minimal, such as education and income maintenance. There were some obvious limitations of the Liberal government's policies, such as the fact that Old Age Pensions were for those aged 70 and over, but average life expectancy at the time was closer to 50. However, it is also apparent that these changes were heavily influenced by the previously outlined criticisms of the New Poor Law by social scientists, especially in relation to Seebohm Rowntree's lifecycle of poverty.

What impact did the First World War have on social policies?

These significant changes to social policies remained largely unchanged for the next 20 to 30 years. There were two main reasons for this. The first was the First World War (WW1) between 1914 and 1918, and the huge financial costs required to pay for the war which had the effect of limiting the development of social policy provision. While there were some increases in the power of the state, these were linked to the wartime effort, such as where industries like weaponry and shipping became 'nationalized', that is the state took some form of control over them. There were also significant increases in income tax for some people, to pay for the war effort. The effects of WW1 in relation to social policy were perhaps most felt after the war had finished, as exemplified by the creation of the Ministry of Health in 1919, and the Housing and Town Planning Act 1919, from which the state funded the building of over 200,000 new houses, and overall between 1919 and 1938, local authorities built over 1.1 million houses (Harris, 2004), which was a huge change from the past and was the beginning of what we now know as council housing. Post WW1, however, the huge financial debt built up by the war meant that development of further social policies was very limited.

The other main reason why there were limited changes in social policies during this period was mass unemployment. As Graph 3.1 shows, while unemployment had decreased after the war started in 1914 as a consequence of the extensive war effort, after the end of WW1 in 1919 unemployment grew to previously unheard of levels. Between 1921 and 1938, unemployment was never below one million people, and reached nearly three million in 1933 (from a much smaller population of approximately 45 million, compared to approximately 60 million today), which is an unemployment rate of over 20% (Harris, 2004).

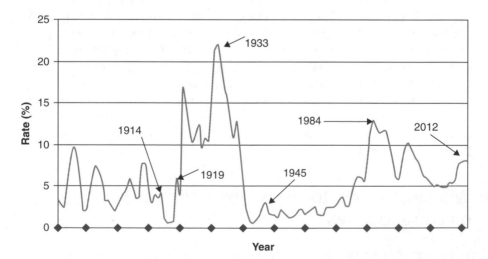

Graph 3.1 Unemployment rates 1881–2012
Source: Denman and McDonald, 1996; ONS, 2013

Question

Look at Graph 3.1 and compare the rate of unemployed during that period with the unemployment number and rate now. How do the two periods compare?

Comparing the rate of unemployment from after WW1 in 1919 to that of 2012 using Graph 2.1, it is clear that unemployment was much higher in the period after WW1. The implication of this was that expenditure on the unemployment scheme that had been introduced in 1911 by the Liberal government grew significantly during this time, as a consequence of high unemployment. This is despite the fact that to deal with the increased expenditure, there were cuts in unemployment benefits, restrictions on who could claim benefits, for example married women couldn't claim, and the introduction of means testing even for those who had social insurance eligibility to the benefit. These had huge implications in terms of lowering living standards of the unemployed.

Real Life Box 3.5 **George Orwell: poverty in the inter-war period**

In two novels published in the 1930s, George Orwell (of *Animal Farm* and *1984* fame) provided accounts of the social effect of mass unemployment and underemployment during the period, in *Down and Out in London and Paris* (1933) and *The Road to Wigan Pier* (1937). While both provide graphic accounts of the misery and hopelessness of the period, *The Road to Wigan Pier* in particular highlights the inequities of the Old Poor Law means test for those reliant on it.

However, the problem of mass unemployment simply overwhelmed the unemployment scheme, and indeed overwhelmed other social policies in general, meaning that the scope for expenditure in other areas was severely limited. So there was very little change in other social policy areas, especially health and education, as social policy was characterized by piecemeal and ad hoc changes, rather than a grand plan for development.

Perhaps more significantly, however, the fact that the government's limited, hands-off approach to dealing with unemployment did not reduce the trend towards mass unemployment reinforced a growing view that rather than being caused of individual failing, unemployment was something that was largely out of the control of individuals. Significantly, this suggested that the minimalist social policies to deal with unemployment were ineffective, and more direct, extensive policies and provision were required.

Why did the Second World War have such an effect on the development of the 'Welfare state' as we know it today?

The impetus towards such a change was provided in 1939 by the beginning of the Second World War (WW2). This war had a much larger impact on society and social policy than WW1, due to it status as a 'total war'. This means that it was a war that had higher levels of mobilization, scale and aims than any war before or since. For example, WW2 lasted 2074 days, which is 513 days longer than WW1, and whereas the number of deaths from WW1 is estimated at 16–30 million people, for WW2 the estimate of deaths is 60–85 million people. This meant that it touched the lives of almost all individuals in British society, through for example conscription (males), employment in war industries (females), evacuation (children and older people) and rationing (all).

As with WW1, WW2 also led to huge increases in government military expenditure to pay for the war, and also to increased government control in areas which it did not previously directly control. Rationing is a good example of this, as the government took control for the distribution of food to the population. This meant that it also had to take control of the means of production of food, including agriculture. Richard Titmuss (1958) has outlined how such effects of WW2's 'total war' impacted on the direction of social policy provision in important ways. For instance, rationing led to food provision being equalized among the population, which in turn led to improvements in health. Additionally, Titmuss identified that WW2 also led to:

> the extension of systems of medical care to the general population, as well as to the army;

> universalizing educational facilities to both army and the general public;

> the need for income-maintenance provision for dependents (wives, children).

The impact of these and other 'total war' changes was to highlight the need for a more comprehensive system of welfare reform to counter the problems that people had experienced during the war and, especially, were continuing to experience, after the war, so that the problems which overwhelmed both the government and individuals after WW1 were not repeated. This desire for comprehensive welfare reform was exemplified by the appointment in

1941 of William Beveridge to chair a committee to look at post-war reconstruction in social insurance and related services. The result of Beveridge's committee is popularly referred to as *'The Beveridge Report'*, which was published in 1942 to huge public if not political support.

Beveridge's Report was a great influence on the design of the post-war welfare state, in terms of its emphasis on cradle to grave welfare as outlined in Chapter 1. Beveridge's report was constructed around the identification of 'five giant evils' which he argued limited the possibility of post-war reconstruction. More significantly, Beveridge directly linked these giant evils to specific social policy areas, and argued for the development of specific policies in these areas. These five giant evils and policy areas were as indicated in Table 3.2.

Table 3.2 Beveridge's five giant evils and social policy

Evils	Policies
Want	Social Security
Idleness	Employment
Disease	Health
Ignorance	Education
Squalor	Housing

Question

Thinking about Beveridge's five giant evils, do you think they are still relevant today?

Of these, Beveridge identified the need for policies to eliminate 'Want' as the main requirement for post-war reconstruction. Beveridge's report was based on the assumption that there would be three main features of any social policy that would be put in place after the war:

1. The introduction of family allowances paid to families with children up to the age of 15, but not for the first child, as wages were expected to cover this.

2. A comprehensive system of health services available to all members of society.

3. The commitment from government to put active policies in place to enable the full employment of the population, and avoid mass unemployment.

Real Life Box 3.6 **Full employment**

What is described as 'full employment' is usually an aim to reach an unemployment level no higher or lower than 3% of the population. An unemployment rate above 3% is seen as being wasteful for the country and the economy. An unemployment rate below 3% is seen as having negative implications as the ready availability of work could increase the power of workers over their employers, and thus lead to things like wage increases and voluntary unemployment.

As can be seen, some of these assumptions were a major break from the emphasis in social policies before WW2. In particular, the assumption that the state should put in place policies for full employment was in complete contrast to the acceptance of mass unemployment seen before the WW2. This effectively made work in the form of paid employment the core to eliminating 'want', meaning that the absence of such paid employment would have significant negative consequences for the effective functioning of any post-war welfare state.

This major change in thinking was built from Beveridge's analysis that the system in place before WW2 had effectively failed, and a new approach was needed. This new approach was encapsulated in the Report's 'Three Guiding Principles of Recommendations'. These were:

1. In making proposals for the future, learning from the past failures was very important, and the war itself provided a unique opportunity for revolutionary change, and *'a revolutionary moment in the world's history is a time for revolutions, not for patching'* (Beveridge, 1942).

2. If policy focussed just on schemes for income security through Want they would fail, as such a focus was not comprehensive enough for social progress. Rather, the road to reconstruction and social progress necessitated a need to define social policies in a broad way, to also include Disease, Ignorance, Idleness and Squalor.

3. Any scheme of social security could only be successful if there was mutual co-operation between the state and the individual. On the state's part, this meant ensuring a stable environment and a national minimum of social security so that individuals could be secure to work and contribute. On the individuals' part, this meant working to contribute to the system, and not relying on the national minimum that the state provided.

Beveridge's proposals were hugely popular with the general population, although less so with the wartime coalition government who were concerned about the cost implications of Beveridge's comprehensive system of social security. However, the end of the war in 1945 saw the election of the Labour government of Clement Atlee and they constructed many social policies largely around Beveridge's 'five evil giants' proposals. This is shown in Table 3.3.

Table 3.3 Linkage between Beveridge's five giants and post-war social policies

Beveridge's evil giant	Government focus	Legislation	Government policies
Want	Social security	1945 Family Allowance Act	➤ Universal child allowance
		National Insurance Act 1946	➤ Sickness benefit ➤ Unemployment benefit ➤ Pension ➤ Maternity and widows' allowance ➤ Guardians' allowance (for orphans) ➤ Death grant (for funerals)
		1948 National Assistance Act	➤ Means tested national assistance for those not entitled to social insurance
Idleness	Full employment	A range of Nationalization Acts and policies to ensure unemployment stayed below 3%	➤ Increased government spending overall ➤ Nationalization of coal, electricity, rail, steel, iron and gas industries, and also the canals, airways and Bank of England
Disease	Health	National Health Service Act 1946	➤ The introduction of the NHS in 1948, making health care free ➤ Comprehensive and universal for all of the population
Ignorance	Education	Implementation of the (Butler) Education Act 1944	➤ Secondary education provided as a right, free and universally ➤ Raising of school leaving age to 15 ➤ Tripartite school system (grammar, secondary technical, and secondary modern) introduced
Squalor	Housing	Housing Act 1949	➤ Over one million permanent new homes built between 1945 and 1951

The specific emphasis on these areas meant they have become known as 'pillars' of the welfare state, as set out in Chapter 1.

An often overlooked additional pillar of Clement Attlee's government's post-war welfare state is the provision for free access to justice, through what we now know as legal aid. Up to and during WW2, there was very limited legal assistance for impoverished defendants in criminal cases, while legal advice for poorer individuals in civil cases (that is where there is a non-criminal dispute between two parties, for example in divorces or housing) relied heavily on the good will of lawyers prepared to work for free (Robins, 2011). Changes made in 1949 gave 80% of the population free access to legal aid not just in criminal cases, but also in civil cases, which was a very significant shift.

Question

The Attlee Government outlined access to justice as one of the three pillars of the welfare state, together with free education and free healthcare. How relevant do you think access to justice is for a welfare state?

These social policies put in place between 1946 and 1951 were a major break from previous systems of social policy, in terms of their scope and comprehensiveness. When people talk about the 'welfare state', it is usually this period of time they are referring to. We can also see the principles of cradle to grave welfare provision outlined in the previous chapter in Table 1.2. Here we can see some important principles of social policy provision being established, such as:

> *comprehensiveness* – to cover the range possibilities (i.e. social security);

> *universalism* – meaning available to all regardless of income (i.e. family allowance);

> *active state intervention* – to meet a social policy goal (i.e. full employment);

> *right to provision* – an entitlement set out in law (i.e. secondary education);

> *free at the point of use provision* – no requirement to pay for provision at the point of use (i.e. health);

> *localism* – extensive local authority involvement in social policy provision (i.e. housing).

The effectiveness of the policies arising from the Beveridge Report and put in place by the post-war Labour government has been extensively debated elsewhere (see for example Gladstone, 2003; Harris, 2004; Fraser, 2009), with obvious contradiction and limitations outlined, such as the fact that social insurance benefits were to be paid at subsistence level, meaning below the basic minimum required for living. However, the key point of interest here is how social policy developed from the minimalist provision before the war, to the more comprehensive systems after the war, and the explicit rationale given for this change. The events outlined above show that the post-war welfare state developed principally as a consequence of the observed and experienced limitations of the previous system of social welfare.

Perhaps what is more remarkable is the fact that such a comprehensive system evolved in a time of true 'austerity', meaning that as a consequence of the huge amounts of money spent on WW2, there was to all intents and purposes no money left for post-war reconstruction. However, the resources were found to put in place a comprehensive system of social welfare to which today's system of social welfare still owes a great deal.

How successful were the post-war 'welfare state' social policies?

The period after the implementation of the Beveridge Report was largely characterized by sustained expansion in social policy areas, especially housing (Taylor-Gooby, 1988). This period of sustained expansion lasted up to the mid-1970s, regardless of which party was in power, and is usually identified as a period of *consensus* in the development of social policy. This notion of consensus is evident in two ways when looking at post-war welfare:

1. Consensus that there was a need for a welfare state.

2. Consensus about the direction in which the welfare state should take i.e. sustained expansion.

Gladstone (1999) provides several arguments which support this notion of consensus. These include the fact that there was no dismantling of the welfare state that had been put in place in the post-war period, despite different political parties coming into power, and continual growth in social policy areas. The system put in place was perceived as largely working in terms of reducing Beveridge's five giants (Gazeley, 2003), with education being a notable exception, and so remained largely intact during this period. A good example of this was in relation to employment, where the period between 1946 and 1973 had the lowest period of unemployment of any historical period, meaning that the goal of full employment, that is unemployment not above 3%, was largely achieved in the three decades or so after the war (Fraser, 2009), as shown in Graph 3.1 above.

Real Life Box 3.7 'You've never had it so good'

In 1957, the then Prime Minister Harold Macmillan made a speech in which he made the claim that 'most of our people have never had it so good'. This was characteristic of the notion of consensus and progress at the time, and that the problems of the pre-war period had largely been solved by the post-war welfare system.

When did the consensus period for social policy come to an end?

This consensus approach to social policy became less clear during the mid-1970s, and certainly after 1979. Then, although there were still increases in social policy expenditure, the increases were noticeably less than before. The mid-1970s saw some important global and national events which impacted on the post-war welfare state. For instance, in 1973 there was a major slowdown in the economic growth of the world (called a recession), and this affected the UK. In particular, there was a quadrupling of oil prices between 1973 and 1974, and significant increases again up to 1976. This had two effects. Firstly, fewer goods were manufactured as there were restrictions on the amount of fuel that could be used. Secondly, this meant that goods and services became more expensive to manufacture and to buy, meaning that people bought fewer goods. The consequence of fewer goods being made and less being bought was a substantial and continual increase in unemployment, specifically at a time when the events outlined above were reducing the government's income.

With the election of Margaret Thatcher in 1979, there was a distinct shift away from Beveridge's guiding principles outlined above, and away from the consensus of the previous 30 years. Rather than a comprehensive system of social welfare being seen as a *solution* to the problem of mass unemployment, Thatcher viewed Beveridge's comprehensive system of social welfare as the *cause* of the problem of mass unemployment. In particular, she argued that the post-war welfare state placed too much responsibility on the state and not enough on the individual. As a consequence Thatcher outlined various policies to change this emphasis, including:

> No focus on active state policies for full employment; unemployment seen as an individual responsibility;

> The introduction of a stricter benefits regime for the unemployed, including the use of benefits sanctions against those deemed to have failed to act in a specified way;

> Reductions in social policy expenditure in specific areas;

> Reductions in specific social policy benefits, such as unemployment benefits;

> Privatization of key nationalized utilities, such as energy;

> Reductions in personal taxation;

> Less universal access to provision; more selective access, such as Housing Benefit;

> Incentives for more private and less state welfare provision, such as private pensions and private healthcare;

> Reductions in local authority responsibility in social policy areas, such as provision of housing.

If we compare these changes to the system envisaged by Beveridge and put in place in the immediate post-war period, we can see that they are significantly different. The shift in emphasis from active full employment policies to unemployment as an individual responsibility is particularly significant, as this was something which underpinned the post-war system. As an example of this emphasis on unemployment, in 1984 unemployment peaked at 3.4 million people, a rate of 12.2%, much higher than the average rate of 3% in the previous 30 years or so, as shown in Graph 3.1 above.

Additionally, the changes show an emphasis on reducing the comprehensives of the Welfare State as well as a shift away from universalism towards selectivism, which means that rather than welfare provision being given to all regardless of means, support is provided only to those without means. In effect, the Welfare State became less comprehensive and more selective in terms of the type and levels of protection of social insurance it provided.

What has been the main focus of social policies over the last 20 years or so?

New Labour was elected in 1997, which was the first change of government for 18 years. To some extent there was a change in government emphasis in social policies. Overall, there was increased government expenditure in social policy areas. Expenditure on health in particular increased to a very large degree, and there were also increases in education. These increases were partly paid for by falls in unemployment, which meant less expenditure on social security payments for the unemployed and more available for other social policy areas.

The increases in education were part of an attempt by the New Labour government to move away from the 'welfare state' as set out in the post-war period, and move towards a 'social investment state' (Lister, 2006). In practice this meant that there was less emphasis on the notion of welfare as a right provided by the state, and more emphasis on the state providing investment in key social policies to enable individuals to take more responsibility for their own welfare. Examples of social policies which emphasized social investment were the increases in education expenditure, and the New Deal employment policies which focussed on providing intensive support for the long-term unemployed to return to work.

It is important to note that this was not a return to 'full employment' policies as seen in the immediate post-war period, rather an emphasis on *active employment* policies, meaning more focus on what the individual could do to regain employment. The emphasis on employment was reinforced by the introduction of the National Minimum Wage (NMW) in 1999, which was part of a strategy to 'make work pay', as poverty from low pay had become an important issue at the time of high unemployment during the previous government.

However, the level at which the NMW was set was arguably too low to make any difference, meaning that those who worked remained in poverty, or their income needed to be increased through additional social policy provision. For this purpose, New Labour introduced Tax Credits, to provide extra money for people who were responsible for children. Disabled workers and other workers on lower incomes also received tax credits. The rationale for this policy from New Labour was that there was a need to increase the income of such groups, as income-wise they had fallen behind other groups.

Question
___

Looking at the groups which tax credits were specifically aimed at, how do they match up to Rowntree's lifecycle of poverty?

Over the last 20 years or so, the growth of tax credits expenditure has been a very significant feature of social policy, as shown in Graph 3.2 below.

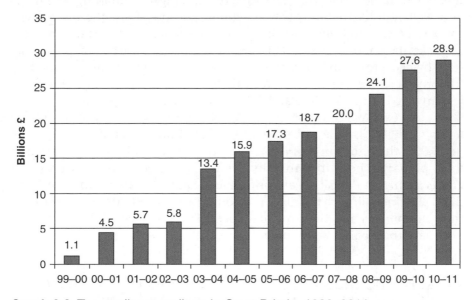

Graph 3.2 Tax credit expenditure in Great Britain, 1999–2011
Source: DWP, 2013

From costing just over £1 billion pounds in 1999–2000, this expenditure had increased in 2010/2011 to over £28 billion, a huge increase over a short period of time. Tax credits are means-tested, meaning that they continued the trend from the previous government of less universal and more selective provision. But they are non-contributory, meaning that you do not have to pay National Insurance contributions to receive them. Their main aim was to top-up the low income of the specific groups set out above.

Question

What does the growth of tax credits shown above say about the extent and nature of poverty in the UK during the period 1999–2011?

New Labour also introduced other important non-contributory benefits, such as Pension Credit, and Winter Fuel Allowance. This was an important change from the welfare state that Beveridge envisaged, in which contribution-based benefits were seen as an important principle for the post-war welfare state.

There was also a definitive shift towards further state down-sizing and privatization through what was called the Private Finance Initiative. This was where rather than the state directly funding the building of important welfare infrastructure such as schools and hospitals, the private sector was allowed to build and then rent the services to the state, in order to make their money back. This meant that large swathes of previously state-owned provision, such as schools and hospitals, became owned by the private sector, which reinforced the thinking that the state should be less involved in the funding and delivery of social policy provision.

A good example of this is the introduction of higher education tuition fees by the New Labour government in 1998. Initially set at £1,000, rising to £3,000, these tuition fees broke the existing principle of free education from primary school to university. New Labour also abolished universal grants for higher education and introduced Student Maintenance Loans in their place meaning that unlike previously when students could get both their tuition fees and their maintenance at university paid, both of these now have to be paid by the student.

What impact has the austerity policies of the 2010 Coalition government had on social policies?

The period of the 2010 Coalition government has been marked by austerity and extensive cuts in welfare provision, with the notable exception of NHS funding. As with the Thatcher government, these policies have been underpinned by a belief that expensive social policies are the cause of increased government expenditure.

The 2010 Coalition approach has been marked by three key principles, as evident in specific policies:

1. In a period of austerity, welfare expenditure is too large and takes too much as a share of government expenditure; as shown by cuts totalling £32 billion in social policy provision.

2. Welfare State provision is too generous, and has led to dependency on the welfare state; as shown by the introduction of a £26,000 welfare cap, and the introduction of the Universal Credit.

3. Welfare State provision is too extensive, and there are areas for which either the individual or the market should take more responsibility; as shown in the Big Society, the increased transfer of social policy responsibility to the private sector organizations such as G4S and Atos, and making receipt of benefits such as JSA more conditional rather than given as a right, plus individuals having to work in order to receive provision.

> ## Question
>
> Thinking about the current emphasis on making receipt of welfare conditional on having to work, does this have a historical precedent in the Old and New Poor Laws?

In addition, it is also notable that unemployment has risen to levels not seen since the 1980s, with no specific emphasis from the coalition on full employment policies.

> ## Question
>
> The Beveridge Report is still seen as relevant today, as evident from the quote below from George Osborne, the 2010 Coalition government's Chancellor of the Exchequer:
>
> *We've been working together on the biggest reform of the welfare system since that great liberal William Beveridge.*
>
> Does the approach of the 2010 Coalition government suggest a move towards or away from Beveridge's welfare state?

Summary

This chapter has explored why your entitlement to cradle to grave social policy exists at all, and as it does today. It is very likely that if you were to go back in time to the era of or before the New Poor Law, you would be surprised by the minimalist form of social policy provision that existed in comparison to today. Conversely, if an individual living at or before the New Poor Law was to visit us today, they would similarly be very surprised at the cradle to grave nature of current state social policy provision. The social policy of today is very different from the social policy of that time, in terms of scope, emphasis, delivery and orientation. These historical differences enable us to make significant linkage between the past and the present nature of social policy:

➤ Social policy does not stand still but develops over time, and can develop quite rapidly over a short period of time, good examples being the reforms at the start of the 20th century, and the post–World War Two reforms.

➤ The historical development of social policies is significantly linked to the research and work of social scientists providing evidence for such development. The most obvious examples of this are the works of social scientists like Charles Booth and Seebohm Rowntree. This means that the development of social policies as we know them today did not just appear from nowhere, but have evolved over a long period of time, and from specific sets of circumstances. The important point about such works is that their findings have stood the test of time, and still remain an important source of reference for current social policies.

➤ While there are diverse ways in which social policies can and have been made and provided, state intervention has been the greatest driver in the development of social policies. This is evident if we look at the way social policies have been transformed by changing legislation and level of provision provided by the state, the NHS being an obvious example.

➤ There is not much in contemporary social policy that has not been experienced historically. Most of the contemporary issues that social policies deal with have a historical precedent, even those which we might tend to think of as modern problems, such as the notion that welfare acts as a disincentive to work, which has historical precedents in both the Old and New Poor Laws. The variation that has existed and continues to exist in relation to dealing with social problems shows that there is always more than one way to deal with any given social problem through social policies. Different governments have chosen different types of policies to deal with essentially the same problem, the most obvious example being different policies to deal with the problem of mass unemployment. This suggests that social problems are rarely solved, they simply reappear in a different form at another time, poverty and low pay being good examples of this.

➤ The post-war welfare state set out by Beveridge and constructed by the Attlee government remains an important reference to contemporary social policy, the existence of the NHS being the most obvious example. Beveridge put paid employment as the core of the post-war reconstruction. This was explicitly in the form of an emphasis on full employment, and meant that high unemployment would have severe negative consequences for the effective functioning of any post-war welfare state built upon Beveridge's principles and assumptions, as we can see today.

In trying to cram nearly 200 years of social history into 10,000 words or so, the account given above provides only a very brief outline of the developments in social policy in the UK. Two consequences of this brevity are simplified explanations for such developments, and the presentation of the emergence of social policies as a 'history without the politics' and as going from the darkness of the Old Poor Laws to the light of the Beveridge post-war welfare state (Gladstone, 2003). Nonetheless, what should have become evident from this chapter is the relevance of Gladstone's claim at the start of this chapter, that a study of the past of social policy is very much relevant to understanding why your entitlement to cradle to grave social policy has developed and exists as it does in its present form today.

Key Point

The cradle to grave social policy that exists today did not just happen but its development occurred over a long period of time to deal with specific social and economic and problems within society.

Useful websites

The Industrial Revolution in action

The website shown below provides a good educational clip of some of the effects and outcomes of the Industrial Revolution. http://www.bbc.co.uk/learningzone/clips/the-industrial-revolution/13933.html

Workhouses in detail

The website http://www.workhouses.org.uk/ provides extensive details of life in the workhouses, including links to surviving workhouse buildings. One such workhouse building is Southwell Workhouse in Nottingham (http://www.nationaltrust.org.uk/workhouse-southwell/), which provides events and activities linked to life in the workhouse.

4

DO YOU PAY TOO MUCH TAX FOR THE SOCIAL POLICY BENEFITS YOU RECEIVE?

The aims of this chapter are to:

1. **Provide an outline of how much tax you pay**

2. **Detail the way that tax pays for social policy**

3. **Compare how much tax you pay with how the cost of the social policy benefits you receive**

4. **Outline important social policy principles related to taxation funded social policy**

In Chapter 1, we saw that social policy is very relevant to you because you both receive it and you pay for it. Expenditure on the five main social policy areas of health, education, housing, income maintenance and personal social services accounts for 70% of total government spending. This is shown in Graph 4.1.

We also saw that taxation in various forms is the main way that the government pays for social policy provision, which represents 82% of all the income that the government receives, as shown in Graph 4.2.

Graph 4.2 shows that tax in various forms is the main source of government income, which the government uses to pay for the social policy it provides. The main types of taxes as shown in Graph 4.2 are:

➤ Income Tax and National Insurance are both taxes paid mainly from what you earn in employment;

➤ Excise duties are taxes paid on some items after they are made but before they are sold (such as cigarettes and alcohol);

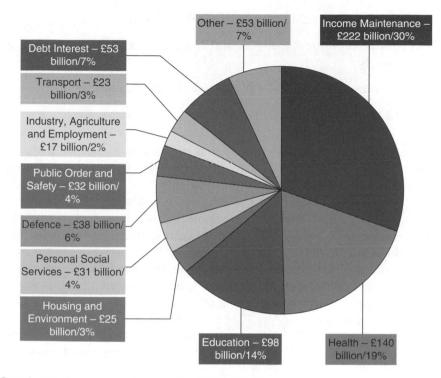

Graph 4.1 Government spending 2014–2015
Source: HM Treasury, 2014

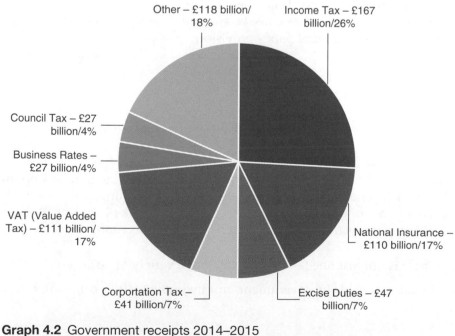

Graph 4.2 Government receipts 2014–2015
Source: HM Treasury, 2014

➤ Corporation Tax is paid by business on their profits;

➤ VAT stands for Value Added Tax and is a sales tax, paid when you buy most things;

➤ Business rates is a tax paid by businesses to pay for local services;

➤ Council tax is paid by individuals to pay for local services.

These various forms of taxation mean that unless you do not work, do not buy anything at all, do not smoke, drink or drive, then you make some contribution to government income, and therefore to paying for social policy. This makes the questions of what is taxation and the amount of taxation you pay for social policy provision highly relevant to you.

This chapter explores the centrality of taxation to social policy. Its principle focus is to provide an understanding of how the taxation you pay funds social policy. Both the amounts of taxation paid and what taxation is used for is often not well understood due to its complexity, so this chapter provides a simplified account of the amounts and process of paying taxation and its use in social policy. This chapter will also consider whether it would be less expensive for you to meet your welfare needs with or without taxation funded social policy. This will then enable important principles related to taxation funded social policy to be discussed.

By the end of this chapter you should have an understanding of what taxation pays for, the amount of taxation that you pay and how much this contributes to the cost of the social policy provision that you use, how much taxation funded social policy costs in comparison to you paying to meet your own welfare needs, and important principles that underpin taxation funded social policy provision.

What is taxation?

In this world nothing can be said to be certain, except death and taxes.

The well-known quote above from Benjamin Franklin (1706–1790) highlights the fact that for some people death and taxation are both as unpopular as each other, and that paying taxation is something that we will all experience at some point in our lives, whether we like it or not. We can also highlight several general characteristics about taxation:

➤ There is not just one tax that we pay, but a variety of taxation;

➤ Taxation is made by government, not by individuals or companies;

➤ Taxation is the principal way that the government pays for the services that they provide;

➤ Taxation is nearly always compulsory, rarely optional;

➤ All individuals are expected to pay some form of taxation;

➤ Failure to pay appropriate taxation is usually punishable by law.

Perhaps not surprisingly, people have differing views on taxation. On the one hand there is the view that taxation is an injustice, as shown below:

Taxation of earnings from labor is on a par with forced labor.

Robert Nozick

This view argues that the compulsory nature of taxation makes it 'unjust' because it forcibly takes money away from people who may not want to give up money that they have earned. This viewpoint implies that individuals should not be compelled to pay taxation, but should be free to spend their money as they like.

On the other hand, there is a view that sees taxation as a 'necessity', as shown below:

Taxation is the price which we pay for civilization, for our social, civil and political institutions, for the security of life and property, and without which, we must resort to the law of force.

Oliver Wendell Holmes Jr

This view argues that taxation works to enable the provision of important public services, which in the absence of taxation would not be provided, and thus would be a major negative for society. This viewpoint emphasizes taxation as something that benefits the development of society.

Question

Which viewpoint do you agree with?

What does taxation pay for?

We saw in Chapter 1 how social policy covers the spectrum of your life, which we can define as cradle to grave social policy, and even beyond this. We also saw in Chapter 3 that the provision of social policy as we know it today has progressed over time from its minimalist provision to a more comprehensive provision, and Graph 4.1 which shows all the functions that taxation principally pays for reflects this more comprehensive provision of social policy. This shows that the five social policy areas of health, education, housing, social protection and personal social services account for approximately 70% of all government spending. Some of these functions are funded in a very comprehensive and extensive way, such as health, while others are only partly funded, such as education.

Graph 4.1 also shows that there are functions other than social policy which taxation pays for, such as defence, transport, public order and safety. Again, some of these functions, such as defence, are funded in a very comprehensive and extensive way while others are only partly funded, such as transport. Some of these are functions which the individual does not or could not provide for themselves, due to either the cost (e.g. defence) or the practicality (e.g. the police), but what links them is that they are essential services for a well-functioning society.

So, the list of things that taxation pays for is fairly large, including not just social policy provision but also other important public services such as defence and transport, which can be described as essential for a well-functioning society.

How does the taxation process work?

To answer this question, we first of all need to separate the taxes shown in Graph 4.2 into two categories. If we exclude the category of 'Other', we can categorize the taxes in Graph 4.2 in terms of taxes paid specifically by businesses and taxes paid specifically by you.

Taxes that are paid by businesses are 'Business Rates' and 'Corporation Tax'. We can ignore these for now. We are interested in taxes that are specifically paid by you, which are 'Income Tax', 'National Insurance Contributions', 'VAT' (Value Added Tax) and 'Council Tax'.

We can calculate in a simplified way an approximate amount you are likely to pay for these taxes, and at the same time explain how the tax system works. This is shown in Table 4.1, which seems very complicated, but is explained in detail below.

Table 4.1 Simplified earnings and taxation 2014–2015

Row	Row calculation	Description	Earnings A	Earnings B	Earnings C	Earnings D
A		**Annual *Gross* Earnings (£)**	10,000	18,615	21,595	26,075
B		Income Tax, Tax Free Allowance (£)	10,000	10,000	10,000	10,000
C =	A–B	Taxable Earnings (£)	0	8,345	11,101	15,547
D		Basic Income Tax Rate	20%	20%	20%	20%
E =	C×D	*Income Tax Paid (£)*	0	1,723	2,319	3,215
F		National Insurance (NI) Contributions Allowance (£)	7,748	7,748	7,748	7,748
G =	A–F	Taxable NI (£)	2,252	10,867	13,847	18,327
H		Basic NI Rate	12%	12%	12%	12%
I =	G–H	*NI Paid (£)*	270	1,304	1,661	2,199
J=	E+I	**Total annual income and NI taxes paid (£)**	270	3,027	3,980	5,414
K =	A–J	***Annual Net Income*** *(After Income Tax and NI) (£)*	9,730	15,587	17,614	20,660
L		Average VAT Paid (£)	1,653	1,653	1,653	1,653
M		Average Excise Duties Paid (£)	754	754	754	754
N		Average Council Tax Paid (£)	1,045	1,045	1,045	1,045
O =	L+M+N	**Total VAT, Council Tax, Excise Duty (£)**	3,452	3452	3,452	3,452
P =	J+O	**TOTAL TAX (£)**	3,722	6,479	7,432	8,866
Q =	A–P	***Post-Tax Income*** (After All Taxes) (£)	6,278	12,136	14,162	17,208
R =	P/A	% Tax Paid	37.2	34.8	34.4	34.0

Table 4.1 shows taxation paid at four levels of earnings in Row A. These four earnings levels have been chosen for specific reasons, as they represent four important earnings points:

a) **Earnings A – £10,000** is the Income Tax threshold for 2014–2015, that is, the earnings level at which you start paying Income Tax. If you earn below this amount, you do not pay Income Tax, but if you earn above this amount you do pay Income Tax.

b) **Earnings B – £18,615** represents the lowest average starting graduate salary for 2013, meaning that it is the lowest amount that the average graduate started earning from employment (Redmond *et al.*, 2014).

c) **Earnings C – £21,595** represents the gross median earnings for 2013, that is, if we divide the working population in half, 50% would earn above this figure and 50% would earn below this figure (ONS, 2014a).

d) **Earnings D – £26,075** represents the mean earnings for 2013, that is, if we calculate the total earnings of all individuals and divide it by the number of working people, sometimes termed the average income (ONS, 2014a).

The earnings figures B, C and D above are for 2013 because they are the latest figures available at the time of publication, but this is not too much of an issue because between 2013 and 2014, there was not much growth in earnings (ONS, 2014a), meaning that the earnings amount would not be much different at the time of publication.

These earnings figures are shown before the deduction of any taxation, which is called *gross earnings*. We can now begin to calculate the amounts of taxation paid at each income level. This should give you an estimate of the amount of tax you pay depending on your income.

Explanatory notes for Table 4.1

You should note that Table 4.1 presents a highly simplified description of the taxation process and the amount of taxation paid, and so you should observe a note of caution for the figures and calculations. In particular, there are a number of assumptions which affect the figures in Table 4.1. These are:

➤ Table 4.1 refers to both *earnings* and *income* as there is a difference between the two terms. Earnings simply refers to the money that you receive from employment, while income refers to the money that you receive from all other sources including

▶

your income. So for example, your income could also include savings interest, investments, and money from benefits, such as Child Benefit. This means that income is usually more than earnings.

➤ The table uses averages throughout. Averages only give a general picture of circumstances, not the *true* account of circumstances.

➤ Due to reasons of differential expenditure, calculations for VAT and Excise duties are not as easy as for the other taxes, so these have been calculated using Crossley *et al.*'s (2009) method of dividing the total amount of each tax paid by the population.

➤ The table assumes that earnings are received at individual level, when actually most people live in households of more than one person. This can reduce the amount of tax that they pay, such as Council Tax, which is a household tax and would be proportionally less the more tax-paying people live in a household. Similarly, the amount of VAT paid for food by households of more than one person will be proportionally less than the amount of VAT paid for food by one person households.

➤ On the other hand, the table overestimates the post-tax cash income, as it does not include all taxes paid, such as insurance premium tax, the licence fee, air passenger duty and savings tax which effectively reduce the amount of post-tax income that an individual has.

➤ See the Keywords at the end of the chapter for a fuller explanation of some of the key terms used.

Income Tax

For Income Tax, at these earnings levels everyone is entitled to what is called a tax free allowance, which is an amount they can earn before tax is deducted. In 2014–2015 this is £10,000 (Row B). Deducting this tax free allowance from individuals' gross earnings gives the amount of their income they actually pay tax on (Row C). This is quite important because many people assume that Income Tax is paid on the full amount they earn, when actually is it paid after this tax free allowance is deducted. At all these levels of earnings, the Basic Income Tax Rate is paid, and this is 20% of their taxable income (Row D). The amounts of Income Tax paid is shown (Row E); note that the amount of tax paid varies depending on the gross earnings level.

National Insurance

The way National Insurance Contributions (NI) is calculated is very similar to Income Tax. Individuals are also provided with a tax free allowance before NI is paid (Row F), although it is less than the Income Tax Allowance. This means that you pay NI earlier than you pay Income Tax, and you may have to pay NI even though you do not pay Income Tax, as seen in the table for the earnings level of £10,000 (Row G). However, the NI Tax Rate of 12% is lower than the Income Tax rate, as shown in Row H. The amount of NI paid over the year for the different earnings levels is shown in Row I, and like Income Tax this varies with gross earnings levels. Another important difference between NI and Income Tax is that while you no longer have to pay NI once you reach the state pension age, Income Tax has to be paid until your earnings no longer exceeds the tax free allowance shown in Row B, which could be at the state pension age upon retirement, or not until death.

The total amounts of Income Tax and National Insurance paid over the year for the different earnings levels is shown in Row J. The amount available to you after deducting these taxes is shown in Row K, and this known as *net income*, or disposable income, meaning income after payment of Income Tax and NI.

VAT

VAT is paid out of your *net income*. It is essentially a consumption tax, as it is only paid once you have bought something, meaning that although in theory it is possible to avoid VAT, in practice it would be hard to avoid paying as most goods and services incur VAT, with the notable exceptions of non-luxury foods and children's clothes. There are also different rates of VAT, but the standard VAT rate is 20%, and the average annual amount of VAT paid is £1,653 (Row L).

Excise duties

Excise duties are often termed 'sin' taxes, as they are applied to things that are seen as bad for the individual or society, such as cigarettes, alcohol, gambling and pollution. They are similar to VAT in that they are effectively a tax on consumption. But they differ from VAT in that while the VAT rate simply represents a percentage of the value of the product when it is sold, excise duties are additionally calculated on the amount of sin that is in the product. So for example, cigarette excise duty is calculated based on the weight of the cigarettes, so the more tobacco there is in the product the heavier it is and so the more the excise duty; similarly the more the alcohol content of product, the more excise duty paid, and the more a car pollutes the environment, the more car tax the owner has to pay. The average annual amount of all excise duties paid is £754 (Row M).

Council Tax

Council Tax is the tax paid to the local authority you live in for local services such as the police, fire, refuse collection, leisure facilities and social care. Councils have to by law provide some of these services, but others are discretionary. The amount of Council Tax you pay is dependent on the value of your house, regardless of whether you own it or not, with housing banded A–H, with A being the cheapest band and H the most expensive band. Council Tax rates also vary between different regions, but the annual average amount of Council Tax paid is £1,045 (Row N). Some people do not pay Council Tax, most notably students.

The combined annual average payment for VAT, Excise duties and Council Tax is shown in Row O. We can add this amount to the amount of Income Tax and NI paid (Row P). This enables us to calculate the *post-tax income*, which is income after all taxes have been paid (Row Q). Row R shows what percentage of the original gross income the amount of Total Tax paid represents for each income level.

Questions

1. What do you think about the levels of Income Tax and NI paid in each instance?

2. What do you notice about VAT and Council Tax?

3. Do you think that the amount of tax paid in each instance is fair or unfair?

How much taxation do I pay?

Despite the caution in the Explanatory Notes above, you should be able to use the simplified account of earnings and taxation shown in Table 4.2 to roughly calculate how much tax you pay, based on the earnings level closest to your own.

Table 4.1 also enables you to make numerous observations about the process of paying taxation and the implication of this process.

➤ Both Income Tax and National Insurance have allowances which means that you do not pay either of these taxes unless you earn above these allowances (Rows B and F).

➢ These allowances significantly reduce the amount of these taxes you pay in proportion to your gross earnings (Rows E and I). For example, anyone earning £10,000 and below pays no Income Tax (Row E) and only £270 National Insurance (Row I).

➢ The majority of people pay the basic rates of Income Tax and National Insurance of 20% and 12% respectively (Rows D and H). Most people do not earn enough to pay the higher rates of these taxes, which are £42,011 for Income Tax and £41,860 for NI. This is known as *graduated taxation*, meaning incomes are taxed at different rates of taxation.

➢ Income Tax is the main known type of tax paid, and with the exception of the £10,000 income level, for all income levels it is the largest amount of tax paid out of all the taxes shown (Row E).

➢ In work, taxes such as Income Tax and National Insurance contribute significant amounts of taxation (Row J), and so highlight the importance of work to the funding of social policy, as set out in the previous chapter. This explains why at times of high unemployment, social policy funding tends to come under stress, as has been recently shown with the austerity of the 2010 Coalition government.

➢ Both Income Tax and NI are specifically linked to your earnings level, which means that the higher your earnings, the more you pay (Rows K). This is known as *progressive taxation*.

➢ For VAT, Council Tax and Excise duties, the amount you pay is not specifically linked to the amount you earn. Instead, they are linked to how much you spend. This is known as *regressive taxation*, which means that those on lower earnings pay the same rate of tax as those on a higher earnings (Rows L, M, N), although in the case of Council Tax, you may get Council Tax Reduction if your income is low. The likelihood is that these amounts will be different depending on earnings levels, as expenditure differs depending on earnings levels. However, the case still stands that such taxes are regressive compared to income tax and national insurance (ONS, 2014b).

➢ Taxation can also be defined in terms of how it is paid. *Direct taxes* are taxes which are imposed directly on a person, as a consequence of their existence, and usually linked to their earnings. Both Income Tax and NI are direct taxes, and they are the main sources of government income. *Indirect taxes* are taxes on consumption and are collected by someone else on behalf of the government, and then paid to the government. In theory such indirect taxes can be avoided. VAT, Excise duties and Council Tax are all indirect taxes.

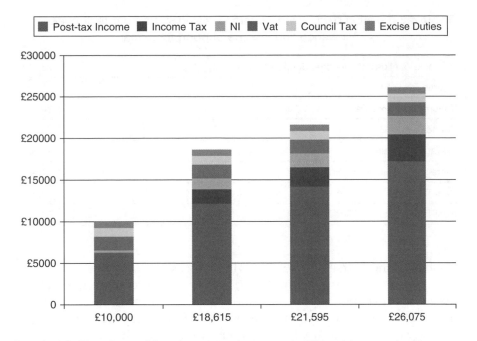

Graph 4.3 Taxation paid and post-tax income at different income levels

➤ Everyone pays taxation, regardless of their income level (Row P), and this is shown in Graph 4.3. Even those who do not pay *direct* work related taxes like Income Tax or National Insurance pay other taxes, as the nature of an *indirect* consumption tax like VAT means that even those who you would not normally think of paying tax, say someone who is unemployed or even an 11 year old, does pay tax, such as in the act of buying a soft drink.

➤ In general, individuals pay about a third of their income in the five main taxes shown (Row R). However, the income group that pays the most amount of taxation as a percentage of their gross income is the group who earn the least. This is because of the impact of regressive and indirect taxes such as VAT, Excise duties and Council Tax.

Do people who receive benefits like Jobseeker's Allowance and Income Support pay taxes?

Table 4.2 shows the amount of taxation paid by individuals receiving Jobseeker's Allowance and Income Support for a year.

Table 4.2 Taxation paid by individuals receiving standard rate Jobseeker's Allowance and Income Support for a year

Jobseeker's Allowance/Income Support Received	£3,764
Income Tax Paid	£0
National Insurance Paid	£0
Council Tax Paid	£0
Average VAT Paid	£1,653
Average Excise Duties Paid	£754
Total Tax Paid	**£2,407**
Total Tax Paid as % of Total Income	**63%**

Table 4.2 shows that a person receiving Jobseeker's Allowance and Income Support at the standard rate of £72.40 a week would receive £3,764 a year. This means that they do not pay *direct taxes* like Income Tax or National Insurance, because the yearly income received from these benefits of £3,764 a year is well below the Tax Free Allowance for Income Tax of £10,000 (Row B) and the National Insurance Contributions Allowance of £7,748 (Row F).

They also very likely do not pay some *indirect taxes* like Council Tax, as they would be eligible for the Council Tax exemption. However, they would be liable for other indirect taxes like VAT and Excise duties. The table shows that these would be a significant amount of the income of someone receiving these benefits. Indeed, using the same method of calculation as in Table 4.1 shows that they pay 63% of their income in these taxes. This is very likely a serious overestimation, but it does highlight the important points that those who receive these benefits *a)* do pay taxes, and *b)* pay a very large amount of their income in taxation overall.

How does the amount of taxation I pay compare to the amount of taxation funded benefits I receive?

To answer this, we have to separate social policy into two types.

There are benefits that are received in the form of cash. These are known as *cash benefits*, and examples of this are Jobseeker's Allowance, Income Support, Housing Benefit, Tax Credits and the State Pension.

There are also social policies that are received in the form of services either free at the time of use or at subsidized prices. These are known as *in-kind benefits*, and examples of this are healthcare, education, free school meals and free childcare.

The average value of cash benefits a person receives in a year is £5,990, while the average value of in-kind benefits a person receives in a year is £6,777 (ONS, 2014b). This totals £12,767 a year. We can compare these amounts to the amounts of taxation paid at all the income levels shown above. This is outlined in Table 4.3.

Table 4.3 Total taxation paid v. total benefits received

Annual gross earnings £	10,000	18,615	21,595	26,075
Cash benefits received	5,990	5,990	5,990	5,990
In-kind benefits received	6,777	6,777	6,777	6,777
Total cash and in-kind benefits received	**12,767**	**12,767**	**12,767**	**12,767**
Total tax paid (Row P in Table 4.1)	**3,722**	**6,479**	**7,432**	**8,866**
Difference between total benefits received and total tax paid	*–£9,045*	*–£6,288*	*–£5,335*	*–£3,901*

As Table 4.3 shows, for all earnings levels the difference between the total tax paid and the total benefits received is negative. This means that at these income levels, most people receive more benefits than the tax that they pay. Furthermore, the lower the gross earnings, the bigger the increase in the final income. This is relevant in the context of the observation above that those at the lower earnings level pay more as a proportion of their earnings in taxation than other income groups. This suggests that overall taxation works in a *progressively redistributive* way, that is it takes resources from the group that has the highest income and gives to the group that has the lowest income, to enable them to live adequately.

Would it be cheaper for me to pay for the social policy benefits I receive myself?

We can calculate an approximate cost per person of each taxation funded social policy provision using the data shown in Graph 4.1. We can do this by dividing the totals shown for each social policy area in Graph 4.1 by the estimated population of 62.3 million people. The results are shown in Table 4.4.

These figures show how much per person it costs to provide each taxation funded social policy benefit. As can be seen, the most expensive taxation funded benefit is income maintenance, while housing is the least expensive. The overall cost of all taxation funded social policy is £8,282 per person, per year. If we look at Column P in Table 4.1, we can see that

Table 4.4 Estimated cost of taxation funded social policy provision, per person, per year

	Social policy cost per person/year (£)
Housing	401
Personal social services	498
Education	1,573
Health	2,247
Income maintenance	3,563
Total	**8,282**

only at the income level of £26,075 do you pay more tax than the total cost of social policy benefits (Column P). At all the other income levels, you pay less tax than cost of taxation funded social policy. This means that the majority of people pay less taxation than the cost of providing social policy.

Again, for the reasons outlined above, this is not a true figure, as some people such as babies do not pay, meaning that the true cost of each provision for each person who does pay taxation is very likely higher. Also, not every person uses all of these services every year, usage will vary depending on age and circumstances, for example education usage is typically between the ages of 5 and 21 years. But the figures do provide us with a rough estimate of how much taxation each social policy provision cost.

Questions

Do you think that the estimated taxation cost for each provision is cheap or expensive?

Do you think that the estimated overall taxation cost is cheap or expensive?

I outlined above the viewpoint that taxation in general is 'unjust', as it does not allow individuals the freedom to spend their money as they wish. This claim has been applied specifically to taxation funded social policy provision, especially through organizations like *The Taxpayers' Alliance*, as part of an argument that such taxation funded social policy is too expensive and could be provided to the individual more efficiently and at less cost through the private market. This would require individuals to purchase equivalent social policy provision themselves, instead of paying taxation. The possible costs of such equivalent private social policy provision is detailed below.

Education

The main private alternative to taxpayer funded schooling is private schooling, either day schooling or boarding schooling. According to Broughton *et al.* (2014), the average cost of a private day school is £12,500 per year. The average fee for boarding is £28,500 per year.

Health

There are two ways in which alternative healthcare could be provided privately, either through Private Medical Insurance (PMI) or on a pay as you use basis. PMI costs less for healthy individuals than it does for unhealthy individuals, costs about 20% more for women than for men, and the costs also increase with age. For a healthy non-smoking male PMI costs approximately £1,000 per year, and £1,200 per year for a healthy non-smoking woman.

These costs are for the most comprehensive PMI treatments available, but it is important to note that PMI generally only provides 'acute' care, meaning care for conditions that are sudden but short term and likely to respond quickly to treatment, such as a broken bone or a hip or knee replacement. It does not however cover emergency treatment and treatment for 'chronic' conditions, meaning conditions that are pre-existing and/or ongoing, such as asthma or multiple sclerosis, nor does it cover routine medical care needed during pregnancy, childbirth or infertility treatment, terminal conditions, and cosmetic surgery; and any previous conditions will also not be covered. The MoneySavingExpert website (http://www.moneysavingexpert.com/insurance/cheap-health-insurance) provides a comprehensive list of exclusions from PMI. Additionally, PMI does not cover routine GP check-ups, which can vary in additional cost from £70 for 15 minutes to £128 for 30 minutes. As with all insurance, claiming for treatment means that premiums increase the next year.

The other alternative way in which health can be provided privately is to pay as treatment is required, essentially pay-as-you-go. This would also be required for those treatments not covered by PMI as detailed above. For example, the prices for giving birth in a private hospital, which is excluded from PMI, would be £7,500–£10,000. The average cost of treatment for a common sports injury, such as cruciate ligament injury, is £6,294, which is more than the premium required for PMI. A list of prices for the most common private healthcare procedures can be found at http://www.spirehealthcare.com/ImageFiles/Bristol/3726%20Spire%20Price%20List%202013.pdf. It is important to note that the cost for these pay-as-you-go treatments are more than the premium required for PMI, and the prices can also vary depending on where you live.

Personal social services
One of the most important personal social services provision is paying for care home residence. The annual average costs of care home residence is £28,000 (www.moneyadviceservice.org.uk, accessed 14 March 2014). This is the cost for someone with no additional care needs, such as requiring nursing care, as this would increase the cost.

Housing
The average rental cost in the UK is £665 per month, totalling £7,980 per year (Osbourne, 2014). A mortgage is slightly cheaper, at approximately £600 per month, totalling £7,200 per year (Rutter and Stocker, 2014). These figures are considerably higher in London.

Income maintenance
The cost of income maintenance as paid through Jobseeker's Allowance or Income Support is £3,728 a year for a single person over 25. This is intended to provide for food and pay bills. For comparison, this would be the minimum level of income that an individual would need to have to provide themselves with the same standard of living.

We can now compare these costs of paying for social policy benefits yourself with the cost of taxation funded social policy benefits. A summary of the cost of these private funded provision is shown in Table 4.5, in comparison to the cost of taxpayer funded provision.

Table 4.5 shows that the costs for all privately funded welfare is more than the cost of taxpayer funded social policy welfare, with the possible exception of health. The range of total costs for private funded social policy provision takes into account the different levels of provision that can be purchased. The lower total of £52,435 assumes that the cheapest options for each type of provision is purchased (private day school, PMI healthy non-smoking male, private care home room, mortgage, JSA/IS

Table 4.5 Comparison cost of taxation and privately funded social policy provision

	Taxation funded cost per person/year (£)	Private funded cost per person/year (£)
Education	£1,573	Private day school – £12,500 Boarding school – £28,500
Health	£2,247	Private Medical Insurance Healthy non-smoking male – £1,000 Health non-smoking female – £1,200
		Private birth – £7,500–10,000
		15 minute GP consultation – £70
Personal social services	£498	Private care home room – £28,000
Housing	£401	Private rental year – £7,980 Mortgage – £7,207
Income maintenance	£3,563	JSA/IS single person (over 25) – £3,728
Total	**£8,282**	**£52,435–79,478**

single person), while the higher total of £79,478 assumes that the most expensive type of provision for each is purchased (boarding school, healthy non-smoking female, private birth, one 15 minute GP consultation, private rental and JSA/IS single person). The difference between these lower and higher cost is £27,043, which is almost as much as the mean earnings.

Real Life Box 4.1 **The $200,000 private cost of delivering a baby**

The 2014 case of a British couple who went on holiday in America while pregnant and had an 11 week premature baby exemplifies the high cost of paying for social policy benefits yourself, particularly health benefits.

In America most health costs are paid for by the individual through taking out insurance and are not taxation funded. This means that those without insurance are expected to meet the costs of any healthcare needed, with some exceptions. Because the British couple did not have insurance they were liable for the costs of the treatments they received when the baby was born, and this was estimated at $200,000, equivalent to £131,000. However, after some controversy, these costs were written off by the hospital.

Table 4.6 compares the difference between the amount taxation paid at the different income levels and the cost of privately funded social policy benefits.

Table 4.6 Difference between taxation paid and cost of privately funded social policy benefits

Income level	Taxation paid	Range of costs of privately funded benefits	Difference: taxation paid and privately funded benefits costs
£10,000	£3,722	£52,435–£79,478	–£48,713 to £75,756
£18,615	£6,479	£52,435–£79,478	–£45,956 to £72,999
£21,595	£7,432	£52,435–£79,478	–£45,003 to £72,046
£26,075	£8,866	£52,435–£79,478	–£43,569 to £70,612

As Table 4.6 shows, the difference between the amount of taxation paid and the cost of privately funded social policy benefits is very large, ranging between a deficit of £48,713 to £75,756 for those on the lower income. This suggests that the cost of providing social policy benefits yourself are much higher that the amount of taxation you pay, and the amount of tax that the majority of people pay as shown in Column P of Table 4.1.

What are the important principles that underpin taxation funded social policy?

The points above enable us to observe several important points about the principles that underpin taxation funded social policy, as detailed below.

Taxation means that everyone pays and receives social policy provision

People not only pay taxation at different levels depending on their income levels, they also receive provision at different levels of social policy provision depending on their circumstances. They are often both taxpayers and recipients of social policy at the same time, even though it might not be obvious that this is the case (e.g. healthcare and education). Even those who are low paid and in receipt of benefits such as Income Support and Jobseeker's Allowance contribute to taxation, as a consequence of indirect taxes which cannot reasonably be avoided.

Buying welfare services yourself is expensive in comparison to taxation funded social policy provision for individuals

For none of the social policy benefits is the private funded cost cheaper than taxation funded cost, with the possible exception of health. Indeed, the difference between the total amount of taxation paid at all the income levels and total costs of private funded social policy is huge. This suggests that for the majority of individuals, relying solely on their gross income to meet their welfare needs is not realistic, and taxation funded social policy provision reduces the deficit that exists between income and costs. A good example of this is the cost of compulsory education over a lifetime. Compulsory education is from the ages of 5 to 18, which is 13 years. In Table 4.4, we calculated the cost of taxation funded education at £1,557 per year, which over 13 years works out at £20,449. We also calculated the cost of private day schooling at £12,500 per year, which over 13 years is £162,500. Therefore private schooling costs approximately eight times more than taxation funded schooling. To put it another way, the cost of 13 years of private schooling is equivalent to the cost of 104 years of taxation funded schooling, which makes it prohibitively expensive for most people.

Taxation funded social policy functions as a 'Savings Bank'

Social policy needs are ongoing at all points of an individual's life, and vary with circumstances. Very often, however, the costs are at the highest when the individual can least afford it, such as for example the cost of education or the cost of care for the elderly. This was something that was specifically identified by Seebohm Rowntree in his 'Lifecycle of poverty' as detailed on Figure 3.1 in Chapter 3. Rowntree's analysis showed that on the one hand, individuals are more likely to be above the poverty line when they initially leave the family home and find work, and again when their children move out of the family home. On the other hand, they are more likely to be below the poverty line when young, when they have children, and when they are old and unable to work. However, these times below the poverty line are also when individuals are more likely to need social policy provision, and also the times when they are less likely to be able to meet the costs of social policy benefits. These times of greatest need below the poverty line are also the times of least resources, which is very problematic for the individual and also for the funding of social policy as it is when individuals are least likely to be able to contribute to the funding of social policy. This problem is overcome by the way that social policy functions as a *savings bank* (Barr, 2001), as shown in Figure 4.1.

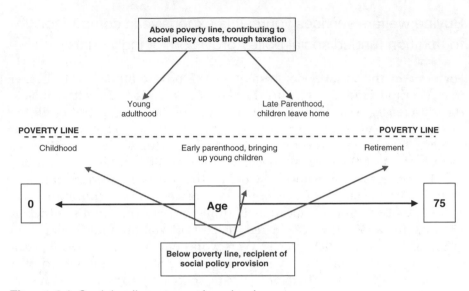

Figure 4.1 Social policy as a savings bank

A savings bank is something that you save into at times of plenty in order to withdraw from on a rainy day. Rowntree's modified lifecycle of poverty above highlights how taxation funded social policy provision works in similar way, as it functions through individuals contributing to social policy cost through taxation at times of plenty e.g. when above the poverty line. This means that at these times you will be using less social policy provision, but contributing more in taxation to funding social policy. Having contributed to funds at times of plenty, you are able to withdraw funds at times of need e.g. when below the poverty line. This means that at these times you will be using more social policy provision, but contributing less to its funding through taxation, but this will be balanced out by the contribution made when above the poverty line.

Taxation funded social policy enables risks to be 'pooled', which reduces the cost to the individual of specific events

Linked to the notion of a savings bank is the way that taxation reduces the risk to the individual. Another important feature of Rowntree's lifecycle of poverty is that it showed that the occurrence of poverty could be predicted upon the stage in life that every person goes through for example, being young, having children and being old. However, there are other specific events which can cause an individual to fall into poverty, such as becoming ill, losing your job or the death of the main earner in the family, which can also impact prohibitively on the individual. These events will not necessarily affect everyone, but there is a chance that at least one of them could affect you at some time. In everyday life, the way we try to reduce the effect of such statistically likely events like these is to take out insurance, similar to insuring your home against burglary or your car against an accident. But insurance for life events could be very expensive and, as we saw with health insurance and perhaps as you have experienced when claiming on an insurance policy, can also have lots of exclusions. However taxation generally reduces the cost of these events, such as having to go into a care home, by spreading, or pooling, the risk among many more individuals that it affects, over a longer period of time. This means that in the likelihood that a statistically predictable event occurs, the cost to the individual at the time it happens is less that it would be if they had to pay it themselves. It would be possible to reduce taxation by reducing the risks that it insures against, for example, by not providing healthcare and leaving it to the individual to provide. This, however, would mean that the individual would have to bear the risk of these events happening, which could have huge cost implications for the individual. So a comprehensive system of social policy funded by pooled taxation tends to reduce these risks that the individual faces.

Summary

The aim of this chapter has been to consider whether you pay too much taxation for the social policy you receive. This is important because taxation is the main way in which social policy is paid for, and is also one of the most contentious aspects of individual lives. There are alternative viewpoints about paying taxation, with some seeing it as a theft and others as a necessary aspect of a developed society.

A key point that the chapter has shown is that everyone pays taxation, regardless of income. This includes the young, the unemployed, the sick and the old. And those who earn the least pay the most as a proportion of their income. This is because of the difference between direct and indirect taxes. This is important to note when we consider the benefits that different groups receive, and that some groups are seen as less deserving than others because they are perceived as not having paid tax. We also saw that while there are some redistributive elements of taxation, overall the taxation system is regressive, meaning that those who earn the least pay the most as a proportion of their income.

This chapter has shown that for most people, the amount of tax you pay does not equal the amount of social policy benefits they receive, but not in the way that most people think. Actually, the amount of tax most people pay is considerably less than the amount of social policy benefits they receive.

This difference between what you pay for in taxation and what you receive becomes even more apparent when we compare the cost of paying for welfare services yourself. This shows that in most circumstances, paying for your welfare needs yourself is prohibitively expensive and you would not be able to meet all the welfare needs that taxation funded social policy provides.

There are important principles of *pooling* and *savings bank* that under-pin taxation funded social policy. These principles mean that the cost of meeting important welfare needs are significantly less than they would be without taxation funded social policy. So in answer to the question posed, most people pay less for taxation funded social policy than they would if they had to meet their welfare needs themselves.

Key Point

For most people the amount of tax they pay is less that the amount of social policies that they receive, especially if we compare the high costs of paying for the equivalent benefits yourself.

Keywords

Gross earnings

Earnings before the payment of any taxation.

Net income

Income available after the payment of Income Tax and National Insurance.

Post-tax income

Income available after the payment of all taxes.

Final income

Post-tax income plus all social policy provision received.

Disposable income

Income available after the deduction of all taxation has been deducted and benefits of all types (*cash benefits* and *in-kind benefits*) have been added.

In-kind benefits

These are also social policies which are received in the form of services either free at the time of use or at subsidized prices, such as healthcare, education, free school meals and free childcare.

Cash benefits

These are social policies that are received in the form of cash, for example Jobseeker's Allowance, Income Support, Housing Benefit, tax credits, and pensions.

Graduated taxation

Taxation for which there are different levels to pay depending on the amount of income that an individual has.

Progressive taxation

Taxation where the outcome is that those who have the lowest income pay the least, and vice versa.

Regressive taxation

Taxation where the outcome is that those who have the lowest income pay the most, and vice versa.

Direct taxation

Taxation which is imposed directly on a person, as a consequence of their existence, and usually linked to their income, such as Income Tax and NI.

Indirect taxation

Taxation on consumption, which is collected by someone else on behalf of the government and then paid to the government, such as VAT and Excise duties; in theory such indirect taxes can be avoided.

5

CAN SOCIAL POLICY SOLVE THE PROBLEM OF POVERTY?

The aims of this chapter are to:

1. **Outline the two main ways that poverty is defined, and discuss the strengths and limitations of these two definitions of poverty**

2. **Detail the official poverty line in the UK, and how it is measured**

3. **Analyse the number of people who live in poverty in the UK, and the main categories of people living in poverty**

4. **Discuss the two main reasons why people are in poverty**

Throughout this book so far, we have seen that tackling poverty has been a major focus of social policy in the past and the present. It has been one of the main reasons for the development of the welfare state, from the Liberal government at the turn of the 20th century to Beveridge's attack on the 'five evil giants', and continues to be an important focus of all current governments. This chapter analyses the reasons for this continued significance of poverty to social policy, and possible ways in which social policy can reduce the levels of poverty that exist.

The chapter starts by defining what we mean by poverty, and the two main ways in which we define poverty. It will then describe in detail both of these main definitions, exploring their strengths and weaknesses, and the implications of using one definition over another. There is an official poverty line in the UK, and the chapter specifies this to determine the extent of official poverty in the UK. The chapter then analyses who are the main categories of people in official poverty, and the particular importance of family status and work to high levels of poverty. An analysis of the reasons why individuals are in official poverty will lead on to a discussion of how effective the current levels of social policy income benefits are at stopping unemployed people falling below the official poverty line and into poverty.

By the end of this chapter, you will understand the two main ways in which we define poverty, and what the official poverty line is in the UK. You will also have an understanding of the extent of poverty in the UK and the risk that certain groups have of falling into poverty. You will also understand how low income from both work and social policy contributes significantly to poverty in the UK, and from this be able to articulate the main issues that social policy faces when trying to reduce levels of poverty in the UK.

What is poverty?

'Poverty' is a very emotive word which for most people has clear implications that something should be done about it. This is why defining what we mean by poverty is very important, as it also enables us to decide the necessary social policies to deal with it. However, this is not as easy as it would seem, as there are a variety of terms which refer to poverty but all with different meanings, such as 'social exclusion', 'deprivation', 'low income', and 'disadvantage'. Despite this, we can categorize these terms as referring to two main types of poverty, '*absolute poverty*' and '*relative poverty*'.

Absolute poverty

Absolute poverty is a type of poverty based on the measurement of the absolute minimum a person requires for biological survival. This means that a person is only defined as being in poverty in the absence of biological necessities such as:

> food;

> water;

> warmth;

> clothing;

> shelter.

The key point about these biological necessities, and therefore the notion of absolute poverty, is that the absence of these biological necessities would ultimately result in death.

In the UK, as most of these needs have to be purchased with money, this type of poverty is often termed 'income poverty'. This type of poverty has the apparent benefit of being simple to observe and therefore easy to measure, as we can easily see who does not have these biological necessities.

This means that we can easily see who is in poverty and who is not, making it easy to put in place social policies to deal with this type of poverty. For some, it also enables a clear distinction to be made between the level of poverty seen in a developed country like the UK to that seen in developing countries, making it obvious that such absolute poverty does not really exist in the UK.

However, there are some important limitations to this type of poverty. Firstly, there is the problem of defining what the absolute minimum should be. Taking food as an example, the absolute minimum has in the past been specifically counted and categorized to give the daily amount of food that a person needs to avoid being in poverty, and today we talk about a person needed a certain number of calories per day. However, the amount of food that a person needs varies from person to person, and also varies depending on the activity being done, with the more physical the activity the more calories required. So an absolute measurement of poverty based on required food would not be able to take these differences into consideration and would be wrong in a significant number of instances if it was applied.

This leads on to a second criticism of absolute poverty types, which is that they provide arbitrary cut-off points of whether or not someone is in poverty. So, to continue with food as an example, the required daily calories for the average male is 2,500 calories, which could act as a cut-off point as to whether someone is suffering from food poverty or not. This would mean that someone who consumes 2,501 calories would not be considered as being in poverty, even though their calorific food intake is essentially the same. To most people, this would seem very arbitrary and harsh.

Another problem with absolute measurements of poverty is they make some heroic assumptions and expectations about what people in poverty should or should not be doing with their time and money. To take the example of clothing, the assumption with absolute poverty is that the clothes that people in poverty buy are of certain quality which lasts for a number of years and that people repair and mend them when they are torn, and only replace them after a certain period of time. However, Oscar Wilde in 1891 made the relevant observation that '*Sometimes the poor are praised for being thrifty. But to recommend thrift to the poor is both grotesque and insulting. It is like advising a man who is starving to eat less.*'

Moreover, if you are living in poverty, the likelihood is that you cannot afford the quality of clothes that those on higher incomes can, so this means that your clothes will very likely last less time and need to be replaced more often. There are also 'incidental costs' which can suddenly and significantly affect the income of an individual on a strict budget, such as if their cooker breaks down. Replacing a cooker would be a huge expense and would impact on their income over a significant period of time. This shows that an absolute measure of poverty does not take into account the reality of living in poverty in terms of the heroic assumptions made about living in poverty.

Linked to this is the fact that living in poverty can also mean higher costs than for those not living in poverty. A good example of this is in relation to paying for household fuel, as there are a variety of ways in which this can be done. The cheapest is paying by direct debit, while the most expensive is paying by a pre-payment meter. Those who tend to pay by a pre-payment meter are those living in poverty, because they cannot afford the large upfront direct debit cost, and need to have a ready supply of money to hand for other things. The effect of this is known as the 'poverty premium' (Westlake, 2011), where those in poverty have to pay many hundreds of pounds more for basic goods, services and heating than the better-off. Other examples of it are shown in Table 5.1.

Table 5.1 Normal costs v. poverty premium

Normal costs	Poverty premium
Direct debit payment	Pre-payment meter
Bulk buying of foods	Single buying of foods
Cash purchases of good	Credit purchases of goods
One-off payment for insurance	Monthly payment for insurance
Use of car for transport	Use of public transport

According to Westlake (2011), this poverty premium means an extra £1,300 a year in costs for those in poverty. An absolute poverty lines assumes that everyone has the same costs and ignores these poverty premium factors, which underestimates the true costs of poverty.

Absolute poverty also does not take into account the things that people might need to improve their well-being, beyond their basic biological needs. For instance, consider for a moment how your life would be if the only things you had money to purchase were the minimum required food, clothing, shelter, water and warmth. This would mean that you would not be able to purchase things for leisure such as books, things for pleasure such as a TV, or things for socializing such as transport. This would very likely impact on your well-being in the long term.

Finally, by their nature, absolute measures of poverty rarely change over time, as they are linked to biological necessities. For example, for some measures of absolute poverty, such as food, the emphasis is still on the biological necessity required for existence. This continued emphasis on a biological necessity is problematic when we consider the fact that standards of acceptable health and food quality have changed over time, meaning that what we thought as acceptable in the past is rarely seen as acceptable now. So the fact that we would not now accept the slum circumstances for housing and sanitation that were seen as acceptable for someone living 150 years ago as detailed in Chapter 3 suggests that biological necessities are an artefact of their time, rather than a factual account of poverty.

Questions

1. Do you think the notion of absolute poverty is relevant?
2. Is anybody in Britain today in absolute poverty?

Relative poverty

Relative poverty is essentially when an individual's standard of living is compared to those around them, or to what others might reasonably be expected to have, not to a set absolute minimum. It is based on the notion that an individual should have a life beyond an existence on the absolute minimum, to enable them to live a life that is at least comparable to what would be considered as acceptable within a society. In contrast to absolute poverty's focus on the absolute biological minimum that a person needs, relative poverty's focus is more about how the living standards of an individual compares to the living standards within a group or society. So if an individual's living standards are below the average living standards within society they would be considered as in relative poverty.

As these average standards are usually above the absolute minimum that a person needs, this can mean that while an individual is not classed as in absolute poverty, they could still be classed as in relative poverty. Peter Townsend's (1979) work in particular has been important in developing the notion of relative poverty as a different from absolute poverty.

A good example of this difference is in relation to absolute housing poverty and relative housing poverty. Absolute poverty's focus would principally be on whether a person has a house to live in; however, relative poverty would also consider the standard of housing that the person lives in and how this compares to the standard of housing of other individuals. This means that the definition of relative poverty is wider than absolute poverty, to include the actual living conditions that an individual is experiencing, as shown below by the list of things that could be defined as relative poverty:

➤ lack of educational opportunity;
➤ absence of material possessions;

➢ inadequate health care;

➢ lack of good quality housing;

➢ denial of civil rights;

➢ lack of social opportunities.

Because the relative definition of poverty changes over time as living standards change, it has the advantage of ensuring that levels of poverty do not lead to such wide gaps between groups. So, for example, if housing standards improve within society, so the definition of relative housing poverty improves, meaning that the housing standards of those in relative poverty maintain the link to the rest of society. This is highlighted in Graph 5.1, which shows how the percentage of ownership of goods within society has changed over time.

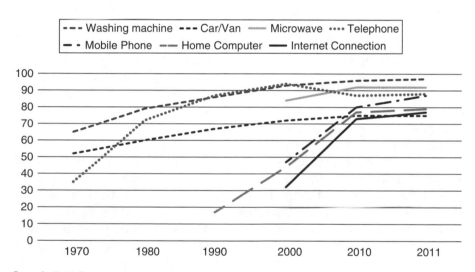

Graph 5.1 Percentage of households with durable goods 1970–2011
Source: ONS, 2012a: Table A45

As Graph 5.1 shows, there are some goods which few people owned 20 years ago, but which are now near universal, such as a home computer, a microwave, a mobile phone and internet connection. It is very unlikely that an absolute measure of poverty would consider the lack of ownership of any of these goods as biologically essential, and therefore not having them would not mean that an individual is in absolute poverty. However, a relative measure of poverty would consider a lack of ownership of these goods as meaning that an individual is in poverty. This is because, to take the ownership of washing machines and microwaves as examples, the fact that almost everyone in society has one of these would imply that the living standards of those who do not have one is below the norms of society, and would be a criterion for considering someone to be in relative poverty. This supports the claim that poverty changes over time and so poverty should be defined in a relative way, linked to the changing standards within society.

An obvious implication of this for social policy is that it requires more extensive benefits than for absolute poverty, as maintaining the link between those in relative poverty and those not in poverty necessitates extensive social provision. This in itself leads to the criticism of the relative poverty approach that trying to maintain the link between the living standards of those in relative poverty and the rest of society can be quite expensive, especially if living standards in general increase in a significant way. Also, as there are always more people classified as being in relative poverty than in absolute poverty, this would also increase the cost, and this is one of the reasons why relative poverty measures are sometimes not adopted by governments.

This is linked to the issue of how often relative poverty standards and measurements should be updated. Some things like housing standards can change very slowly, but others can change very quickly. The most interesting observation from Graph 5.1 is the huge growth in ownership of recent goods such as access to the internet, mobile phones and home computers. And it is clear that something like internet access is now a very important requirement for work, school and access to a whole host of other services, including accessing social policy benefits, in a way that it was not five years ago. For example, having internet access at home for children has been linked to higher attainment at school compared with those who do not have internet access at home (Boffey, 2011). And not being able to pay bills by the internet means paying £440 more each year than for those with internet access (Smithers, 2014). This suggests the need to constantly update relative poverty measures, which can be time-consuming and expensive to do, and makes it difficult to understand what relative poverty is today, as opposed to relative poverty last year.

Relative poverty's emphasis on the quality of living standards is also not as easy to understand as absolute poverty, as evident from the explanations above. Most people think of poverty in terms of whether someone has a lack of a specific thing now, not in terms of the overall quality of something and the way that this quality impacts on their life. For example, it is easier to describe poverty in relation to education in terms of simply not having an education, rather than the quality of schooling that an individual receives, even though this can be very important to the outcomes. This is one of the reasons why perhaps most people might think that in comparison to other countries, there is no education poverty in the UK, as schooling exists for all. This is made even more difficult by the fact that the relative definition of poverty needs constant updating as described above.

It can also be difficult to get agreement on the difference between those things that are essential to an individual relative to the rest of society, and those things that are a luxury for individuals. Most people would perhaps accept that having an internet connection is important for individuals in society, but Graph 5.1 also shows that the vast majority of the population also have a mobile phone. However, for some people having a mobile phone is not an essential but a luxury, and so for them to link not having a mobile phone with poverty is not a true reflection of poverty, even though most individuals in society have one. The exercise below should emphasize the difficulties in determining what is essential and what is non-essential.

Real Life Box 5.1 **Essential or non-essential items for living?**

➤ Look at the list of things below, and decide which category in the table each item falls into (write the number of each in the table).

➤ Compare your answers with a friend.

➤ Did you get all the same items in the same category?

1. Able to afford carpets and other floor coverings

2. Having a refrigerator, freezer or fridge-freezer

3. Able to buy second hand clothes

4. Giving pocket money to children

5. Able to afford trips out with school

6. Eating meat at least once a week

7. Owning a car

8. Having a washing machine

9. Having a TV

10. Having broadband internet connection

11. Having Sky or similar subscription

12. Having a landline telephone

13. Having a mobile phone

14. Having a microwave

15. Having access to clean water

▶

16. Able to afford to have friends/family for a meal once a month

17. Not living in overcrowded housing

18. Having a place to live

19. Having central heating

20. Able to do a leisure activity once a week

21. Having a holiday abroad once a year

22. Eating out once a month

23. Going to the barbers/hairdressers once a month

24. Having a games system i.e. PS2, Wii

25. Able to buy new clothes

Essential	Non essential but important	Non essential and not important

While you might have agreed on which category some items belonged to, it is very unlikely that you agreed on all the items. This highlights the problematic nature of categorizing which things are essential to an individual relative to the rest of society, and which things are a luxury for individuals. This is important because when things that some might perceive as a luxury are classified as relating to poverty, then ownership of them can breed resentment towards those deemed to be in poverty from those not deemed to be in poverty.

The final criticism of a relative measure of poverty is the fact that, by its very nature, relative poverty is almost impossible to eradicate. This is because no matter how much a society improves, some people will always have less than others, and so always be relatively worse off. This means that in relative terms, poverty will always exist, even in a well-off society. This contrasts the usability of a relative measure of poverty over an absolute one, which can provide a definitive account of when poverty is eradicated (Townsend, 1979).

It should have become obvious to you by now that deciding on the number of people in poverty depends on the way that poverty is defined. An absolute definition of poverty will result in fewer people defined as being in poverty than a relative definition of poverty. And of course, the chosen definition also has implications for the type of social policies that are put in place. This becomes very evident when we look at the way that the government defines poverty in the UK.

Question

What are the different implications for social policy of adopting an absolute or a relative measurement of poverty?

How is poverty defined in the UK?

The UK government has a specific definition of poverty, which is:

Low income households are defined as *households* with *income below 60% of the median*, as reported in the Households Below Average Income statistics.

The two emphasized points above are key to understanding this definition, as they refer to the following:

➤ *Income below 60% of the median income* – poverty for the government is defined in terms of income, or specifically the lack of income. The median means dividing the population in half in terms of their income, which would give the income level which 50% of people are above, and 50% are below. Having 60% of this median translates into an income that the lowest 30% of the population have. This is shown in Figure 5.1.

➤ *Households* – the measurement of poverty is at the household level not the individual level. A household can consist of one person or numerous persons, and where it consists of more than one person, all the incomes are added together. This means that the whole income of the household is taken into consideration when deciding if a person is living in poverty. This is important because a person could have an income below the poverty level, but because they live in a household where someone else earns considerably above the poverty level, they would not be considered to be in poverty.

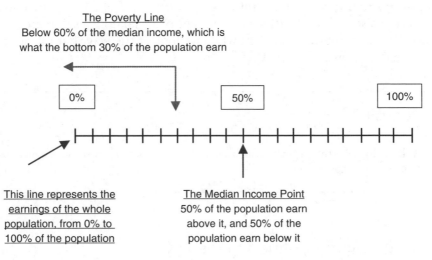

Figure 5.1 The official poverty line

The median earning figures given in Table 4.1 in Chapter 4 are for the earnings from employment only. A different figure has to be used to calculate the poverty levels, to include not just earnings, but all income, including income from social policy benefits. This is called *total income* and includes income from all sources, from all members of the household, before deductions of Income Tax and National Insurance, and including any tax credits and some benefits in-kind.

Using the latest government data available from 2012–2013 (DWP, 2014b) shows median *total income* at £440 per week. 60% of this median *total income* is £264 per week, which works out at £13,728 per year. This is the maximum income level of the lowest 30% of households, as shown in Figure 5.1. It is the income level that the government uses to determine who is in poverty, meaning that anyone living in a household with an income below £264 a week OR £13,712 a year is classified as being below the poverty line, and therefore in poverty.

The £264 per week official poverty line – inclusion and exclusions

Included in the poverty line total income amount are:

➤ *net* earnings from employment;

➤ all Social Security and tax credits *cash benefits*;

➤ the cash value of certain forms of *in-kind* benefits (e.g. free school meals, Healthy Start vouchers and free school milk and free TV licence for those aged 75 and over);

➤ income from occupational and private pensions;

➤ profit or loss from self-employment (losses are treated as a negative income);

➤ investment income (e.g. interest onshares and savings);

➤ maintenance payments, if a person receives them directly;

➤ income from educational grants and scholarships (including, for students, top-up loans and parental contributions).

Excluded from the poverty line total income amount are:

➤ income tax payments;

➤ National Insurance payments;

➤ domestic rates / council tax payments;

➤ contributions to occupational pension schemes;

➤ all maintenance and child support payments, which are deducted from the income of the person making the payment;

➤ parental contributions to students living away from home;

➤ student loan repayments.

Does the official poverty line reflect absolute or relative poverty?

There are two reasons why we could describe this official poverty line as reflecting absolute rather than relative poverty. The first is that the figure does not reflect the average income in any sense, but a figure well below the average. This means that anyone below the poverty line and therefore in poverty has a living standard which is significantly below that of the average person in the population.

The second reason is the nature of the cut-off point. Using such a cut-off point suggests that someone is in poverty if their income is below £264 per week, but not in poverty if their income is £265 per week. This suggests that poverty can be clearly defined in terms of an absolute level of income that is required to exist, with little consideration for the quality of life that such income could purchase.

On the other hand, the poverty line above could also be described as relative, as to some extent the level of existence that it enables is above the basic subsistence levels described above for absolute poverty. This means that, for example, instances of individuals starving are rare, although this is sometimes due to the additional support that is provided by social policy benefits, such as through Tax Credits. This poverty line amount is also modified year by year as income levels change, meaning that there is some relative relationship between the income of the population and those below the poverty line.

Overall, the official poverty line reflects elements of both absolute and relative poverty definition, but the fact that it is well below the average income of the population leans it more towards absolute poverty than relative poverty.

How many people are officially in poverty?

We could use the official poverty line of £264 per week to calculate how many people are below the poverty line, and therefore officially in poverty. However, there is a significant problem with using this poverty line as it stands. This is the fact that it does not take into account that different people live in different household sizes, and this can affect the amount of income that they need. We can assume that a household with a single person in it needs less income than a household with two adults and two children, as having children has a significant impact on the costs of a household, but the official poverty line above does not reflect this significant impact.

Income equivalization

To take account of this, we need to modify this poverty line for the different needs that different household sizes face. This is called 'income equivalization', and means that income is adjusted to take into account household size and composition. So, the more people living in a house, the higher the income requirement is, and the fewer people living in the house, the lower the income requirements is (see Jin *et al.*, 2011: 73 for a more detailed explanation). Table 5.2 shows the income equivalence scales for the official poverty line income of £264 per week.

Table 5.2 Equivalized income scales

People in household	Equivalence	Poverty line income
Couple	100%	£264.00
Single adult	67%	£176.88
Additional adult	33%	£87.12
Child aged over 14	33%	£87.12
Child aged under 14	20%	£52.80

Table 5.2 shows that £264 per week represents the poverty line for a couple household. For a single person household the poverty would represent 67% of £264, which is £176.88. For each additional adult or child over 14 it would be £87.12. For a child under 14, it is £52.80. We add or subtract these figures from the £264 poverty line depending on the household size, as shown in the calculations below.

Real Life Box 5.2 **Calculating the equivalized poverty line**

Example 1: Single adult household

Single adult	= 67%	= £176.88
Equivalized poverty line		**= £176.88**

Example 2: Couple household with one child over 14 and one child under 14:

Couple	= 100%	= £264.00
+ Child aged over 14	= 33%	= £87.12
+ Child aged under 14	= 20%	= £52.80
Equivalized poverty line		**= £403.92**

Example 3: Single parent household with one child under 14:

Single adult	= 67%	= £176.88
+ Child aged under 14	= 20%	= £52.80
Equivalized poverty line		**= £229.68**

The equivalized calculations show that generally the more people in a household, the higher the poverty line amount, and vice versa. Using the equivalized calculations, we can now provide a more accurate calculation of the amount of people in poverty, linked to their household size.

The government officially states that the number of people in poverty in the UK totals 9.7 million people (DWP, 2014b). This represents approximately 15% of the population. Of these, the majority is households with children, which perhaps should not surprise us considering what we know from Chapter 3 about Rowntree's lifecycle and risk of poverty. Pensioner households also had a high incidence of poverty.

Real Life Box 5.3 **Are you above or below the poverty line?**

Using the figures from Table 5.2, calculate what the poverty line is for your household.

➢ Is this above or below the income level of your household?

➢ Are you above or below the official poverty line?

Are there more people in poverty than the government says?

Accepting that the official number in poverty represents all of those in poverty is problematic for an important reason. This is because the official poverty line represents an income figure before housing costs (BHC). This means that from their income, individuals would still be expected to pay any housing costs such as rent or mortgage, but not council tax. This is problematic for a number of reasons:

➢ Whereas something like food cost may not vary greatly in similar households, the cost of housing can vary greatly depending on where you live and the type of accommodation. Two households living in similar housing in London and Birmingham would very likely be paying very different housing costs. This means that the amount of income they would have after their housing costs would be different, which would also impact on their living standards.

➢ Another issue is due to the way increasing housing costs are paid, which can distort the number of people in poverty. For example, the rent for someone who receives Housing Benefit might be increased by

£10 a week. If this increased amount is paid in full by Housing Benefit, this means that the income of the person has gone up by £10 a week, as income from income maintenance benefits is included in the calculating the official poverty line. If this person's *disposable income* before the rent increase is just below the official poverty line, say £250 a week, this extra £10 would take them above the official poverty line, and therefore officially no longer in poverty. However, this £10 would go straight to their landlord, meaning that in reality, their *disposable income* has not increased. They would still have the same actual amount of income to spend as they had before their rent increased, and therefore their living standards have not improved. The principle is the same for those paying a mortgage, where an increase in *disposable* income that takes a person above the poverty might be wiped out by an increase in mortgage costs (Jin *et al.*, 2011).

➤ A final problem is the difference in *disposable income* between those who own their homes outright and those who do not. Imagine two people who earn the same amount, but one person has paid off their mortgage and the other is still paying their mortgage. If we calculate their incomes before housing costs, they would both have the same income, and therefore standard of living. It is only by calculating their incomes after housing costs that a difference in living standards become apparent, as the person paying the mortgage would have a lower disposable income and therefore a lower standard of living. Pensioners are a good example of a group where this difference is important, as while 70% of over 65s own their homes outright, 30% do not, and when housing costs are taken into account pensioner poverty falls from 20.4% to 16% (HomeOwners Alliance, 2012)

Real Life Box 5.4 **Housing costs**

1. Calculate your total income

2. Now calculate how much you spend per week, month or year on your housing costs

3. Now deduct your housing costs from your total income

   ➤ How much of your total income does housing costs represent?

   ➤ Are your housing costs the highest costs you have, out of all your costs?

   ➤ Does deducting your housing costs from your total income make a major difference to how rich/poor you feel?

For these reasons, determining the poverty line before housing costs (BHC) are paid is seen as problematic. Instead, determining the poverty line after housing costs (AHC) is seen as a more accurate measurement of poverty, and of the number of people in poverty. If we use the income AHC figure, then the poverty line reduces to £224 per week, which is £40 per week less, or 15% lower. We then have to calculate equivalized income figures as explained above, and these are shown below in Table 5.3.

Table 5.3 Equivalized income poverty lines, AHC

Household type	Equivalized weekly poverty line AHC	Equivalized yearly poverty line AHC
Single adult with no dependent children	£150.08	£7,804
Couple with no dependent children	£224.00	£11,648
Single adult with two dependent children under 14	£239.50	£12,459
Couple with two dependent children under 14	£313.60	£16,307

Question

Do these AHC poverty lines seem more reasonable to you than the BHC poverty lines in relation to the household type?

Using AHC significantly changes the amount of people living in poverty in the UK. The amount of people in AHC poverty in the UK now totals 13.2 million people (DWP, 2014b). This is 3.5 million more people than the government's official number of people living in poverty. It is approximately 21% of the population, which is one out of every five people. The AHC poverty line is the figure that is used in the graphs and data below, unless stated otherwise.

Question

Does the amount of people living in AHC poverty surprise you?

Which groups are most likely to be poor?

There are two main factors that determine which groups are most likely to be in poverty. These are the household type that an individual is living in, and their work status.

Household type

Graph 5.2 shows the levels of poverty by household type.

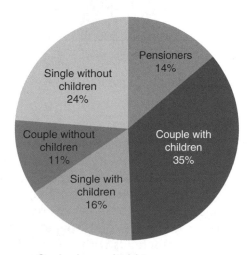

Graph 5.2 Who is poor? – by household type
Source: DWP, 2014b

We can see that couples with children are the households that have the highest levels of poverty. The level of poverty for a couple household with children (35%) is three times that a couple household without children (11%). Indeed, if we add all the households with children in poverty ('Couple with children' and 'Single with children'), we can see that households with children make up the majority of households in poverty, at 51%. So having children presents a significant risk of living in poverty.

Single person households without children also have high levels of poverty (24%), and together with couple households with children, these make up 35% of those in poverty. This suggests that living alone and not having children also has a significant risk of poverty. We can look at this in more detail by comparing the levels of poverty between all households with children and all households without children. This is shown in Graph 5.3, which compares the levels of poverty with the population levels of the different family types.

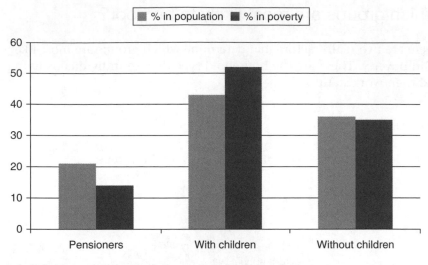

Graph 5.3 Household population v. household poverty
Source: DWP, 2014b

Graph 5.3 shows that while pensioners make up 21% of the population, they only make up 14% of those in poverty, meaning that the risk of being a pensioner in poverty is lower than we could expect from their population. This is also the case for households without children, where they make up 36% of the population, but 35% of those in poverty. On the other hand, households with children make up 43% of the population, but 52% of those in poverty. This means that households with children have a higher likelihood of being in poverty than other household types.

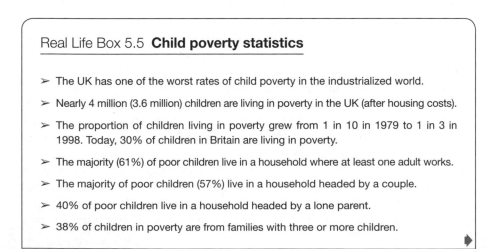

Real Life Box 5.5 **Child poverty statistics**

➢ The UK has one of the worst rates of child poverty in the industrialized world.

➢ Nearly 4 million (3.6 million) children are living in poverty in the UK (after housing costs).

➢ The proportion of children living in poverty grew from 1 in 10 in 1979 to 1 in 3 in 1998. Today, 30% of children in Britain are living in poverty.

➢ The majority (61%) of poor children live in a household where at least one adult works.

➢ The majority of poor children (57%) live in a household headed by a couple.

➢ 40% of poor children live in a household headed by a lone parent.

➢ 38% of children in poverty are from families with three or more children.

◀ 'Ending child poverty by 2020' has been a specific aim of social policy since 1999 from all governments. For example, the Labour governments of 1997–2010 increased expenditure on provisions such as tax credits, while the 2010 Coalition government introduced the Child Poverty Act 2010, which places a legal responsibility on the government to effectively end child poverty by 2020/21. Since 1999, when the Labour government pledged to end child poverty, 550,000 children have been lifted out of poverty. However, the 2010 Coalition government's tax and benefit changes will result in an increase in child poverty by 2020, meaning that the target set out in the Child Poverty Act will be missed (Brewer *et al.*, 2011).

One of the main reasons for this is the levels of poverty in single parent households. Single parent households make up 8% of the population, but 16% of those in poverty, which means that living in a single parent household significantly increases the chances of being in poverty.

So if we look at who is poor by household type, we can see that households with children make up over half of those living in poverty, and this level is higher than we could expect from the amount of such household types. Even more specifically, we can see that those living in a single parent household experience a very high level of poverty when compared to their population in society.

Work status

The other important factor in determining who is poor is individual's work status. Graph 5.4 below shows the levels of poverty by work status.

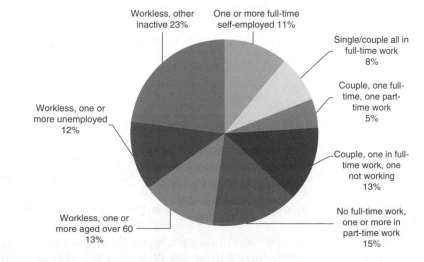

Graph 5.4 Poverty by work status
Source: DWP, 2014b

Graph 5.4 shows that the largest group of people in poverty are those who are 'workless, other inactive' (23%), meaning people who are of working age but not in employment or unemployed, and not necessarily required to find employment. This includes students, those looking after the family or home such as single parents with very young children or full-time housewives, and those temporary sick, long-term sick, or retired early. It is important to note that a significant number of these 'workless, other inactive' individuals will be in receipt of social policy benefits as described in Chapter 2, such as single mothers with very young children having entitlement to Income Support, students in receipt of student loan and grants, and long-term sick and disabled in receipt of Employment and Support allowance.

The next highest group of people in Graph 5.4 is those working part-time (15%), while a couple with one person working full-time has the same level of poverty as someone not working aged over 60 (13%), very likely pensioners. Eight per cent of households where everyone works full-time are in poverty. If we add up all groups where at least one person works full time, this accounts for 37% of those living in poverty. Research also shows that most children who live in poverty are in a household where at least one person works (McVeigh, 2010). This suggests that there is a significant link between work and poverty, and working full-time does not guarantee being out of poverty.

The level of poverty for households due to unemployment is 12%, almost the same level as for those who work full-time self-employed. This suggests that being unemployed is not strongly linked to being in poverty. But again, if we compare the 12% poverty rate for those who are unemployed with the current 7% rate for those who are unemployed then we can see that being unemployed significantly increases the risk of being in poverty.

These points suggest that both being in work and unemployment are linked to being in poverty, and we can explore the reasons for this below.

Why are so many working people in poverty?

Graph 5.4 above suggests that being in work is not a guarantee of being above the poverty line, even for those working full-time. Indeed, there are more households in poverty where one person works than where no one works. The specific reason for this is to do with the level of income that work provides.

The lowest amount that an individual should legally be paid for work is set by government via the National Minimum Wage (NMW), although this is not always adhered to (Ramesh, 2013). The rates of minimum wage are shown in Table 5.4.

Table 5.4 National minimum wage rates 2014

21 and over	£6.50
18 to 20	£5.13
Under 18	£3.79
Apprentice rate	£2.73

As can be seen, the rates of the NMW differ depending on age and type of job. The principle of the NMW is that it provides a 'wage floor' below which no one is legally allowed to fall (Pennycock and Whittaker, 2012). According to the Low Paid Commission, there are approximately 1.3 million jobs which pay at the NMW (Low Pay Commission, 2014). Table 5.5 compares the level of *gross earnings* (e.g. before deduction of income tax and national insurance) provided for someone working 37 hours a week with the official poverty line before housing cost of £264 calculated above, for the year 2014.

Table 5.5 NMW earnings levels (2014) and poverty line BHC

NMW category	Rate	Gross weekly earnings (37 hours)	Amount below poverty line of £264 before housing costs (BHC)
21 and over	£6.50	£240.50	−£23.50
18–20	£5.13	£189.81	−£74.19
Under 18	£3.79	£140.23	−£123.77
Apprentice rate	£2.73	£101.01	−£162.99

So we can see that none of the minimum wage rates pay at above the official poverty line before housing costs, with most paying significantly below this official poverty line. There are two important points to note when considering this fact:

1. Firstly, the calculations in Table 5.5 for NWM earnings are for *gross* earnings, that is earnings before tax is paid. However the BHC official poverty

line of £264 is for *net* income, meaning this poverty line is after income tax and national insurance have been paid. So if the figures we calculated in Table 5.5 were for *net weekly earnings*, they would be lower, meaning that the figures in the last column for the amount that earnings are below the poverty line of £256 would be greater than those shown.

2. Also, we have used the official poverty line before housing costs, not the poverty line after housing costs, as it is hard to calculate specific after housing costs income for each instance. However, what we know from above is that using the official poverty line after housing costs significantly increases the amount of poverty that is experienced by individuals.

These two points suggest that the earnings from the NMW are significantly less than the official poverty line, and highlight low pay as a significant factor in why so many people in work are poor, taking into consideration the 1.3 million jobs which pay at the NMW. Moreover, the proportion of jobs at the NMW increased from 4.4% in 2012 (Low Pay Commission, 2012) to 5.1% in 2014 (Low Pay Commission, 2014), suggesting that such low pay and therefore poverty has increased over the last few years.

There are also numerous jobs that pay just above the NMW which impacts on the numbers officially in poverty. Overall, according to KPMG (2013) there are 5.24 million jobs which pay below a wage required for a basic standard of living, called the 'living wage'. This accounts for 21% of all employees in the UK, or one in five working people. A wage of £8.55 per hour in London and £7.45 per hour elsewhere is required for the NMW to become a 'living wage', which suggests that the NMW as it stands represents an absolute definition of the minimum required to overcome poverty rather than a relative definition of the minimum required to overcome poverty. The fact that the NMW tends to rise more slowly than living costs rise (Davis *et al.*, 2012) means that this gap between the income from the NMW and what is required for a basic standard of living will become even wider over time.

This high prevalence of low-paid employment also means a requirement for increased expenditure on social policy top-up benefits such as tax credits that we saw in Graph 3.2 in Chapter 3, and also increases in benefits linked to low income such as Housing Benefit. This highlights that social policy benefits have increasingly been needed to subsidize the income of the growing numbers of those on low pay.

It should be remembered from Chapter 3 that the link between work and poverty is not new; it was something that was specifically outlined by Seebohm Rowntree in his distinction between *primary poverty* (poverty due to earnings below subsistence) and *secondary poverty* (poverty due to earnings above subsistence but wasteful spending). Rowntree identified, contrary to conventional thinking at the time, that it was primary poverty that was the main cause of poverty. The impact of low wages on poverty outlined above suggests that primary poverty is still a major problem within society.

Why are so many people on benefits poor?

Social policy benefits are a very important source of income for those classed as unemployed, indeed in most instances it is their only source of income. Despite this, as we saw above, those unemployed have a very high risk of being in poverty, suggesting that social policy is not very good at stopping the unemployed from falling into poverty, and this is explained below.

Social policy provides numerous in work and out of work benefits which can enable people to avoid falling below the poverty line. These include *cash benefits* such as Working Tax Credits, Child Tax Credit, Housing Benefit, State Pension, Disability Living Allowance, Incapacity Benefit, Statutory Sick Pay and Child Benefit. It also includes *in-kind benefits* such as education, healthcare, free school meals and free childcare. This means that 'most people spend much of their lives either receiving or paying for social [policy] – often both at the same time' (McKay and Rowlingson, 2009: 304), and this is important in enabling them to overcome the predictable life risks that could lead to poverty.

For those unemployed, there are two main benefits which provide an income level. These are Jobseeker's Allowance (JSA) or Income Support (IS), and entitlement is to one or the other, but not both. Both are means tested, meaning they are only paid if income is below a certain level. The amounts of both JSA and IS vary with age and household type, and Table 5.6 compares these amounts to the equivalized poverty line income after housing costs. We can use the AHC figure here because entitlement to these benefits typically also means that there is entitlement to Housing Benefit to pay rent.

An important point to note is that for those households with children, they would also be entitled to other cash benefits such as child benefit or tax credits, which would increase their total income AHC significantly. But for a household without children, there would not normally be any other cash benefit entitlement to increase their total income AHC, meaning that all normal bills and costs would need to be paid out of their income of £57.35.

Table 5.6 Jobseeker's Allowance and Income Support entitlement and the equivalized poverty line AHC 2013

	Weekly Jobseeker's Allowance/ Income Support entitlement	Weekly equivalized poverty line income AHC	Weekly amount below equivalized poverty line AHC
Lone parent, over 18, two children over 14	£72.40	£297.92	–£225.22
Couple, both over 18, two children under 14	£113.70	£313.60	–£199.90
Couple, both under 18, with one child under 14	£86.65	£268.80	£183.00
Lone parent, under 18, one child	£57.35	£194.88	–£137.53
Couple, both over 18, no children	£113.70	£224.00	–£110.30
Single, under 25, no child	£57.35	£150.80	–£92.73
Single, over 25, no child	£72.40	£150.80	–£77.68

Real Life Box 5.6 **Could you live on £57.35 per week?**

As Table 5.6 shows, the level of entitlement to Jobseeker's Allowance or Income Support for those who are single is £57.35 per week. Do you think you could live on £57.35 per week?

The key point that Table 5.6 shows is that for none of these household types is their income from the main social policy benefits above the equivalized poverty line after housing costs. Indeed, for the majority it is significantly less. The fact that the main benefit level is below the poverty line goes a long way in explaining why being unemployed is a significant cause of being in poverty. This means that for those unemployed, social policy benefits do not enable them to exist above the poverty line. Instead, such benefits reinforce their disadvantaged status of being unemployed by providing an income level which is well below the poverty line.

Question

Match up one of the households in the Table 5.6 above with your own circumstances. Do you think you could live on the income that would be provided to you?

Is the amount of poverty falling or rising?

'Monitoring Poverty and Social Exclusion' (MacInnes *et al.*, 2013) is an annual report published by the Joseph Rowntree Foundation that tracks changes in poverty from year to year. It provides a summary of five and ten year trends in poverty.

According to the report, over the last five years there have mainly been falls in the levels of poverty related to health and education. However, there have been significant increases in levels of poverty related to income and work. For example, incomes have fallen over the last five years, meaning that levels of income poverty have risen. And as part of the *austerity* programme of the 2010 Coalition government, benefits levels have been frozen, meaning that the income of those who rely on them have also been frozen. Overall, the report states that the recession and the 2010 Coalition government's austerity response to it have led to some significant deteriorations in poverty for some groups, and will continue to do so for the next couple of years.

Evidence to support this is the rise in the use of foodbanks and other types of 'food aid' in the UK over the last five years, a rise which can be seen as a consequence particularly of increasing problems of low income (Lambie-Mumford *et al.*, 2014). There have also been continual increases in the numbers of households in fuel poverty over the last 10 years in the UK (Bolton, 2012), and this is something that is specifically linked to low income households.

Furthermore, the 2010 Coalition government introduced a number of measures that will reduce the income of those reliant on social policy benefits. The main one has been limiting rises in benefits to 1% a year, which has meant that the income of those on benefits has fallen further behind the rest of the population. There has also been the benefit cap, which limits overall benefit entitlement to £26,000 a year, and mainly affects those not in work with large families. The Universal Credit has also been introduced to 'ensure that work always pays and is seen to pay'. It aims to do this by providing a higher level of income for those who move from social security benefits such as Jobseeker's Allowance into work.

Real Life Box 5.7 **The Living Wage v. the Citizen's Income**

As identified above, low income from work and low income from social policy benefits are two important reasons why levels of poverty in the UK are high. To overcome these issues, two main policy suggestions have been put forward

The Living Wage

The Living Wage is an idea promoted by the Living Wage Foundation. The simple idea is that those in employment should be paid a minimum amount to enable them to lead a decent life. The level of the living wage in 2014 is set at £9.15 an hour in London and £7.85 an hour in the rest of the UK. As can be seen, these Living Wage rates are considerably higher that the National Minimum Wage. A key argument of the Living Wage Foundation is that where employers pay the living wage, this means that less money is paid out in benefits to subsidize low pay. At the time of writing, 1,000 employers have signed up to pay the Living Wage, most notably, Barclays, Nationwide, ITV, Chelsea Football Club, HSBC and Channel 4. The Living Wage has received some political support, but remains wholly voluntary on the part of employers.

See: http://www.livingwage.org.uk/

The Citizen's Income

The Citizen's Income is the idea of everyone having the entitlement to an unconditional amount of money each week or month. This entitlement would be given as an automatic right, would be tax free and would be without a means test. So, for example, for those not working, there would be an automatic entitlement to a certain level of income from benefits. This is different from the current system, where entitlement is usually decided by having to undergo a means test. Those working would still be entitled to receive the Citizen's Income, and would pay taxation at a set rate only on what they earn. The main argument for the Citizen's Income is that it would simplify the benefits system by making it immediately apparent what people were entitled to, and would also limit the disincentive for work through the reduction in benefits received.

See: http://www.citizensincome.org/

Summary

In this chapter, we have explored the extent and context of poverty in the UK. This has not been easy as poverty is something that can be defined in more than one way. However, the above suggests that poverty is still a significant issue for social policy in the UK, and we can make the following specific observations about poverty in the UK:

➣ The government's official poverty line is set at £264, which is the total income per week of the bottom 30% of the population.

> Using the government's own official poverty line before housing costs, there are 9.7 million people living in poverty in the UK.

> However, if we calculate poverty after housing costs, there are 13.2 million people living in poverty in the UK, which is 21% of the population.

> Households with children are most likely to be in poverty than other types of households.

> Those in work are more likely to be in poverty than those not in work.

> Low pay in general is an important reason why so many people in work are in poverty, as evident from the low level of the NMW in relation to the official poverty line.

> Social policy benefits for those unemployed provides an income which is significantly below the poverty line, and so means that reliance on such benefits results in living in poverty.

Whether we take the level of poverty at the very low official poverty line before housing costs, or the level of poverty after housing costs, the fact remains that poverty is still a significant issue for social policy so many years after the welfare state set out to deal with it. Indeed, it is very likely that William Beveridge would be shocked by the levels of poverty that exist in modern Britain, with his vision of the welfare state as a safety net to stop people from falling into poverty undermined by both the numbers and the causes of poverty. Thus, Beveridge's aim that work should be the best route out of poverty is something we have seen is definitely not the case in contemporary UK.

However, the analysis above does point to two specific ways in which social policy could work to reduce poverty in the UK. The first is to ensure that work does pay, meaning it provides a level of income that is at least at the official poverty line. This could be done, at no extra increase to social policy expenditure, by increasing the level of the NMW to at least the level of the official poverty line. This would also reduce the amount of 'dependency' on social policy expenditure by reducing the huge amount of in work benefits paid, such as Working Tax Credits, and Housing Benefit paid to those who work but whose income is below the poverty line.

At the same time, if social policy is to be a safety net and stop people from falling into poverty, its level of entitlement needs to be increased to at least the level of the poverty line. This would immediately eliminate the risk that falling into unemployment means falling into poverty. For some, having social policy benefits at a very low level is important to incentivize into work those unemployed who are 'underserving' and 'shirkers'. However, Chapter 3 has taught us that such an emphasis on 'less eligibility' is not grounded in reality and simply reinforces poverty for the majority of those who are in fact 'deserving' from the fact that they work, and therefore defeats the initial and ongoing objective of social policy which is to reduce the risk and levels of poverty in the UK.

Key Point

Poverty remains a significant issue for social policy as there are between 9.7 and 13.2 million people living in poverty in the UK, most of which is caused by either inadequate income from work or inadequate income from benefits.

6

SHOULD ENTITLEMENT TO SOCIAL POLICY BENEFITS BE JUST FOR SOME PEOPLE OR FOR EVERYONE?

The aims of this chapter are to:

1. **Outline the differences between selective and universal entitlement to social policies**

2. **Compare and contrast the advantages and disadvantages of universal and selective social policies**

3. **Analyse whether universal or selective social policies provides the most effective social policy outcomes**

4. **Analyse whether recent changes in social policies are universal or selective in nature**

So far in this book we have seen that there is a multitude of social policies which all individuals are entitled to throughout their lives. These can be *cash benefits* which effectively involve cash being given by the state to individuals, such as Jobseeker's Allowance; or these can be *in-kind benefits* which provide individuals with a benefit which is not money but a service, such as education. The key point is that all individuals and groups are entitled to and in receipt of some benefits at some point in their lives, and you are very likely to be receiving some such benefits as you read this.

There are a variety of social policy benefits that you are likely to be entitled to and receiving at this point in time, such as higher education and higher education tuition fees. There are also others that you are not likely to be entitled to now and are not receiving but which you might receive at a later date, such as the state pension. There are also other benefits that you might have been entitled to in the past, but are no longer entitled to, such as NHS dental treatment. And there are also social policies that you may never be entitled to and so never receive, such as Child Benefit if you don't have children or your income is above a certain amount.

Your entitlement to such benefits is dependent on a variety of factors. For example, it may be due to age, having a certain level of income, being a parent, being disabled, being ill, being pregnant, being in work, or being in education. The reason for such specific entitlement is sometimes obvious, such as those related to being disabled, but in other instances it is less obvious why some groups are entitled to some benefits and others are not. An example of such less obvious entitlement that you might have experienced is NHS prescriptions, where some people get their prescriptions for free and others, maybe you, do not.

Some of these benefits are available to all on a continuous basis, regardless of who you are and how much income you have. An example of this is the NHS. This type of entitlement to social policies is called *universal* entitlement or universalism.

For some other benefits, entitlement is dependent on specific circumstances such as illness (e.g. Income Support), low income (e.g. Working Tax Credit), or disability (e.g. Personal Independence Payment). Additionally, entitlement to such benefits is dependent on the level of individual or family income, meaning that below a certain income level, there is entitlement, and above a certain income level there is not entitlement. An example of this which you might have experienced is Higher Education Maintenance Grants. This type of entitlement to social policies is called *selective* entitlement or selectivism.

This chapter explores the main differences between universal and selective entitlement to social policy benefits. The specific advantages and disadvantages of each type of entitlement will be explored in detail. Housing will be a particular focus of this chapter, as it is a social policy area that has undergone a significant shift in entitlement over the last 30 years. This chapter will also highlight a general and important contemporary shift in policy away from universalism towards selectivism for all groups (children, young people, families and older people), and its implications for social policy. By the end of this chapter, you will have an understanding of differences between universal and selective entitlement to social policy, and the implications of each for the actual effectiveness of the social policy benefits you receive.

What is universalism?

We can define universalism as where entitlement to a social policy is available for the whole target population on the principle of equal access. This means that regardless of your income level or your ability to pay, entitlement is available to you. The NHS is the purest form of universalism for social policy benefits, as it is available to all regardless of need. However, universalism can also refer to where a benefit is provided for a specific group and there is equal access to all within the group. Examples of this type of universalism are education up to the age of 18 (children and young people), the 15 hours of free childcare (children), the basic state pension (older people), and tuition fee loans for university (students). As the name suggests, these benefits are given universally to all members of the specific group. Individuals can choose whether or not to take up these benefits, but the point is that they will be provided if the individual chooses to take them up.

Advantages of universalism

There are various advantages which universal social policies have. The first is that they are easy and simple to understand. This is evident in something like the NHS, where everyone understands that they are entitled to healthcare that is free at the point of use.

Linked to this is a second advantage, which is that universal benefits mean that many more people are able to, and choose to, use a universal service. Education up to the age of 18 is a good example of this, as almost all children are in school, although the fact that this is a compulsory requirement may be a reason for this. As a consequence of this universalism, more people are insured against the specific risk that the benefit is designed to counter.

A third advantage is that universal services cost very little to administer. As almost all people are entitled to universal services, there is no need to devise costly systems to determine who is entitled, what they are entitled to, and for how long.

A fourth advantage of universal services is that they can lead to greater social cohesion. This works in two ways. Firstly, providing free childcare to everyone means that almost all children use the service, so they mix with each other and are more socially aware of each other. This can apply to both the parents and the students. The second aspect is that as everyone is getting the same benefit, there is no jealousy or distrust towards those receiving from those not receiving.

Disadvantages of universalism

Providing social policies that are universal does have some disadvantages. The first is the cost. As we saw in Figure 1.1, 'Income Maintenance' has the highest expenditure of all social policies, and the main reason for this is expenditure on universal state pension, as shown in Figure 2.1, which is the most expensive social policy benefit to provide. 'Health' and 'Education', which are also both essentially universal services, are the next most costly social policy services, as a consequence of being available to all.

Another disadvantage is that universalism can mean that some people who could afford to provide for themselves also get entitlement. This is evident in, for example, universal free childcare, which is something that some people could afford and would buy anyway. This means that universal benefits often wastefully duplicate and replace services, which increases the overall cost of social policy.

This means that, thirdly, there is less money available to spend on people who are really in need, as the amounts of benefits are spread too thinly on too many people and so cannot be provided specifically and at a higher quality to those who really need it.

The final argument against providing universal social policies is that to do so means providing something for nothing, as individuals do not have to do anything to be entitled to provision. This is evident in something like the basic state pension, where it is possible to get a pension despite not having contributed directly into the system.

What is selectivism?

In contrast to universalism, selectivism refers to where social policies are provided only to those who have met specific entitlement criteria beyond being a member of a particular group. The main criterion that has to be met is usually having an income level above or below a certain point, such as for Income Support, Jobseeker's Allowance, Housing Benefit, Higher Education Loans or Child Benefit. Entitlement can also be in terms of having made contributions, such as for Statutory Maternity Pay and Statutory Sick Pay. Or entitlement can be dependent on long term individual circumstances, such as disability (Personal Independence Payment) or being a carer (Carer's Allowance). As the name suggests, a benefit is given selectively to only some of the particular group, not to everyone in the group.

Advantages of selectivism

There are various advantages that selective social policies have. The first is that it means that there is more efficient targeting of resources on those who are most in need. So for example, disability benefits are only provided to those with a disability who meet specific conditions, such as being disabled over a long term (at least three months), and not to those who have a short-term disability. Such targeting can be a more efficient way of allocating limited resources, and can save money.

Also, by only targeting those who need it, extra resources can be provided to those who need it the most. An example of this is higher education loans, which provides different levels of benefit depending on the parental or household income of the applicant. This means that those who live in lower income households get more, and those who live in higher income households get less.

Thirdly, such selectivism is a form of redistribution, as resources are transferred from those with the most to those with the least, such as in relation to Income Support.

Finally, as not everyone gets the benefit, such selectivism is cheap in comparison to situations where everyone gets the benefit, and so selectivism saves money where resources are tight, such as in relation to Housing Benefit.

Disadvantages of selectivism

Providing social policy benefits that are selective has some specific disadvantages. The first is that they are very difficult to understand and administer. This is due to the rules and regulations they have. Sometimes this means that individuals do not understand what they are entitled to, and sometimes not even those who administer the system understand it either. An example of this is the system for Child Benefit, which requires individuals to understand both the benefits systems and the taxation system, which as we saw in Chapter 4 is not an easy thing to do. Another relevant example is anyone who has ever filled in a Housing Benefit application will know that it is not an easy form to fill in, as it is very complex and lengthy.

As a consequence of not being easy to understand, many do not get what they are fully entitled to. Or if they are required to apply, they do not apply because they are not aware of how to apply. This is evident for Carer's Allowance, which very few carers receive. As such social policies are usually for those who are in poverty, this lack of take-up can reinforce their poverty.

A third disadvantage is that the complexity of such selectivism can lead to higher instances of error from both benefit recipients and those in charge of the system, such as where individuals do not receive benefits that they are entitled to, or do receive benefits they are not entitled to (DWP, 2010). This is because selectivism requires complex systems of administration and surveillance to check who is receiving what, and the more complex a system the more the possibility of error, as evident with Jobseeker's Allowance. For instance, the manual used by the Department for Work and Pensions to help them apply benefit rules correctly has 8,690 pages worth of instruction, and the guidance for Tax Credits staff runs to 1,447 pages!

Not surprisingly, this complexity has led to errors, and where such errors occur, this can lead individuals to become frustrated and discouraged and to not apply for other benefits that they might be entitled to.

Real Life Box 6.1 **How high is benefit fraud and error?**

Benefit fraud and error are often cited as major problems with social policy benefits in the UK.

The UK government estimate of total benefit fraud for 2013/14 totals £1.2 billion. This represents 0.7% of the total income benefits expenditure (DWP, 2014c).

In contrast, the amount of benefits paid out in error totals £3.6 billion, or 2.2% of the total income benefits expenditure. The majority of these errors caused benefits to be overpaid by £2.2 billion, but a significant amount of these errors caused benefits to be underpaid, totalling £1.4 billion (DWP, 2014c). Interestingly, this figure for underpayment is less that the amount of total benefit fraud above, meaning that the amount of benefits lost to fraud is very similar to the amount of benefits which individuals were entitled to but did not receive.

As a comparison, the government estimates that total fraud across the whole of the economy amounts to £73 billion a year. This means that benefit fraud represents 2% of the estimated total annual fraud in the UK. In comparison, tax fraud costs £14 billion, or 19% of total fraud. So in both the amount and percentage terms, tax fraud is a much bigger issue than benefit fraud. This is shown in Graph 6.1.

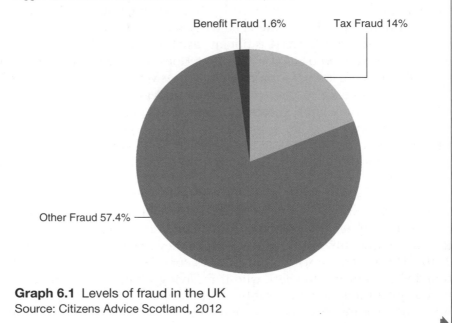

Graph 6.1 Levels of fraud in the UK
Source: Citizens Advice Scotland, 2012

Where fraud and error does occur, according to the DWP (2010) the main cause is the variety of changes in circumstances which individuals are expected to report and the complex relationships between different benefits and tax credits which make it very difficult to comply with the rules, even when they want to do so, and this is a key factor in customer error. For example, in the Tax Credits system a significant cause of complexity is the need for individuals to guess what their income will be, which then has to be confirmed at a later date. For individuals with uncertain work and hours and whose job may change during the year, this can often be a source of error, and can result in claimants 'falling into' fraud.

Fourthly, and linked to this need for complex systems of administration and surveillance is cost. Selective benefits can be very expensive to administer, and indeed can be more expensive than simply giving everyone the benefit.

A fifth disadvantage of such selectivism is that it can lead to a lack of social cohesion and the stigmatization of those who receive it. This is because if benefits are seen as going only to those who are poor and who are not able to contribute to the system, this clearly identifies those recipients as being different from those not in receipt of benefits. Disability benefit is a good example of this, where over the last 20 years or so there has been a prevailing mood that those who receive such benefits are 'skivers' and cheating the system, and so not really entitled to what they receive. This is despite the fact that, as with all selective benefits, recipients have to undergo a specific test to be classified as disabled, which has actually become more extensive over time.

Real Life Box 6.2 **Higher education grants**

Prior to 1990, the government gave all students at university a maintenance grant to cover their living costs, and there were no tuition fees to pay. As a universal grant the only criteria was acceptance on a university course, and the grant was non-repayable. Over time the value of the grant has been reduced, and now grants are not universal but selective, meaning that only some students get them. Universal maintenance grants have effectively been replaced by selective student maintenance loans, as the amount that an individual gets varies depending on family income (Wyness, 2010).

Questions

1. Do you think that higher education grants should be universal or selective?

2. Do you think that all students should get the same amount of maintenance loans, regardless of family income?

These main advantages and disadvantages of universal and selective social policies are summarized in Table 6.1.

Table 6.1 Main advantages and disadvantages of universal and selective social policies

	Universal	Selective
Advantages	Easy and simple to understand	More efficient targeting of benefits on those who are really needy
	Costs less in administration, therefore more money to provide the benefit	Means more extra benefits can be provided for those most in need
	More people entitled so high take up	Redistributes resources from the rich to the poor
	Leads to greater social cohesion, as less jealousy and distrust of those receiving	Cheap in terms of the amount of provision that needs to be provided
Disadvantages	Inefficient, goes to some people who do not need it	Administratively complex and so expensive systems required to monitor
	Reduces funds available for more needy causes and groups	Lack of understand of entitlement from those who most need it so low take-up, which reinforces poverty
	Expensive in terms of amount of benefit needed to be provided	Complexity leads to errors in benefit entitlement
	Means that some people get something for nothing	Specific targeting of benefits at some groups leads to stigmatization and lack of social cohesion

What is the evidence for and against universalism and selectivism?

We can explore some of these arguments for and against universalism and selectivism through an analysis of actual benefits that individuals claim.

Which is the most expensive?

As outlined above, universal benefits would seem to be more expensive from the fact that everyone gets some benefit, while only some people get selective benefits. However, when considering the cost of benefits, we also have to take into consideration the costs of administering the benefit, such as the checks required to determine whether an individual is entitled or not to a benefit, and to help people to claim the benefit in the first place. This is especially important where selective benefits like Income Support are targeted at some of the poorest who are least likely to understand the complexity of the benefits system, and so need assistance to first of all know what they are entitled to and secondly to claim what they are entitled to.

For a universal benefit, such administration costs are minimal as there are minimal qualifying criteria. The experience of receiving NHS treatment exemplifies the simplicity of universal benefits, as most treatment is typically received with no specific requirement on the individual to do anything.

On the other hand, the administration costs for a selective benefit can be very high, depending on the complexity of rules that determine who gets a benefit. Anyone who has ever filled in a student maintenance loan or grant application will know how long, complex and time consuming the forms are, and this detail has to be analysed to ensure that the correct benefit is given out. This means that, according to the National Audit Office (2011:19), while selectivism can reduce public spending through the targeting of support, the costs of administering selective benefits tend to be higher than for universal benefits even where benefits have similar target groups. For example the DWP estimates that administering selective Pension Credit costs £47 per claim, compared to £14 per claim for the universal State Pension. A more recent example of this is the change in 2014 of Child Benefit from being universal to being selective. This is a change which the HMRC estimated as costing approximately £118 million in administration costs over five years (Kennedy, 2010). The reason for this is the need to assess a variety of factors such as present circumstances, changes in circumstances, the amount required to be paid, age of children, and the income levels of all earners in the household.

Which provides the most effective social policy outcomes?

Selective benefits are seen as more effective as a consequence of the fact that they are specifically targeted at those who need it. This assumes that everyone who is entitled to the benefit is actually receiving it. However, if we look at how many people take up selective benefits in comparison to universal benefits, we can see that this rarely happens, as shown in Graph 6.2, which provides official estimates of the maximum percentage of entitled people who take up particular benefits.

The figures for Child Benefit in Graph 6.2 are for when it was universal, and this allows us to compare it to the take-up of selective benefits. As can

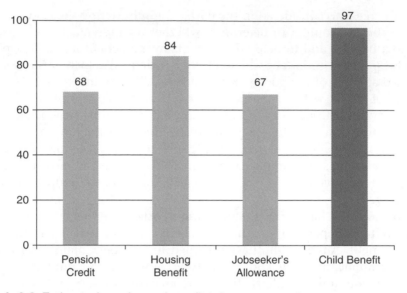

Graph 6.2 Estimated maximum benefit take-up percentages
Source: DWP, 2012a: HMRC, 2012

be seen, universal child benefit has the highest take-up of all the benefits, at nearly 100%. The maximum take-up of Jobseeker's Allowance is 67%, which means that approximately one third of people who are entitled to it are not receiving it. This would certainly affect the effectiveness of the benefit in terms of its stated aim of reducing poverty, bearing in mind that the selective benefits shown above are specifically targeted at those who are on a low income, and therefore most in need of it. This means that a significant proportion of the poorest of the poor do not receive what they are entitled to, and HMRC (2012) estimates that up to £12.3 billion of selective benefits are left unclaimed each year. This would seem to undermine the effectiveness of selective benefits significantly, as one of their main advantages is meant to be that those who need the benefit the most get it.

Real Life Box 6.3 **From selective to universal free school meals**

From September 2014, all children at school in Reception, Year 1 and Year 2 became entitled to free school meals. This was a change from a selective benefit to a universal benefit, as previously entitlement to free school meals was dependent on having a low ▶

◀ income. The government justified the shift by arguing that universal free school meals were more effective in terms of:

➤ Improving the health of children;

➤ Improving the behaviour of children;

➤ Improving the results that children achieved.

This claim of greater effectiveness for universal free school meals over selective free school meals was supported by research that compared those who received different entitlement to free school meals. The research found that universal entitlement provided better value for money than selective free school meals, principally in terms of improving the results of children (Kitchen *et al.*, 2012).

Another argument for selectivism is that the money saved from providing for everyone can be used to provide more for those who really need it. However, the take-up figures above suggest that a significant number of people are worse off with selective benefits, and would be better off if they had received a lower amount of universal provision. This suggests that selectivism can actually contribute to the poverty of some who it specifically targets, as a consequence of the low take-up of selective benefits. On the other hand, universal benefits would seem to be more effective because they provide a guarantee that everyone gets something, suggesting that universal provision is the most effective way to meet the welfare needs of all low income households (Morelli and Seaman, 2005). Experience has also shown that when a benefit goes from being universal to being selective, the level of benefit rarely increases. Instead, it goes the other way, and becomes less than when it was universal. The experience of the change from universal student grants to selective student grants described above exemplifies this.

Which is fairer?

The argument that selective benefits are fairer is based on the claim that they are redistributing resources from the rich to the poor. Also, selectivism aims to keep the costs of benefits as low as possible, meaning it provides a fair overall cost for taxpayer funded social policies. Selective benefits can also be specifically targeted at groups in need, so benefits are fairly provided depending on needed.

On the other hand, universalism's claim to fairness is based on the greater social cohesion which it encourages, from the fact that everyone gets something, therefore creating a fairer society. The fairness argument is reinforced by the fact that as all people pay something into the tax system to fund social policies, as we saw in Chapter 4, so they are entitled to receive something out. The experience of the NHS also supports this, as a universal service to which everyone is entitled it is the most popular institution in the UK (British Future, 2013), despite the fact that, from a selective viewpoint, it is unfair that those who can afford to pay for their own healthcare can get free NHS healthcare. This also supports the claim that universal benefits lead to greater social solidarity.

The recent change from universal to selective Child Benefit highlights another aspect of the fairness claim. This is that for selective benefits, families in very similar positions can be treated very differently. This is because the means test that is usually applied to determine eligibility provides an arbitrary cut-off point, above which there is no or limited entitlement. So for example, with Child Benefit, a family with someone earning £50,000 would keep all their Child Benefit, while a family with someone earning £50,001 would have their Child Benefit reduced, even though the two circumstances are effectively the same. This can lead to a perception of unfairness, which may increase the potential for fraud and abuse, and therefore the cost, as people feel that they have to cheat the system to make it fairer to them. This is in contrast to universal benefits where families in similar positions are treated the same, which suggests a certain type of fairness.

What does the example of council housing going from universalism to selectivism show us?

Council housing is a social policy benefit that has undergone a radical shift away from universalism towards selectivism over the last 40 years. At present, the main benefit for housing is Housing Benefit, which is a selective benefit. As we saw in Graph 2.1 in Chapter 2, Housing Benefit accounts for 11% of all Income Maintenance expenditure, totalling nearly £25 billion a year.

Those entitled to Housing Benefit have to be on a low income, and the benefit they receive enables them to pay their rent in full or in part, regardless of whether they are in social housing or private housing, with the notable exception of students. This means that it is a benefit which subsidizes rents, and as rents increase so does the amount of Housing Benefit that individuals claim.

Housing Benefit has its origins in the 1970s. Prior to this, social policy expenditure on housing did not subsidize rents. Instead, most social policy spending on housing subsidized the building of houses. The government paid a direct subsidy to councils for houses they built, which they then rented to tenants. The direct subsidy for building houses which councils received also enabled them to charge their tenants relatively low rents (Glennerster, 2009). This meant two things. Firstly, that councils built a significant number of houses each year in comparison to private house builders, and had a large number of houses to rent. Secondly, as a consequence of this, councils were able to provide housing on a less selective, more universal basis, not just to those on a low income, and this meant that those living in council housing were from a broader and more diverse mix of society than we think of today.

This changed in 1972 and housing became financed more like we know it today. There were no longer subsidies to councils for building houses. Instead, the subsidies went directly to people to pay their rent. This had the consequence of reducing the number of houses that were built by councils, as such house building was no longer subsidized. As fewer houses were built by councils, so there were fewer houses for them to rent out. This reduction in council housing was reinforced by the 'Right to Buy' policy, which meant that councils had to sell large amounts of their housing stock, particularly the best housing stock, meaning that they had less quality social housing available. This in turn meant that the criteria for those who could receive council housing were tightened, as there were fewer houses to go around. This made council housing more selective in terms of who became entitled to it, particularly those who were most in need. In effect, council housing moved away from being a universal social policy benefit available to a broad and diverse mix of the population to a selective service only available to those most in need, as we know it today.

We can see a number of the disadvantages we outlined for selectivism above occurring in the changes for council housing from universalism to selectivism. In terms of *expense*, Housing Benefit is the benefit which effectively replaced council house building subsidies. Out of all social policy benefits, it is the social policy benefit for which expenditure has increased the most over the last 15 years or so, in comparison to other benefits (Full Fact, 2011). The change to Housing Benefit is also something which has worsened the problem of growing house prices (HomeOwners Alliance, 2012) and over time made housing more expensive for all.

The current Housing Benefit expenditure of nearly £25 billion per year would finance the building of a lot of universal housing that would be available to more people. However, the change from the universal subsidizing of house-building for all to selectively subsidizing rents for some has meant less houses being built, and this shortage has directly led to increases in the cost of housing for those wanting both to rent and to buy. This has made housing less *effective* in terms of housing being available to all, and also in terms of reducing poverty, as we saw in Chapter 5 the effect that housing costs has on the increase in poverty.

Finally, in terms of *fairness*, selectivism has led to council housing only being available to poorer sections of the population, who are typically on Housing Benefit. This has meant that council housing is now available only to the very poor, rather than to a broad mix of people, and as a consequence has become a stigmatized benefit. Richard Titmuss made the observation that 'services for the poor end up being poor services' (Titmuss, 1968), and this is something we can definitely see in the shift from universalism to selectivism in council housing.

Are social policies in the UK universal or selective overall?

It should have become apparent from reading above that social policies in the UK are a mixture of universalism and selectivism. As we saw in Chapter 3, up to World War II, most social policies were selective, but that the universalism of World War II's 'total war' led to the creation of various universal services, particularly the NHS, but also in comprehensive schooling, full employment, housing, and personal social services and social security. This moved social policy towards a more universal nature, although there were still some important selective provisions, such as the contributory requirements in the National Insurance Act 1946. This meant that universalism was a key feature of the post-war welfare state, and survived largely intact up to until 1979.

However, since then there has been a noticeable drift away from universalism towards selectivism. This is exemplified by the fact that in 1979, when the Thatcher government came to power selective benefits accounted for less than 16% of the social security expenditure, but by 1997 this had doubled to 32% of expenditure, and rose further to 36% of expenditure by 2007–2008 (Walker, 2011: 137). The introduction of Tax Credits by New Labour is an important reason for this recent change, because as we saw in Graph 3.2 in Chapter 3, Tax Credit expenditure has increased significantly. There was some universal provision put in place by New Labour, such as the Winter Fuel Allowance for pensioners, 15 hours free childcare and Sure Start centres, but this was not as large as the increase in selective provision.

Have the 2010 Coalition government's social policies been universal or selective?

The austerity social policies of the 2010 Coalition government has reinforced this shift away from universalism towards selectivism. Universal social policies include the raising of the income tax threshold to £10,000 for all, and the introduction of free school meals for all up to the age of 7. However, there have also been some important selective policies, such as the Pupil Premium, Help to Buy, and the Bedroom Tax.

Real Life Box 6.4 **The Bedroom Tax**

The Bedroom Tax (officially known as the Spare Room Subsidy) was implemented in 2013 by the 2010 Coalition government. Its main aim is to increase the number of larger houses available to larger families in the social rented sector. This is done by applying a charge for every un-occupied spare bedroom that a house has, if the person is claiming Housing Benefit to pay some or all of their rent.

So for example, if a single person lives in a two-bedroom social rented house, they have to pay a surcharge for the extra room. The charge is 14% of the rent for one spare bedroom room and 25% of the rent for two spare bedrooms. So, someone with one 'spare bedroom' whose rent is £100 per week has to pay at least £14 of the rent themselves to their landlord. Someone who has two or more 'spare bedrooms' whose rent is £100 per week has to pay at least £25 of the rent themselves to their landlord.

The alternative to paying the surcharge is to move into a smaller house, which is the main intention of the policy, so that a larger family can move in to the larger house. There are exemptions from the bedroom tax, such as pensioners and people living in some types of supported accommodation, but generally it applies to most people. In terms of universalism and selectivism, though, the Bedroom Tax has made a selective benefit, social renting, even more selective in terms of restricting the type of accommodation that people can live in, and the amount of benefit that people receive. This means that social rented housing will probably become even more restricted to the very poorest than it has been in the past.

There have also been significant changes to existing social policies to make them more selective, such as in relation to benefits for disabled people, Child Benefit, the increase in student tuition fees, and the introduction of the Universal Credit, which despite the name, is not universal but actually selective. There has also been much debate in the 2010 Coalition government about making other current universal benefits for the elderly selective, such as the free eye tests, free prescriptions, free bus passes and Winter Fuel Allowance. As Lawson (2013) observes, the argument is that in times of austerity, the concept of universalism is something that we cannot afford, but instead, benefits must be selectively targeted at those most in need.

Summary

Those who argue for universal social policies claim that they are easier to understand for most people, which means that they cost less in administration, and they enable more people to claim, and lead to greater social cohesion in society.

Those who argue for selective social policies claim that they cost less in terms of provision required, are better at targeting those in need, are a more efficient allocation of scare resources, and are fairer to those who pay for social policy.

This chapter has explored these claims of each in some detail, specifically in terms of cost, effectiveness and fairness. This analysis has shown us that while universalism and selectivism each has specific advantages, selectivism limits social policies in more acute ways. The analysis of the change in council housing from universalism to selectivism underlines the limitations of social policies that emphasize selectivism over universalism.

This is significant because there has been a general trend away from universal social policies towards more selective social policies, and the austerity policies of the 2010 Coalition government have intensified this trend in a number of ways. The analysis presented here suggests this trend will limit social policies in the future in significant ways.

Key Point

Both universal and selective benefits have advantages and disadvantages, but there has been a trend over the last 30 years towards making social policy more selective, which has some important limitations for the effectiveness of social policy.

7

WHICH WELFARE NEEDS SHOULD SOCIAL POLICY BE RESPONSIBLE FOR MEETING?

The aims of this chapter are to:

> Outline the two main types of welfare needs that exist

> Detail how and why these different types of welfare lead to different social policies

> Highlight how current social policy is focussed on meeting needs, and the implications of this current focus for the effectiveness of social policy

As we saw in Chapter 3, William Beveridge's identification of the 'five evil giants' of want, disease, ignorance, idleness and squalor continues to be an important reference point for the cradle to grave welfare state that exists today. The consequence of this is evident from the fact that modern day social policy is still largely built around meeting income maintenance, health, education, employment housing and social care needs. This means that an understanding of welfare need is very important to our understanding of how social policy in general functions. This chapter discusses the different types of welfare needs that you can have and the important factors that influence which types of needs social policies meet.

The chapter starts by defining and distinguishing between the two main types of welfare needs, and how welfare needs differ from welfare wants. It analyses the implications of adopting either of these different types of needs in social policies. There is also a focus on the different ways that the different areas of social policy meet needs, and how current social policy is focussed on meeting welfare needs. The chapter uses health needs as a way to exemplify the consequence of social policy meeting needs in a narrow rather than in a broad way.

By the end of this chapter, you should have an understanding of the two main types of welfare needs, and understand how welfare needs differ from welfare wants. You should be able to outline the ways that different areas of social policies meet needs, and what underpins such decisions. Finally, you should understand what the implications are for social policies of specific focus on meeting need in a narrow way.

What is need?

Your day is made up of many single and interrelated acts, small and large. For example, it is very likely that during a day, you will eat something, talk to other people and go to sleep. Other things that you might also do are watch TV, read, go online, go to the shop, or even study.

If we think about these acts that make up your day, we can see that there are some things which we have to do. An obvious thing that you have to do is eat, the simple reason being that without food, we would not exist, and there are various other things we have to do to continue living, such as drinking water, keeping warm and sleeping. Therefore, we can define need simply as things which are essential to continuing to live.

However, defining need in this simple way is problematic for two important reasons. The first is that there are also things we choose to do which are not essential to continuing to live, but which we very likely could not do without. An example of this is having social interaction, such as talking or just being with other people, as loneliness over a long period of time would be very troublesome to the majority of us. Love is another good example of this, as in theory we could survive without love, but in practice it would be very hard. The other problem is that if we only had the things that are essential to our lives, we would probably not have a very good quality of life. So for example, imagine what your life would be like without books, TV or the internet, all things not essential to our existence but important to our quality of life and therefore our well-being.

This shows that while it is possible to define need as limited to things that are essential to continuing to live, there are other things such as love and books which can also be very important to improve the quality of our lives and so can also be important needs.

What is a welfare need?

Defining a welfare need is not easy. This is for the same reasons given above, that a welfare need is something that can be defined in more than one way. On the one hand, we can talk about a welfare need as something which is a necessity for life and without which your life would be unsustainable. So an absence of money would be something which means we are not able to buy the things we need to continue to live, and if we think about health, constantly being unwell would also be something which would affect our ability to continue to live. These types of welfare needs are also things which we see as real and concrete, and therefore as need which are easily met.

On the other hand, we can also define a welfare need as something which has the potential to enhance our quality of life. So for example, if we think about education, this is something that enables us to acquire learning and understanding which could enhance our life in the future. These types of needs are not things which are a necessity for life, but they enhance our welfare in terms of quality, in both the short term and the longer term. Another example of this might be books, or even TV, as without these things, you would still be alive, but your quality of life would be diminished. These types of needs can also be abstract things like feeling loved or self-development, and so are not as easy to meet as the other type of need.

Defining welfare need in terms of being either something which is a necessity for life or something which enhances the quality of our life enables us to distinguish between two different types of need. By looking at the Case Studies in the box below and answering the questions set, we can distinguish in more detail between these two types of welfare need, and consider if one type of need is more important than the other.

Real Life Box 7.1 **Case study: what is the welfare need?**

1. Identify the need(s) of each individual below

2. Decide whose need is greater and why

Case Study 1

Jessica is a pensioner and lives alone in a one bedroom bungalow, and has done so since her husband died three years ago. Last winter was a particularly cold winter and her heating bill was more than double what it was the previous year. She managed to pay it by dipping into savings. She is worried this year that she will not be able to pay it, so has decided to only turn the heating on if the temperature reaches zero degrees outside. She needs about £200 to enable her to have the heating on throughout the winter.

▶

◀

Case Study 2

Joe is a final year student at university, who has worked throughout his time of study. This has enabled him to buy books and pay his transport costs. Unfortunately he has been falling behind in his work because he has needed to work throughout his time at university. He is finding the third year particularly hard to match the demands of work and study. Because he has not worked as much, he has not had money to pay transport or to buy books. This has meant that he has fallen behind and is in danger of failing modules. If this happens, he will have to quit the course as we would not be able to afford to redo a year. He has already applied for student hardship and received the maximum amount. He needs another £200 to pay for transport and buy all the books he needs for the year.

The case studies above highlight two different types of welfare need. In Case Study 1, we can see that Jessica's need is something which arguably has an immediate life-threatening consequence to it. This is in contrast to Case Study 2, where it is arguable that the need present is not life-threatening to Joe, but is a need which is important for Joe's quality of life in the longer term. This contrast in the case studies enables us to classify welfare need into two main types, *subsistence needs* and *participatory needs*.

Subsistence needs

Subsistence needs are those which are concerned with the immediate avoidance of serious harm or death. Examples of this are needs related to food, water, health, and as we see in the Jessica's case study above, warmth. The negative consequences of these needs not being met are often immediately apparent for the individual, and also for the community in which they live, and so the need has to be met immediately. This makes this type of need relatively easy to define and determine when it has been met, and means that this is the type of need that is often the primary focus of social policy.

Participatory needs

Participatory needs are those which improve the quality of life of individuals. For example, if we talk about having education needs as in Joe's case, we can describe a need for education as something that enables him to live a life that is fulfilled and meaningful in a variety of ways. Defining needs as something that improves our quality of welfare is significant because the need is typically seen as something to aspire to, and which has long-term implications for our welfare.

The negative consequences of participatory needs are not necessarily immediate, but may be felt in both the short and long term by both the individual and the society in which the individual lives. This means that the need that Joe has now is something which could impact on the rest of his life in a significant way. In Joe's case above, an obvious short-term consequence of his need for education not being met is frustration, which could translate into unhappiness.

The longer-term consequences could be six months later when he applies for a job, or six years later when he applies for a promotion and is refused as a consequence of not having the relevant qualification. If he is denied either as a consequence of his needs not being met now, this could have a detrimental effect on his participation in society. Moreover, such lack of participation can also impact on society, in the sense that Joe's potential contribution to wider society is limited by his needs not being met, which impacts on the wider development of society. This highlights that participatory needs are more complex to understand and define, and therefore meet, than subsistence needs.

Does everyone have the same welfare needs?

What the case studies also show is that different people can have different needs at different points in their life. So for example, while Jessica's need is for heating, Joe's need is for education. This highlights that needs can change over time and with circumstances. However, it is probable that when Jessica was Joe's age, she had the same needs as he has now, and when Joe reaches Jessica's age, he will have the same needs as she has now. This is a point that Doyal and Gough (1991) make when they argue that there are eight human needs that are 'universable', that is they are common to all individuals regardless of who they are and where they live in the world. Doyal and Gough's universable human needs are:

➤ survival/health;

➤ autonomy;

➤ water/nutrition;

➤ housing;

➤ health services;

> security;

> education;

> reproduction.

Question

Which of Doyal and Gough's needs do you agree are universable, and which are not?

You may or may not agree with all of Doyal and Gough's list of universable human needs, but it would be very surprising if you did not agree with at least one thing on the list, such as survival/health, water/nutrition, housing, health services or security, while the others might be more debatable. This does indeed suggest that there are some needs which everyone has, regardless of who they are or where they live. The key point here is that acceptance in any way of Doyal and Gough's list of universable human needs also has a very important implication in relation to social policy. This is that all humans, regardless of who they are and where they live, have some needs which have to be met, as a consequence of simply being human. This places an obligation on societies to ensure that such needs are met, and this is where the relevance of social policy in general and specific social policies become apparent.

However, it is important to note that this is not the same as saying that all universable welfare needs are the same for everyone. For example, if we take 'health services' from the list above, while both male and female may have health needs, these needs are somewhat different, and this means while needs can be universable to all, they can also be particular to the individual.

Are welfare needs different from welfare wants?

Social policy's focus is on meeting needs, which as we have seen above can be difficult to define. Something else that makes need difficult to define is distinguishing needs from wants, which is not the focus of social policy (note that this is different from Beveridge's 'Want' outlined in Chapter 3 which referred specifically to income maintenance needs).

It is fairly easy to distinguish wants from subsistence needs, but less easy to distinguish wants from participatory needs. This is because they can both improve the quality of our welfare. We defined a participatory need as something which improves the quality of our lives, and we can similarly define a welfare want as something which could improve the quality of our lives. An obvious distinction between the two is whether what we are talking about is something that we could realistically live without. For example, in relation to our health, gym membership is something which would very likely improve the quality of our health, but we do not actually need gym membership to improve our health, and our health is not necessarily diminished in its absence; rather it is something which we would like to have but which we can live without, and so is a want, not a participatory need.

However, this distinction is not always so clear cut, and the box below emphasizes this difficulty in distinguishing between the two.

Real Life Box 7.2 **Health needs or health wants?**

Look at the list of health treatments below.

1. Could any of these be classified as wants rather than needs?

2. Are they need or wants for the individuals concerned?

Glasses	Alcoholism treatment
Tattoo removal	Male or female sterilization
IVF treatment	Lung cancer treatment caused by smoking
Dental treatment	Birthmark removal
Dementia treatment	Vaccination for flu
Varicose veins treatment	Gastric band treatment for obesity

The box highlights that it is not easy to distinguish between a want and a participatory need for some health treatments. For example, while some people may see tattoo removal as a want, there have been cases where a tattoo that a person had several years earlier has restricted their ability to get a job. In such instances, it is clear that having the tattoo is impacting on their participation within society, which then means that its removal becomes a participatory need for them. Similarly, while gastric band treatment for obesity may be seen as something that individuals can live without, and therefore a want, for the individual it may be the difference between simply survival and participation within society, and so is a participatory need for them.

It is important to note that all the treatments in the box above are available on the NHS in certain instances. This means that a treatment that you may have identified as a want is something that has been identified as a relevant social policy need for some individuals. This reinforces the point made above about the difficulty of distinguishing between wants and participatory needs.

Questions
_____

1. Are welfare wants as important as welfare needs to human well-being?

2. Are there instances when social policy should meet wants, not just needs?

How do the different definitions of welfare need shape social policies?

So we can categorize two distinct types of welfare needs:

> *Subsistence* needs can be narrowly defined as concerned with the avoidance of harm or death, usually in the immediate future.

> *Participatory* needs can be more widely defined as concerned with the quality of life and lack of participation in society, both immediately or in the longer term.

We can see how these different definitions of need shape actual social policy areas by looking at Table 7.1, which summarizes the differences between subsistence and participatory needs for specific social policy areas.

As Table 7.1 shows, there are major differences in the way that subsistence and participatory needs shape social policy areas. Just to take health as an example, a subsistence emphasis on absence of illness is very different from a participatory emphasis on physical mental and social well-being. These differences show that an emphasis in policy on meeting subsistence needs can mean significant differences from a policy that emphasizes meeting participatory needs, as detailed in Table 7.1.

Which type of need is the most important for social policy to meet?

Table 7.1 below shows that there are major differences in the way that subsistence and participatory needs shape social policy areas, and this brings

Table 7.1 How different subsistence and participatory needs shape social policies

	Subsistence needs	Participatory needs
Health	Having the absence of illness e.g. not having cancer, heart disease etc.	Having complete physical, mental and social well-being e.g. having good physical and mental health
Education	Having basic literacy and numeracy e.g. being able to read and count	Being able to undertake lifelong learning and development e.g. being able to continuously acquire new knowledge and skills
Housing	Having basic shelter e.g. having somewhere to live	Having safe, secure and stable accommodation e.g. having affordable and good quality housing
Income maintenance	Having an income level that mean means you do not live in absolute poverty e.g. an income that is just above the poverty line	Having an income level that means not living in either absolute or relative poverty e.g. the living wage
Personal social services	Having basic care needs met e.g. being safe, clean and secure	Having emotional and personal care needs met e.g. having social interaction and participation within society

us to the question of which type of need is the most important for social policy to meet.

The obvious first response to this is that subsistence needs are most important, as they can have immediate negative consequences, as in the case study for Jessica above. This would mean that the focus of social policy should be on meeting these type of needs.

However, the nature of participatory needs means that their importance should not be overlooked. As in the case study for Joe, not meeting a particular participatory need can have long-term negative impact on an individual's welfare, and this impact can also be felt in the wider community. Moreover, a participatory need not being met can have a domino effect in terms of also diminishing an individual's other related participatory needs. This is a point that Maslow's (1943) 'hierarchy of needs' makes, as shown in Figure 7.1.

Maslow's 'hierarchy of needs' presents five sets of needs which individuals have, and which are ordered in a specific way. The needs presented are needs that all humans have, and not just some individuals. At the bottom of the figure are the needs which we have termed subsistence needs (food, water etc.). This is followed by various needs we can identify as participatory to different degrees, such as family, love,

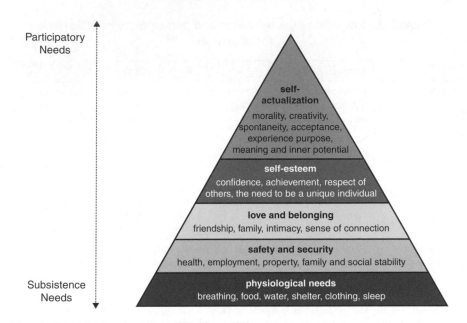

Figure 7.1 Maslow's 'hierarchy of needs'
Source: Adapted from Maslow (1943)

achievement, confidence and sense of connection. At the top is the ultimate participatory need, 'self-actualization', which is where an individual is in total control of their existence and the way their life functions.

Maslow ordered the needs in this way because it represents the order in which needs have to be satisfied, meaning that a higher level of needs cannot be met unless the lower order has already been met. So for example, meeting the need for 'love and belonging' is only possible after 'safety and security' has been met. However, unless all of these needs are satisfied, human life is not as fulfilling as it could be. This is because these needs are not separate but are interlinked, meaning that failure to meet a need in one aspect has implications for other higher aspects of needs.

Question

Consider what you think would be the difference in outcomes if a baby was brought up:

a) with only their subsistence needs of adequate food, warmth, clothing and shelter met?

b) with their participatory needs of love, social interaction, communication etc. also met?

The important point from Maslow is that while subsistence needs are an important starting point for meeting needs, they should not be seen as the only needs that have to be met. Participatory needs are also important in order for individuals in society to feel self-fulfilled, and therefore contributing as much to society as possible. We can sum up this difference between just meeting subsistence needs and meeting both subsistence and participatory needs as the difference between merely 'survival' and 'surviving and thriving', as summarized in the quote below from Maya Angelou:

My mission is life is not merely to survive, but to survive and thrive.

Question

Which level of Maslow's hierarchy of needs do you think is relevant to you now?

We can discuss this implication for social policy of an emphasis on subsistence needs or participatory needs by looking at health. We can define health in two main ways relating to subsistence or participation. A subsistence definition of health focuses solely on the absence of illness. So only if a person is evidently ill are they seen as having health needs. A good example of this is where an individual has cancer, and so it is clearly evident that they are ill.

On the other hand, the World Health Organization (WHO, 1946) defines health as 'a state of complete physical, mental, and social well-being and not merely the absence of disease and infirmity'. In this definition, health is seen as wider than just illness, and considers the ability of individuals to participate in society. A good example of this is obesity, which is something that affects individuals' ability to participate in society in particular long-term ways.

If we defined health only in subsistence terms to limit treatment to those with immediate necessity such as cancer, there would be numerous other health conditions which would not be eligible for treatment, such as obesity. In the short term, denying treatment for such non-immediate conditions would be less costly and save money for the health service. However, obesity impacts on the individual in a variety of ways that limits their welfare, especially over the longer term, such as increasing the risk of heart attacks, diabetes, high blood pressure and mental illness. It is these long-term impacts which mean that the costs of obesity in the UK are growing and are predicted to reach up to £50 billion by 2050 (National Obesity Forum, 2014). This highlights that limiting health resources only to narrow subsistence needs and not for meeting wider participatory needs can have longer-term costs for social policy which are above and beyond the initial cost of dealing with them.

We saw an example of this is Chapter 5 in terms of employment and poverty, where the focus in policy both is on in work and out of work benefits that are at or below the poverty line, which means that there are millions of people living below the poverty line, just about able to meet their subsistence needs of food and shelter, but not their participatory needs of social interaction, self-respect and confidence. The clear implication of this for social policy is that unless the focus of policy is on ensuring that both subsistence and participatory needs are met as fully as possible, then individuals within society will not reach their full potential and capabilities. Where this happens, the effectiveness of social policy is limited in terms of its overall aims of improving the welfare of individuals.

Does social policy meet welfare needs in a subsistence or participatory way?

As outlined in Table 7.1 above, there are major differences between an emphasis on subsistence and participatory needs, and Figure 7.2 summarizes these differences in terms of the extent that social policies meet participatory or subsistence needs for the five main social policy areas.

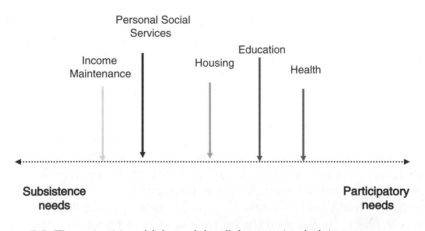

Figure 7.2 The extent to which social policies meet subsistence or participatory needs

Figure 7.2 shows that social policy meets some welfare needs in a more participatory way, and meets others in a more subsistence way. The area of social policy where needs are met in the most participatory way is in relation to health. This is because access to most health needs is available to all in a universal way, and free at the point of use throughout their life. This means that most individuals are able to maintain a good quality of health, which enables them to participate in other aspects of society. There are also important preventative health measures, such as vaccinations and smear tests, which not only improve the subsistence health of individuals, but are preventative and so enable individuals to improve their overall well-being. However, there are some aspects of health policies which are not available to everyone in this manner, such as prescriptions, optical care and dental care, and these limits mean that health is not fully participatory. And mental health services are often called a 'Cinderella service', meaning that they are often more of a luxury than a reality for many individuals.

Social policy meets education needs in a mainly participatory way, but not to the extent of health needs. This is despite the fact that education from the ages of 5 to 18 is compulsory, and access to education during these ages is also available to all in a universal way, and free at the point of use. This means that in general, overall literacy (i.e. reading and comprehension) in most of the UK compares well with other countries, although overall numeracy does not compare so well (Wheater *et al.*, 2013). However, the introduction and extension of tuition fees and maintenance loans for university education has limited the ability of individuals to meet their needs beyond 18 years old, as for example, there are less students applying for university than before the increase in tuition fees, and particularly fewer mature students applying to university than before (Independent Commission on Fees, 2013). This suggests that the ability to pay rather than their actual need has become an important deciding factor for many.

Real Life Box 7.3 **Education: a compulsory need**

It is interesting to note that education is a need which is seen as so important to the welfare of individuals, that it is a legal requirement to acquire it, as evident from the legal requirement to go to school from the ages of 5 to 16. Additionally, in 2015 the school

▶

leaving age in England is increased to 18, meaning that all young people up to this age are not simply able to leave school but have to choose between staying in full-time education, undertaking work-based learning such as an Apprenticeship, or part-time education or training if they are employed, being self-employed or volunteering for more than 20 hours per week. There is no other welfare service which is compulsory to this extent.

The way that social policy meets housing needs is a mixture between subsistence and participatory needs. On the one hand there is support in the form of income benefits such as Housing Benefit to ensure that the subsistence need for housing is met, and most people do have some form of housing. Housing policy also enables people to buy their homes, through the *Right to Buy* and the *Help to Buy* policies, which provide subsidies for those buying homes. However, homelessness is also evident, which suggests that not all individuals' subsistence needs are being met. For example, according to Crisis (2014), 112,070 households applied to their local authority for homelessness assistance in 2013/14, which is a 26% rise on the previous year.

Also, for those who rent from private landlords, Housing Benefit is paid at a rate well below the average rent for the area in which they live, and this means that they are not able to access the highest quality housing, thereby limiting their ability to meet their participatory needs.

Real Life Box 7.4 **The difference between subsistence and participatory housing needs**

The essential difference between subsistence and participatory housing is summed up succinctly in the quote below from Raquel Rolnik (2013), a United Nations Special Representative:

> The right to housing is not about a roof anywhere, at any cost, without any social ties. It is not about reshuffling people according to a snapshot of the number of bedrooms at a given night. It is about enabling environments for people to maintain their family and community bonds, their local schools, work places and health services allowing them to exercise all other rights, like education, work, food or health.

In terms of participatory needs, in 2012–2013, 3% of households in England were overcrowded, and 22 million homes failed to meet the decent homes standard, meaning that they were below adequate standard for people who lived in them (DCLOG, 2014b). This shows that many people's participatory housing needs are not being met.

The range of social policies for personal social services is wide, with responsibility for children such as through child protection services, older people through personal care services, and services for disabled people. However, like mental health services, personal social services is also often called a 'Cinderella service', due to the lack of funding that exists for it, and often functions in a state of crisis. An example of this is the failures in child protection that resulted in the death of several children, such as Baby P, Daniel Pelka and Victoria Climbie. This limits its potential to meet participatory needs, and instead means that it is often only able to meet subsistence needs.

Income maintenance is the social policy area that has the highest expenditure, but is more subsistence than participatory. This is mainly due to the fact that the majority of income maintenance expenditure is on pensions, meaning that there is very little available to spend on other benefits, as we saw in Chapter 2. Also, as we saw in Chapter 5, the official poverty line is set very low, and so the main benefits that are meant to relieve poverty, such as Income Benefit and Jobseeker's Allowance, are set at a level that is below the poverty line. This means that income maintenance benefits are much more subsistence in nature than they are participatory.

Has the 2010 Coalition government's emphasis in social policy been on meeting needs in a subsistence or a participatory way?

As set out in Figure 7.2, social policy meets some welfare needs in a way that is more participatory, while others are met in a way that is more subsistence. The financial constraints of the austerity policies of the 2010 Coalition government have had a significant impact on the way that social policy meets needs. This is because the argument that the 2010 Coalition government put forward for its austerity social policies was that it could only afford to meet needs in a subsistence way due to lack of financial resources, as meeting social policy needs in a participatory way is much more expensive than meeting social policy needs in a subsistence way.

So for example, in the years 2010–2014 expenditure on income maintenance benefits such as Income Support, Jobseeker's Allowance and Personal Independence Payment for disabled people fell by £18 billion. And expenditure on personal social services for social care for children and adults fell by £15 billion, all of which reinforced the subsistence nature of these policy areas as shown in Figure 7.2.

However, at the same time, expenditure in some areas has increased, such as expenditure on health which increased by nearly £13 billion, and expenditure on pensions increased by £10 billion (Duffy, 2013). And even within social policy areas, there were some areas where some expenditure increased at the same time that other expenditure decreased, for example while expenditure on higher education decreased, expenditure on schools increased (Duffy, 2013), as evident from the introduction of universal Free School Meals to those age 5 to 7 in 2014 and the £1 billion spent on Free Schools. Housing is another area where while expenditure on benefits such as Housing Benefit decreased significantly, expenditure on other benefits such as Help to Buy increased.

This means that overall the impact of austerity has affected some social policy areas more than others, and so the impact of austerity on the participatory nature of areas such as health has been limited. However, for areas such as income maintenance and personal social services, austerity has reinforced their subsistence nature. Moreover, the different ways that the 2010 Coalition government has applied austerity to different social policy areas shows that governments can and do choose the ways in which they want social policies to meet needs. It also highlights that the 2010 Coalition government's emphasis in general is on social policies that meet needs in a subsistence rather than a participatory way.

In particular, the 2010 Coalition government has outlined three specific ways in which social policy needs can and should be met in a more subsistence way at a time of austerity. These are:

> charging;

> rationing;

> choice.

We analyse below how these processes work in health as a way to exemplify how they work in other social policy areas in general. The benefits and limitations of each in terms of meeting needs are also discussed.

Charging

Charging is where an individual is expected to pay for a taxpayer funded social policy benefit that meets their need. A good example of charging is prescriptions. Also, if you are a higher education student, you are directly experiencing charging through paying tuition fees. Charging is also evident in personal social services, where individuals with an income above a set limit are expected to pay for some or all of their care home costs.

More recently, there has been a call to introduce a flat rate charge for GP consultations as a way to reduce demand and save costs for health (Cawston and Corrie, 2013) (as we saw in Chapter 4, private healthcare already charges for visits to a GP). Cawston and Corrie (2013) estimate that such a consultation charge of £10 per visit could raise £1.2 billion in additional revenue for the NHS. According to Aziz (2013), the introduction of charges for GPs would impact significantly on the NHS meeting health needs, with people going less to their GP, and some groups in particular, such as those on low incomes, choosing not to go at all. This would mean that in the longer term, any additional revenue raised made would be limited by the increased cost of additional healthcare required for more serious conditions that emerge. There has also been a proposal to introduce charges for mobility devices such as crutches and neck braces (Campbell, 2014).

In terms of the NHS, while some people get free dental treatment, prescriptions, glasses and hearing aids, a significant number of NHS patients in England pay for these. The most evident form of charging for health is prescription charges in England. In Scotland, Wales and Northern Ireland there are no prescription charges. There are several exemptions to prescription charges in England, such as under 16s, pregnancy, and receiving certain benefits, such as income support or income based Jobseeker's Allowance. At the time of writing, prescription charges in England were £8.05.

One of the main arguments for prescription charges is they provide additional income for the NHS, as prescription charges raise £450 million of additional funding for the NHS (Cawston and Corrie, 2013). Another important argument is that they save money for the NHS by limiting the number of prescriptions that individuals use. In this sense, it is argued that they mean that only genuine health prescription needs are met rather than wants.

However, there are a number of arguments against charging for healthcare. The first is that they limit the comprehensive nature of the NHS, as it means that those who cannot afford the cost of prescriptions will not access the prescriptions, and so their health will deteriorate. This means that comprehensive healthcare becomes the preserve of those who can afford it, rather than being based on need. This could have a longer-term cost to the NHS, if the inability to afford required prescriptions means that a person's healthy condition deteriorates. This is especially the case where an individual has a chronic condition that requires repeat prescriptions over a long term, such as multiple sclerosis or mental illness, whereby the costs of prescriptions could significantly increase over time (Prescription Charges Coalition, 2014).

Question

Would having to pay £10 every time you went to see your GP affect your decision to go to see them?

Rationing

Rationing occurs where the amount of a welfare service provided is less than the demand for it. A good example of this is in relation to council housing, where there are more people who want council housing than there are council houses. Where this happens, this means that the service is not able to immediately meet all the demand for it, and so can put in place a way to determine whose needs should be met, a rationing mechanism. In the case of council housing, this is done through a waiting list, which works to allocate the limited amount of housing that is available.

Rationing has always been a way to limit demand for specific welfare needs, especially in the NHS. The issues of rationing in the NHS has come to the fore as more people live longer and so more illnesses become evident. For example, dementia is an illness which 20 years ago was not the issue it is today. Also, as treatments have got better, so more people are being kept alive who would previously have died. Severely premature babies are a good example of this, as improvements in health technology mean that premature babies than 20 years ago are more likely to be born alive, even at 23 weeks (McVeigh, 2014). Over recent years, procedures such as cataract operations and knee replacements have become more in demand with the ageing population, and these treatments have become especially subject to rationing.

Rationing in healthcare through waiting lists is something that you may have come across, and which functions to delay treatment that you are entitled to in the absence of sufficient resources. This is only one of three types of rationing that occurs, as shown in Table 7.2.

Table 7.2 Types and examples of healthcare rationing

Rationing type	Example
Delay of treatment	➤ putting individuals on NHS waiting lists for treatment ➤ making long-term medical referrals to experts to determine if treatment is needed
Dilution of treatment – giving people less service	➤ having to wait for GP appointments ➤ reduction in nurses on wards
Denial of treatment – restricting access to certain treatments and drugs	➤ denying treatment to some groups such as smokers ➤ denying access to expensive drugs from NICE (National Institute for Health and Care Excellence) guidelines

Source: Adapted from http://www2.rgu.ac.uk/publicpolicy/introduction/socadmin.htm

Real Life Box 7.5 **NICE (National Institute for Health and Care Excellence)**

NICE is an independent government body that provides national guidance and advice on whether health and social care interventions should be available on the NHS or through social care bodies. Effectively it decides whether a treatment is rationed or not. These decisions affect medicines (such as for cancer), treatments (such as for Alzheimer's disease) or new technologies (such as for surgery).

The aim of NICE is to ensure that a universal level of treatments is available, regardless of where you live. This does not mean that all treatments are available to everyone, but that only the treatments that meet a certain level of cost-effectiveness are available to all.

NICE decides whether to approve an intervention based on how much it costs and how much it improves the life of patients. This involves judgements about *how long* (in months or years) the intervention will add to a person's life, as well as whether the intervention improves the *quality of life* for the person during the treatments. This means if a drug is cheap but not very good, it probably will not be approved by NICE. But if a drug or treatment is expensive and good it can be approved by NICE.

The decision that NICE made on two cancer drugs exemplifies how this works. The first is known as Herceptin, a treatment for breast cancer, and in 2006 NICE approved its use on the NHS. Herceptin costs approximately £21,800 per patient per year.

The second drug is known as Avastin, a treatment for bowel cancer. Avastin costs approximately £20,800 per patient per year, and in 2010 NICE rejected its use on the NHS. So although it is cheaper than Herceptin, it was rejected on cost-effectiveness grounds.

These NICE decisions mean that if a health authority does not provide Herceptin to a patient who is eligible, it can be taken to court to force treatment. On the other hand, a health authority does not have to provide Avastin, but it can do if it chooses to do so.

Rationing as a way to limit demand for specific welfare needs has a number of disadvantages over charging, the main one being that it does not necessarily put off people who need a benefit from seeking it. A summary of the advantages and disadvantages of rationing welfare is shown in Table 7.3 services.

Table 7.3 Advantages and disadvantages of rationing welfare services

Advantages	Disadvantages
It weeds out those who do not really need assistance	It is ethically suspect to deny services to those who need it
More cost effective, as decisions are made by those who understand system	More expensive in the longer term as it leads to pent up demand
Less wastage of provision	Decision making is often on cost grounds, not on basis of needs
Provides an honest and straightforward way to allocate limited provision	Decision making is bureaucratic, undemocratic and not easy to understand by most
Reduces dependency on welfare state	Blunt tool of decision-making, those less able to articulate needs less likely to receive services

Choice

Choice in welfare services refers to giving you more responsibility for how your needs are met. This is mainly in terms of how your welfare need is met, an example of which is in education, where parents have the choice to send their children to a variety of different schools such as local authority, free schools or academies. Another example of this choice that you are very likely to have come across is evident in the provision of higher education. Such exercise of choice is argued to limit demand for welfare services by matching needs precisely to demand, therefore limiting wasteful expenditure and services that exist and so are not needed.

Patient choice has been expanded considerably in the NHS over the last 20 years to the extent that it now dominates the health agenda (Bosanquet *et al.*, 2010). In practical terms, this has meant the development of the NHS Choices website (http://www.nhs.uk/Pages/HomePage.aspx), which enables patients to compare hospitals by information such as waiting times, re-admission rates and comments and ratings from patients. Patients are also now able to 'Choose and Book' their first hospital appointment at their chosen hospital once they have a confirmed referral from their GP, something which you may have done. More recently, with the introduction of the NHS and Social Care Act 2012, some NHS services such as adult hearing, diagnostic tests and wheelchair services have been given over to different providers to give patients the choice of services they are able to use.

Bosanquet *et al.* (2010: 25) argue that there is evidence that the main benefit of using choice to limit demand for health needs is that it enables patients to access the specific services that they need, and this means that services that are not needed are not accessed, and so not provided.

However, the major limitation of using choice to limit demand for health needs is the lack of information that an individual has over what would be the best choice. This would mean that the potential for the wrong choices to be made is increased, and the individual would be blamed.

A significant way that choice has been enabled in healthcare is through the use of vouchers, such as for glasses, and more recently for wheelchairs. The 2010 Coalition government introduced vouchers to enable individuals to buy their own health treatments (Ramesh, 2011).

Choice in healthcare specifically and social policy in general is something which governments of all types have introduced in welfare services over the last 40 years. This is explored in more detail in the next chapter.

Summary

This chapter has shown that defining precisely what constitutes a welfare need is not as straightforward as we might think, for the simple reason that there is more than one type of need. So subsistence needs refers narrowly to things which our existence depends on, while participatory needs refers more widely to things that are not necessarily essential but which are nevertheless very important for our quality of life and therefore our well-being. Similarly, trying to distinguish welfare wants from participatory needs is not easy, especially for those with the want. Despite these difficulties, if we accept that some welfare needs are universal, meaning that everyone has these needs regardless of who they are or where they live, then this places an obligation on societies to ensure that such needs are met, and this is where the relevance of social policy in general and specific social policies becomes readily apparent.

This chapter has also shown that the difference between subsistence needs and participatory needs also has important consequences for the nature of social policies, as there are major differences between social policies that emphasize subsistence needs and social policies that emphasize participatory needs. We can see that some social policy areas, such as health, meet needs in a more participatory way and others, such as income maintenance, meet needs in a more subsistence way. Where the emphasis in policy is on meeting subsistence needs, Maslow's 'hierarchy of needs' highlights to us that unless the focus of policy is on ensuring that both subsistence and participatory needs are met as fully as possible, then individuals within society will not reach their full potential and capabilities. Where this happens, the effectiveness of social policy is limited in terms of its overall aims of improving the welfare of individuals.

While governments often outline financial constraints as the most important factor in determining the subsistence or participatory nature of social policies, the austerity policies of the 2010 Coalition government show us that governments can and do choose the ways in which they want social policies to meet need. In particular, the 2010 Coalition government's emphasis is on social policies that meet needs in a subsistence rather than a participatory way, particularly through increased charging, rationing and choice.

Key Point

We all have welfare needs, and social policies meet welfare needs in either a subsistence or a participatory way, which has an important impact on the overall social policy aim of improving the welfare of individuals.

8

WHO SHOULD PROVIDE SOCIAL POLICIES?

The aims of this chapter are to:

1. Outline differences between social policies provided by the state, private companies, voluntary/community organizations and individuals

2. Outline the specified advantages and limitations of these different ways of providing social policies

3. Understand the notion and the significance of the shift to a mixed economy of welfare for current social policies

This book has shown that you receive a wide range of social policy benefits to meet the wide range of welfare needs you have. This means that you have entitlement to some very important benefits such as the NHS, Jobseeker's Allowance, Child Benefit and Student Maintenance grants. Most of these benefits are provided by the state, either directly from central government (meaning the government that runs the country such as the 2010 Coalition government, as for the NHS) or from local government (such as the local council, as for Council Tax Benefit). This means that state provided social policy benefits are vast and varied in extent and scope, and are relevant to meeting the welfare needs of all individuals at some points in their lives.

However, not all social policies are provided by the state and there are some which are met by private companies. Examples of this are private education, private healthcare and private care homes. Another example is a private pension, and it may be the case that at the same time individuals receive both a state pension and a private pension from a private company.

Some social policies are also provided by voluntary and community organizations, such as those run by charities or community groups.

Obvious examples of such voluntary and community social policies are the child protection services provided to vulnerable children and young people by the NSPCC, housing provided to homeless people by Shelter, and food provided by foodbank organizations such as The Trussell Trust.

And some welfare needs are also met by individuals, care being an obvious example. Care provided by individuals can either be short term or long term for a variety of reasons, such as sickness, disability, mental illness or age. According to Carers UK, there are 6.5 million carers in the UK, who can be family, friends, neighbours or the community.

This highlights that while the state is the most important provider of the many social policies you receive, it is not the only possible provider, and there are in fact a variety of others providers of social policies you receive.

This chapter analyses differences between the state, private companies, voluntary/community organizations and individuals as providers of social policies. It specifically focuses on education policy to outline the advantages and disadvantages of each type of provider. However, the reality is that rather than social policies being provided solely by one type of provider, they are often provided by a mixture of different providers. This is known as the *mixed economy of welfare*, that is, where total welfare provision is provided by a combination of state, market and voluntary/community and individual providers. The chapter analyses the rationale and limitations of this shift towards the mixed economy of welfare over the last 40 years or so.

By the end of this chapter, you will be able to explain and discuss the differences between social policies that are provided by the state, private companies, voluntary/community organizations and individuals, and outline the strengths and limitations of each. You will also be able to articulate the significant changes that have occurred in the provision of social policies over the last 40 years, including an understanding of the notion of the mixed economy of welfare, and its importance to current social policies.

What are the differences and specified advantages between the providers of social policies?

State social policies

As detailed above, for most people the state provides the vast range of the social policies that they receive. State provided social policies are in the form of various benefits, such as:

> *direct cash benefits* – in the form of money, such as Jobseeker's Allowance, Child Benefit, Housing Benefit, Carer's Allowance, student maintenance grants, student maintenance loans;

> *indirect cash benefits* – such as NHS prescriptions, NHS dentistry, HE tuition fees, Council Tax reduction;

> *in-kind benefits* – in the form of services, such as NHS healthcare, housing, education, care homes;

> *the regulation of welfare conditions* – such as the National Minimum Wage, school standards through OFSTED, and fair access to higher education through the Office for Fair Access (OFFA);

> *part-payment for a benefit* – such as the childcare tax credit, Help to Buy for house buying.

Such benefits can be purely funded and provided by the state through taxation so there is no direct charge to the individuals, such as most NHS hospital services. Or they can be funded but not provided by the state, such as housing provided through the payment of Housing Benefit to private landlords and housing associations. They can also be provided by central government, meaning the government that runs the whole country such as the 2010 Coalition government, or local government, meaning the government that runs a local area, such as a local council.

Real Life Box 8.1 **The difference between central government and local government**

The state can provide social policies either through central government or local government, also referred to as local councils. Both central and local government are elected, but central government is elected to govern the whole country, while local government is elected to govern a particular part of the country. The powers of central government are also much greater than those of local government. So for example, while central government can make new laws, local government cannot do this. And while central government can create new taxes to pay for what it does, local government cannot do this. Instead local government relies for most of its funding on grants from central government.

Examples of social policies that are provided by central government are the NHS and most income benefits such as Jobseeker's Allowance and the State Pension.

When people think of what local government does, they perhaps think of dustbins and dog pooh, but local government does much more than that. Examples of social policies that are provided by local government are council housing, Housing Benefit, social work and social care. An interesting point of difference between central and local government to note is that the benefits central government provides are generally standardized and the same for all, while the benefits local government provides are generally variable depending on where a person lives.

◀

A good example of this is in relation to Council Tax, which is the main local tax that you will pay local government. Firstly, the amount of Council Tax varies in different parts of the country. So in 2014–2015, a Band A (which is the lowest band) Council Tax in Birmingham was £862, while in Liverpool it was £1,056. Secondly, local councils can only keep some of their Council Tax receipts, and have to give some to central government, who then redistribute it to councils on a needs basis. This means that Council Tax is only a very small amount of the money that local government spends.

There are four main advantages for state provided social policies. The first advantage is that the state provides benefits which in most circumstances the individual would not be able to afford due to the high costs. A good example of this is the cost of compulsory education over a lifetime, as shown in Chapter 4. In Chapter 4, we calculated the cost of state provided education at £1,557 per person per year, which for 13 years of education between the ages of 5 and 13 works out at £20,449. In comparison, we also calculated the cost of private day schooling at £12,500 per year, which over 13 years is £162,500. Therefore private schooling costs approximately eight times more than taxation funded schooling. To put it another way, the cost of 13 years of private schooling is equivalent to the cost of 104 years of taxation funded schooling, which makes it prohibitively expensive for most people. This highlights that state provided social policy decreases the cost of social policy provision to the individual, in comparison to where social policy is expected to be provided solely by the individual.

The second advantage is that because entitlement to most state benefits is from the criteria of need rather than the ability to pay, this ensures that the basic minimum needs of most people in society are met, regardless of whether they have the financial means to pay. For example, while access to the NHS is limited for some conditions, the NHS does provide a wide range of comprehensive healthcare for free, even for conditions that cost a lot to treat, such as heart conditions, and this ensures that most people are able to access healthcare for a range of conditions. This ensures that most of the health needs of the population are met, and so a basic level of health within society is established.

Related to this is the fact that the state also provides benefits that other organizations cannot or will not provide as it is not cost effective for them to do so. For example, the state provides income maintenance benefits such as Jobseeker's Allowance and Income Support for those unable to work. These benefits are paid to enable individuals to maintain a certain standard of living, usually to those in circumstances where they have little chance of directly paying back what they have received. In the absence of such benefits, one alternative to individuals would be to borrow from other individuals, or to borrow from other organizations, for example in the form of loans, but this is not a realistic alternative for any significant period of time. Therefore, the provision of such state provided benefits enables individuals to maintain a minimum standard within society at time of need, when other sources of assistance would either be not available or would be prohibitively expensive to access.

Linked to this is the fact that such an emphasis on minimum standards in state provided social policy leads to some level of equality within society, especially where the state regulates certain welfare conditions. For example, OFSTED regulates standards in state schools to ensure that all children receive education that is of a minimum standard, but does not regulate private schools. Examples of other organizations which perform similar regulatory functions are the Care Quality Commission for care homes, and the Health and Safety Executive. Regulation which protects workers' rights, such as the *National Minimum Wage* and the *Working Time Directive* also work in this way. The state can also regulate in terms of what individuals can do. So for instance it sets the age of consent for sexual intercourse and for smoking at 16, while the age at which alcohol can be sold to individuals and at which they can vote is 18. And there is also social policy legislation which sets up organizations that are concerned with limiting discrimination and inequality among groups, such as the Equal Pay Act 1970, the Equality Act 2010 and the Marriage (Same Sex Couples) Act 2013. In the absence of such an emphasis on minimum standards, the likelihood is that there would be less equality within society.

Real Life Box 8.2 **The Working Time Directive**

The Working Time Directive is a regulation that means that most workers cannot be forced to work more than 48 hours a week, unless they specifically choose to do so. This works out at a maximum of 9.6 hours a day for a five day working week, and it is illegal to force someone to work more than these hours.

The Working Time Directive was brought in to stop employers forcing employers from working long hours. An example of where it had a particular effect was in relation to junior doctors, who sometimes were forced to work up to 70 hours a week. This could mean that they would be working while tired, and so increase the likelihood that they made mistakes with patients' treatments.

▶

So the Working Time Directive highlights two important advantages of state provided social policy. On the one hand, it functions as both a safety mechanism for employees and patients, which ensures that a minimum standard of service is provided. On the other hand, it also gives workers rights which mean that there is equality in terms of the working conditions that exist.

Private companies and social policies

In some instances, some individuals choose to pay a private company to meet a welfare need that they might receive from the state, such as education and healthcare. In other instances, individuals have to pay a private company to meet a welfare need because of the lack of availability of state provision, such as for private rented housing, or because it is not provided to them by the state, such as some types of health treatments like dental treatment or optical treatment, or even university education. For most private social policies, to receive the benefit the individual has to be able to pay, although in some instances provision is subsidized by the state. The key difference between private and state social policies is that the main objective of private social policy providers is to make a profit from the social policies they provide. This profit is then paid to those who work for the company.

A specified advantage of the private provision of services is that it is an efficient way of matching and meeting the demand for welfare services, as people will only pay for welfare services that they need. So for example, people will not pay for care if they do not need it, and will not pay for education if they do not need it. This means that private welfare services are a good way to separate welfare needs from welfare wants, which is not something that state welfare services are necessarily good at.

Private welfare services also give individuals the power of choice in determining their welfare, in terms of both whether or not to have a welfare service and which welfare services to have; such choice improves individual welfare (Botti and Iyengar, 2006). This means that it is individuals who have the power in determining how their welfare needs are met, because if one private company does not meet their needs adequately, they can buy their needs from another company. So for example, if a person does not like the education that they receive, they can buy education from another private provider. This means that private companies have to be acutely aware of and responsive to the needs of customers.

As a consequence of this, private welfare services are rationalized as less wasteful than public welfare, because private companies have to be as efficient as possible to make as much profit as possible. This efficiency can be in terms of the way the service is provided, or the price that is charged for the service. So for example, the cost of social care is less in the private sector than it is in the public sector (Fotaki *et al.*, 2013) as they use fewer employees to do more work. Private healthcare is also rationalized as less wasteful because there is no need to set up complex systems to determine who is entitled to what, as with means-tested public welfare, as what determines entitlement is simply the ability to pay.

Private healthcare can also reduce the strain on state welfare. So for example, private healthcare is sometimes used to reduce the waiting list on the NHS, either through the government paying for individuals to have private treatment, or individuals choosing for themselves to pay for treatment. For example, the NHS funds a range of treatments from private Independent Sector Treatment Centres, such as hip operations, scans, cataract surgery and knee operations. In this sense, private welfare can complement and reduce the pressure on state provided welfare.

Real Life Box 8.3 **Private universities**

There are now four private universities in the UK:

➢ The University of Buckingham;

➢ Regent's University London;

➢ The University of Law;

➢ BPP University of Professional Studies.

A major difference between these private universities and other state funded universities is that they offer courses that last two years, rather than three years. This means that they teach courses throughout the year, including during the summer, so courses are less expensive than three year courses from other universities. This exemplifies the rationale that private sector welfare can be less expensive that state provided welfare.

Another difference is that they tend to provide less variety of courses than other universities. This exemplifies the notion that private welfare is a very efficient way of meeting demand for welfare services, as they only provide the degrees that individuals want.

Voluntary/community organization social policies

Voluntary and community organizations provision of social policy is different from state welfare because most of the funding comes from donations, charitable activities such as fundraising and charity shops, or income from services they provide, such as housing services in the case of housing association.

Voluntary and community organization, like private companies, may directly charge for the services that they provide. However, voluntary and community organizations are different from private welfare because their main objective is not to make money from the provision of the welfare service, but to meet the need. This means that any surplus money that the organization makes has to be paid back into meeting the needs of the organization, not paid out to those who work for the organization.

Voluntary and community organizations are usually set up to meet one specific welfare need, rather than a variety of welfare needs. So for example, a housing association's focus is mainly on meeting housing needs. An organization like The Prince's Trust is concerned with meeting the welfare needs of young people, the Samaritans provides support and advice to those feeling in distress or despair, and Macmillan Cancer Support provides welfare to those who have been diagnosed with cancer. Although all of these are big organizations with paid employees, the majority of charities are very small, local volunteer-run organizations, and for the majority of voluntary and community organizations it is volunteers rather than employees who make up the majority of people within their organizations.

The main specified advantage for voluntary and community provided welfare is that as they are set up to meet a specific welfare need, such organizations can be very effective at meeting the needs they are specifically set up to meet, and can become specialist in the area that they are concerned with. For example, when people think of homelessness, Shelter is one of the main organizations that comes to mind, and similarly when people think of dealing with child abuse, the NSPCC is a very prominent organization. For older people, Age UK is an organization which provides a range of services for older people, including information, advice and advocacy services, day centres and lunch clubs, home help and 'handyperson' schemes, and IT and other training, and they also carry out research which aims to provide a comprehensive service for older people.

Because such organizations are largely self-funded and fundraise, keeping cost down is a fundamental element of their survival. This means that they are able to provide welfare services that are very cost effective. The fact that they are not concerned with making profits also contributes to this cost-effectiveness, as the price they charge for a service reflects the true cost price, without a profit element added. For example, the cost of renting from a housing association is usually less that the cost of renting from private landlords.

Real Life Box 8.4 **The largest voluntary group in the country**

All state schools in England, Wales and Northern Ireland have to have a governing body, run by a mixture of people known as school governors. These are made up of parents, staff, the local authority, members of the community and other school partners. In theory, anyone can become a school governor, as parent governors are elected by the school. Being a school governor is a voluntary position, in that it is unpaid. There are approximately 300,000 school governors in England, which is the largest voluntary group in the country (Whitby, 2011).

School governors have a range of responsibilities, such as monitoring and evaluating school performance, holding the head teacher to account and setting budgets and staffing responsibilities. This large range of responsibilities means that school governors come from a variety of professions, such as teachers, doctors and lawyers.

The work of such volunteers means that the cost of schooling to the state is reduced. Also, the variety of skills that such school governors have ensures that the welfare need is met in a very effective way. And the fact that members of the local community, such as parents, are part of the governing body means that they have a specific interest in the ensuring the best outcomes from their volunteering activity.

The fact that such organizations do not need to make a profit means they can be more innovative and responsive is terms of the welfare services that they provide and the way that they provide them. This can include developing more effective ways to provide welfare needs. For example, 'care farming' is a form of therapy developed by the voluntary and community sector where agricultural landscapes are used to promote mental and physical health in a variety of groups, such as psychiatric patients, those suffering from mild to moderate depression, people with learning disabilities, those with a drug history, disaffected youth or elderly people, as well as those suffering from the effects of work-related stress or ill health arising from obesity (Hine *et al.*, 2008). Care farming has been taken and used by a variety of state organizations, such as health bodies, youth organizations and probation trusts working with offenders.

Finally, such voluntary welfare can also be a good indicator of new, unmet need, and so may lead to the requirement of the state to provide new welfare provision. For example, the rise of food banks is an example of where voluntary organizations are meeting new, unmet demand for welfare provision.

Individual social policies

Individual welfare is usually provided as care, by friends, family, neighbours or the community. It is similar to voluntary/community welfare as it is provided by volunteers generally without payment, but differs as it is not provided by an organization, but by individuals. This is why it is sometimes referred to as informal welfare, as there is often no formal agreement to provide a service; it often happens from circumstances or expectation. For example, when a disabled child is born into a family, it is a circumstance that happens to the family. In this circumstance, depending on the level of disability the family may feel that they are able to care for the child, and so choose to provide the care. However, it may also be the case that because the state welfare provision is not available, the family may not have an option but to provide welfare for the child. Also, the type of care provided by carers is wider than by that provided by voluntary and community organizations, involving not just personal care, but also emotional support, financial support, physical help, administering medication, and other practical support.

The advantages for individual welfare are similar to the advantages for private/voluntary welfare in terms of being good at meeting unmet need, and being innovative and responsive to care. However the main advantage for individual welfare is that it seen as very cost effective. For example, for a seriously disabled wheelchair user, the cost of residential care is £700–£800 a week, which works out at between £36,400 and £41,600 a year. However, the cost of care in the home by a family carer for the same individual is between £10,400 and £15,600, which is an average saving of around £26,000 a year (Heywood and Turner, 2007). This is why it is estimated that the unpaid care provided by informal carers saves the state approximately £119 billion a year (Carers UK, 2011), a huge amount of money.

Real Life Box 8.5 **The benefits of grandparent care**

Grandparents are becoming an increasingly important source of care for families, especially where two parents work or where a family is headed by a lone parent who is required to work. A study by Burn et al. (2014) showed that grandmothers who take care of their grandchildren stay more mentally agile than those who do not look after grandchildren.

This suggests that caring can have beneficial results not just for the individual but also for society. In particular, it also highlights the fact that individual welfare can save money not just for the state, but also for the individual, as such care for grandchildren would otherwise need to be paid for by the individual or the state.

What are the limitations of the state, private companies, voluntary/community organizations or individuals providing social policies?

While each type of welfare provider has specific benefits, there are also limitations that are evident for each. These limitations are shown in Table 8.1.

As can be seen in Table 8.1, each type of social policy provider has specific limitations. These limitations at times overlap with each other, and at other times are similar to the limitations of other types of service providers. For instance, a major limitation of state provided welfare is the lack of choice that it gives to individuals, but the choice that is provided by private providers is also problematic as this can increase the overall cost of the welfare service. The key point here is that no particular type of welfare provider is perfect, they all have limitations which you need to be aware of.

Can social policies be delivered by a combination of providers?

So far this chapter has described different types of ways in which social policies can be delivered. It has done so by separating out the different social policies of welfare providers, and analysing the different types of welfare providers as distinct from each other.

However, your experiences of social policies should have told you that this is far from reality. Actually, social policies are often provided by a mixture of service providers, and it is very rare to find a social policy that is only provided by one of the types of provider shown above. For example, if we think about housing, this is provided by a mixture of state, private and voluntary/community organizations, as evident in council houses, private rented housing, and social housing from housing association. Even more specifically, if we look at rented housing, we can see that for Housing Benefit, it is often the case that while the state funds the benefit, it is private companies through private landlords who provide the house, or voluntary/community organisations through housing associations. NHS dentistry is provided by self-employed dentists who receive a fee from the NHS for the work they carry out, and many parents also use their Childcare Tax Credit to buy nursery care from nurseries run by private companies. And although universities receive most of their funding from the state, they are registered as charities, which means that they are not part of the state but are organizations with charitable aims and objectives.

Table 8.1 Limitations of different types of welfare providers

State welfare services	Private welfare services	Voluntary/Community welfare services	Individual welfare services
Does not provide a real choice to service users e.g. NHS is the only health system available	Private welfare can be expensive e.g. the cost of private day school is £10,200 per year	Only able to meet needs in a limited sense e.g. generally limited size of organization means that not able to meet needs extensively	Reliant on good will of individuals e.g. circumstances can change which mean that care is no longer possible
Not good at responding to needs or preferences of individuals e.g. Housing Benefit limits the type of housing that an individual can live in	High costs excludes some groups from receiving services at all, especially those most in need e.g. only some groups can afford private healthcare	Only meets needs as defined by group, patchwork coverage, exclusions e.g. welfare needs are only met if a group is set up to meet need, not necessarily if need exists	Care provided is not necessarily the highest standard e.g. friends and family not qualified to provide relevant care
Lack of power for users e.g. school places are allocated to individuals, not chosen by individuals	Focus on limiting the cost of welfare service, not on the quality of the service e.g. private housing quality can be poor due to unwillingness of landlords to spend money to improve quality	Replication of provision leads to inefficiencies e.g. existence of lots of small voluntary/community organizations which repeat service provision available	Care not well funded and supported e.g. individuals may not be able to afford the necessary equipment to provide the best care
Too bureaucratic, leads to inefficiency e.g. long process required to claim benefits such as Jobseeker's Allowance and Income Support	Inefficient as too many small private providers means duplication of service e.g. lots of different care providers means that each have different administration costs	Reliant on unreliable income e.g. funding can dry up if donations are not made, which means that service is not reliable	Assumption that carers always have best interest of individuals at heart e.g. ignore the possibility of neglect and abuse in care situations
Very inefficient in terms of cost e.g. social care provided by the local authority is more expensive than social care from private providers	Leads to different quality of service for different user e.g. expensive healthcare treatments only available to those who can afford it, cheap healthcare to those who cannot afford it	Lack of need to make a profit leads to service inefficiencies e.g. services providers do not have the incentive to reduce costs to make a profit	Strains of providing care can be very high e.g. stress of caring can lead to break up of relationships
Paternalistic, meaning assumes that welfare professionals rather than service users know best e.g. doctors decide the treatments that an individual has, rather than the individual	Undermining of universalist principle e.g. service provision becomes fragmented as only some groups receive welfare, so leads to lack of social cohesion	Reliance on volunteers means service quality may not be good e.g. volunteers not necessarily experts in meeting specific welfare need	Sacrifices required by carers is very high e.g. may need to give up work which impacts of economic situation in household and therefore level of care

Similarly, for something like the Work Programme for the long term employed, it is private companies and voluntary/community organizations that provide the service while the state pays for the service they provide. The state also provides a significant amount of funding to voluntary and community organizations. And as outlined above, the state often pays private or voluntary companies to carry out operations on NHS patients, and some social policy benefits can also be dominated by providers other than the state. For example, 78% of all residential homes for looked after children, or those in care, are non-public, and only 22% of such homes are provided by the state (Stanley and Rome, 2013).

This means that rather than social policies provided solely by one type of provider, they are often provided by a mixture of different providers. This is known as a *mixed economy of welfare*, that is, where total welfare provision is provided by a combination of state, market and voluntary and individual providers. A good example of the mixed economy of welfare is in education and particularly in primary and secondary schools, and this is discussed below.

How does the mixed economy of welfare work in primary and secondary schooling?

An obvious distinction in primary and secondary schools is between state schools (also called state maintained schools) and private schools (also called public or independent schools). The majority of schools in the UK are state, and the likelihood is that you went to a state school, rather than a private school, as approximately only 7% of people are privately educated, and 93% educated in state schools. The major reason for this is that while state schooling is taxation funded and therefore free at the point of use, private schools have to be paid by the user, and can cost up to £28,500 per year for boarding school, as detailed in Chapter 4. This division between state schools and private schools is fairly straightforward and easy to understand.

However, there are at least three other types of primary and secondary schools in addition to private school and state schools, and these are shown in Table 8.2.

As Table 8.2 shows, while there are obvious differences between private and state schools, there are also major differences between schools which we tend to think of as state schools. These differences can be in terms of who owns the school, who employs the staff, whether pupils have to follow the national curriculum, and the admission policy of the school.

This means that even where schools are funded by the state (either through central government or local government), there are significant

Table 8.2 Different types of primary and secondary schools

	State maintained schools	Private schools	Voluntary schools	Academies	Free schools
How is the school funded?	State through local government i.e. city council	Payment of school fees	Combination of state through local government (i.e. city council), charity and religious organizations	Combination of state through central government (Department for Education), and private funders	State through central government (Department for Education)
Who owns the school?	State through local government	Private company	Charity or religious organization	School governing body, which can be universities, FE colleges, education charities, businessmen	School governing body, which can be parents, teachers, existing educational charities, universities, community groups
Who employs staff?	State through local government	School	School governing body	School governing body	School governing body
Is the National Curriculum followed?	Yes	No	Yes	No, but some subjects must be taught	No, but some subjects must be taught
Who sets the admission policy?	State through local government	School	Can be set by school e.g. religious organization	State through central government	State through central government
Does OFSTED regulate the school?	Yes	No	Yes	Yes	Yes

differences in ownership. So charities or religious organizations can own Voluntary Schools. Universities or colleges, education charities or businesses can own Academies. And parents, teachers, and community groups can own Free Schools. This exemplifies the notion of the mixed economy of welfare, the fact that welfare services are provided by a combination of state, market and voluntary providers, rather than by a single type of provider.

What are the advantages of the mixed economy of welfare for social policies?

There are two main advantages for having a mixed economy of welfare rather than one based on a single type of welfare provider for social policies.

The first advantage is that having such a variety of providers working in combination means that services are able to overcome the limitations of each type of provider as shown in Table 8.1, therefore making welfare services more complete in terms of meeting needs. For example, a major limitation of state provided provision outlined in Table 8.1 is the lack of choice it gives to services user, something that the mixed economy of welfare's different array of providers for junior and primary schooling above overcomes. Similarly, a limitation outlined above for private welfare is that the high cost excludes some groups, but the state provision of state and voluntary primary and secondary schooling alongside private schooling above overcomes this. And for voluntary provision, a major limitation is that it is only able to meet needs in a limited sense, but this is overcome in the mixed economy of welfare by the provision of other types of welfare providers. In this sense, it can be seen that the mixed economy of welfare enables services to be complemented and therefore be more comprehensive in terms of meeting needs.

The second advantage of the mixed economy of welfare is that it enables shifting and diverse needs to be better met than a reliance on one type of provider, particularity state provision. So for instance, the different types of providers above provide services that are different from the state in many ways, and different from each other as well. Because people have different needs, they are able to choose the best provider that matches their needs, rather than be stuck with a one size fits all service that is not meeting their need. The obvious example here is in relation to religious schools, where some parents feel the need to educate their children in a particular religion, and wish to send their children to a school with a particular religious ethos. Also, private schools tend to have lower class sizes than state schools, and for some people this is an important education need for their child (Murray, 2011). And as other providers are seen as more responsive to need than having only state provision, so they are better able to respond to changing needs as they happen.

What are the limitations of the mixed economy of welfare?

There are five main limitations of the mixed economy of welfare. The first is that the mixed economy is not necessarily less expensive than providing welfare by one provider, it can actually be more expensive. For example, the Free Schools policy has been estimated as costing over £1 billion more than if the provision had been provided by the state. And as we saw, private schooling can be much more expensive per person than state funded provision. This extra cost is often not taken into account, and this means that the true cost of such a mixed economy is often overlooked.

Such a mixed economy can also mean that there are differing standards with different types of providers. For example, while all state maintained and academies have to meet set nutritional standards for school meals, private and free schools are exempt from these standards, which means that those who go to private and free schools could be eating school meals at a lower standard than those in other schools. Similarly, private schools do not have to be inspected by OFSTED, and so there is no analysis of whether their teaching meets national requirements that other schools have, such as in relation to the quality of teaching. So such a mixed economy can lead to a difference and disparity in national standards, rather than the same standards for everyone.

Another limitation is the amount of choice that such a mixed economy can provide. From the above there are at least five different choices of schooling that a parent can make. However, this choice means that individuals have to carefully consider the differences between each type, and this can take considerable time, as the implication of making a wrong choice can be significant for their child. Having to make such an important choice can overwhelm individuals, especially when it has such important long-term consequences, meaning that they can make the wrong choice (Botti and Iyengar, 2006). So rather than the wide range of choice of varying quality that the mixed economy provides, it might be better to simply provide a single service that is of good quality for all.

Such a mixed economy can also be bureaucratic in terms of administration, from all the different rules for each type of provider. So for example, in Table 8.2 above different types of state school have different admission policies, which all have to be overseen and regulated. This means that the level of administration required is quite large in comparison to a system that only has one admission system and would therefore be easier to understand. Such a bureaucratic system also increases the cost of the provision, as the administration needs to be paid for.

The final limitation of such a mixed economy is that it reduces the potential for social cohesion within society. So for example, private schools tend to be populated by those with wealth above the average of society, while religious schools are populated by those with a certain level of religiosity. This means that these groups are less likely to mix with other individuals within society, and so there is less likely to be social interaction that leads to social cohesion.

How important is the mixed economy of welfare to current social policies?

The mixed economy of welfare is not a new concept, it is something that has been around since the beginnings of the welfare state as we saw in Chapter 3. What is new is the extent to which the mixed economy, and in particular the drive towards private providers in the delivery of welfare, has become increasingly prominent since the election of the Thatcher government in 1979. This has been through a process of extensive privatization, in which state services are sold to private individuals. The obvious example of this is the privatization of state housing though the 'Right to Buy' policy, as set out in the Chapter 6. Another example is in social care, where in 1979, 64% of residential and nursing care services were provided by the state, but by 2012 this had fallen to just 6%. Conversely, the private sector provided 5% of home-care services in 1993, but by 2012 this had risen to 89% (Fotaki *et al.*, 2013: 4).

This process of increasing the mixed economy of welfare through privatization was continued by the 1997 New Labour government, as a consequence of which there has been a 55% increase in privately-provided NHS care, and almost 10% of NHS care is provided by private providers (Fotaki *et al.*, 2013).

More recently, the introduction of Free Schools outlined above by the 2010 Coalition government is an example of the extension of the mixed economy to education. Moreover, the 2010 Coalition government also handed over the administration of The Work Programme, which provides personalized support for claimants who need more help looking for and staying in work, to private companies such as A4e and G4S. These companies, together with Atos, Serco, and Capita are among the best known private providers of public services. They provide a wide range of public services across the public sector, costing over £4 billion in 2012–2013 (National Audit Office, 2013: 12).

And in the NHS and Social Care Act 2012, the provision of health services was opened up to 'any qualified provider', meaning that rather that the state being the primary provider of NHS services, the intention is to open up to other types of providers, particularity private providers. These changes mean that the mixed economy of welfare is becoming more prominent now that it has been in the recent past of social policy.

The 2010 Coalition government also placed greater emphasis on welfare being met through the 'Big Society', which has meant a prominence in policy of voluntary and community organizations meeting more of the welfare needs that the state is currently responsible for, such as for housing. And the Big Society also gave emphasis to individual welfare as a way for individuals to meet their own welfare needs, for example those outlined above, rather than the state taking responsibility for meeting such welfare needs.

This means that over the last 40 years, the emphasis on mixed economy of welfare has seen less state responsibility for meeting welfare and more responsibility for private providers, voluntary and community organizations and individuals.

Summary

When people think of who provides social policies, they tend to think of the state as the main provider of such policies. It is true that the state is the most important provider of some very important social policies, such as for healthcare and education, and there are some very important advantages of state provided social policies. However, individuals may choose or may have to receive social policies from other providers, such as private companies, voluntary/community organizations or even other individuals, and these also have some important advantages. While all of these different providers have significant advantages over each other, a key point to note is that no particular type of welfare provider is perfect, they all have their limitations which you need to be aware of.

It is also important to be aware that, actually, social policies are often provided by a mixture of service providers, and it is very rare to find a social policy that is only provided by one of the types of provider outlined above. This means that the reality is that social policies are provided in a 'mixed economy of welfare', where total welfare provision is provided by a combination of state, market and voluntary and individual providers. The analysis of education is a good example of this, and this also highlights that the mixed economy of welfare can have important advantages over a single provider of social policies, such as in relation to overcoming the limitations of different providers. However, the analysis of education highlights that the mixed economy of welfare also has some important limitations, such as in relation to cost, standards, choice and bureaucracy.

Despite these limitations, the mixed economy of welfare has become more prominent in the delivery of social policies over the last 40 years or so, particularly the drive towards private providers in the delivery of welfare. This has been continued by successive government, particularly the 2010 Coalition government, and this has seen less state responsibility for meeting welfare and more responsibility for private providers, voluntary and community organizations and individuals.

Key Point

While social policies can be provided by the state, private companies, voluntary/ community organizations and individuals, the focus has been towards a combination of these providers for social policies in what is called the mixed economy of welfare.

9

WHAT DOES THE FUTURE HOLD FOR SOCIAL POLICY?

The aims of this chapter are to:

1. **Outline the major social and economic changes that have happened in society since the development of the post-war 'Welfare State'**

2. **Discuss how these changes are affecting social policy now, and how they will possible affect social policy in the future**

3. **Detail important social policies that have been put in place to deal with these changes**

One of the most important points about social policy that has hopefully become apparent from this book is that social policy never stands still but is constantly changing, and can change significantly in very short periods of time. This affects not only what we receive as social policy benefits, but also what we pay out for social policy benefits. A good example of a recent major change to what we receive in social policy benefits is the modification to Child Benefit to make it selective rather than universal. And a good example of a major recent change to what we pay out for social policy benefits is the charging of tuition fees for higher education that was previously provided for free. These changes mean that in some social policy areas, there has been a significant shift away from the post-war 'Welfare State' as set out in the Beveridge Report in 1942. One of the reasons for this constant change in social policy is that the society that we live in now is socially and economically hugely different from the time of the Beveridge Report, and social policy has had to change to reflect these different times. So we should expect social policy to constantly change as we live in a constantly changing society.

This chapter describes some of these key social and economic changes that UK society has undergone over the last 70 years since the Beveridge

Report, and is predicted to undergo in the near future. Specifically, it outlines four main types of changes which are occurring. The chapter will discuss how these changes are not only impacting on social policy now, but also how they have potential important effects on social policy in the future, both positive and negative. It also outlines some key social policies that have been put in place to deal with the changes in these areas. The chapter focusses specifically on the area of personal social services to highlight some of the important social policies that have been put in place to deal with these changes, as a way to consider the effect that these changes are having on the future social policy.

By the end of this chapter, you will have an understanding of key social and economic changes occurring in society, and the impact that these changes could have on social policy in the future. You will also be able to identify some key social policies that have been put in place to deal with the changes in these areas, and what these policies indicate about the future direction of social policy.

What are the major social and economic changes occurring within society?

There are four main areas of changes which are occurring within society, and which will affect social policy in the future. These are:

> Work

> Family

> Technology

> Demography

Work changes

One of the most important assumptions that the Beveridge Report made for the post-war welfare state was that all governments would maintain high employment in the economy, and specifically that they would ensure that there was *full employment*. For Beveridge, full employment was important as it was the way that the welfare state would be paid for, through taxation as set out in Chapter 4. Full employment for Beveridge meant a social policy aim of ensuring an unemployment rate no higher than 3% of the population.

In the first 30 or so years after World War II, Beveridge's assumption of full employment was a reality, as set out in Graph 3.1 in Chapter 3, as the unemployment rate rarely if ever rose above 3%. An important reason for this was the need for extensive reconstruction after World War II, which led to many jobs being created, but there was also a range of active social policy measures which ensured full employment, such as the government providing subsidies to businesses to invest, the nationalization of industries such as coal and steel to maintain employment, and the Keynesian approach of government as set out in Chapter 10. During this period of full employment there was a significant possibility of a job for life, meaning either the possibility of working for the same company throughout your life, or being able to find employment so easily that you were effectively employed throughout your life.

However, Graph 3.1 also shows that the full employment of the post-war years is no longer present, and unemployment has been well above 3% for most of the last 30 years. Indeed, more recently in the aftermath of the financial crisis of 2008, unemployment has been as high as over 8%, which is equivalent to 2.7 million people. Had the unemployment rate been 3% during this period, the unemployment rate would only have been around 1 million people, which is a significant difference. Young people aged 18–25 in particular are one group who, in comparison to the high employment immediately after World War II, have been significantly affected by high unemployment over the last 30 years, and are now more likely to be unemployed than other age groups. This high unemployment rate has meant that the possibility of having a job for life is no longer the reality for many people, with employment more insecure and frequently changing.

Question

What is the current employment rate, and how does it compare with the employment rate after World War II?

The need to reconstruct the UK following World War II meant that the type of jobs available were mainly in manufacturing. Manufacturing jobs are those involving the production of new products from raw materials or from components, for example engineering, mining and production. Manufacturing jobs are usually in a factory or factory type setting but can also be in a home, as long as products, not services, are created. Graph 9.1 below shows how there has been a shift away from manufacturing jobs since 1948.

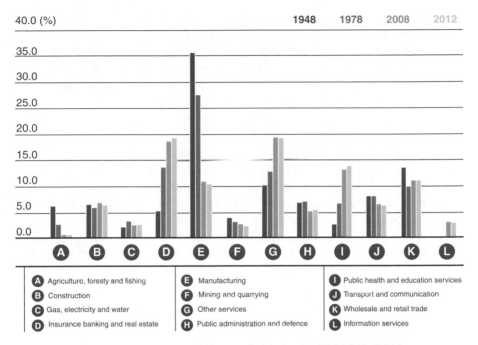

Graph 9.1 Changes in types of jobs available in the UK 1948–2012
Source: ONS, 2013a

From Graph 9.1 we can see that there have been a number of important changes in the types of jobs available since 1948:

➤ In 1948 manufacturing jobs (Column E) accounted for over 35% of all jobs in the UK economy, and were by far the largest type of jobs available. By 2012, this had reduced to just over 10%, well below several other types of jobs.

➤ There has been a shift towards service sector jobs, which are jobs that produce services rather than goods (Columns D, G and I). The service sector includes education, finance, hospitality, communications, health care, utilities, wholesale and retail trade, and transportation.

➤ For example, in 1948, 5% of jobs were in banking (Column D), but in 2012 it was nearly 20%.

➤ Similarly, in 1948 10% of jobs was in other services (Column G), but it was nearly 20% in 2012.

Overall, Graph 9.1 shows that there has been a major shift away from manufacturing jobs towards service sector jobs in the UK, a shift which has been the greatest shift of any major nation in the world (Chakrabortty, 2011).

This change from manufacturing jobs to service sectors has important implications for the wages that people earn. This is because while the pay for those in service sector jobs like banking and finance can be very high, in actual fact service sector employment is generally less well paid than similar manufacturing employment (Kennedy *et al.*, 2013). This means that if you have two people doing similar level jobs in manufacturing and the service sector, the manufacturing job will generally be paid more than the service sector job.

This change in the type of jobs available has also changed the nature of jobs available. While manufacturing jobs tend to be mainly full-time, service sector employment has higher levels of part-time work (OECD, 2001), and the increase in service sector jobs in the UK has seen a linked increase in part time work to nearly 7 million people (ONS, 2014c). Moreover, according to the ONS (2014c), there are 4.5 million people who are self-employed, which is the highest number ever. There are also more female workers than ever before (ONS, 2014c), and the increasing use of zero-hour contract jobs.

Real Life Box 9.1 **Zero-hour contract jobs**

A zero-hour contract job is where a person is employed by a company, but without a guarantee of the hours that they are required to work. In a standard job, a person is given a set number of hours that they are expected to work each day, week or month. But with a zero-hour contract, there are no set hours given. Instead the employee is expected to be on call as and when the employer needs them, and is only paid for when they work. Zero-hour contracts do not normally include sick pay.

Zero-hour contracts are a relatively new phenomenon. According to the Office of National Statistics, there are at least 600,000 people on zero-hour contacts, which is 2% of the workforce, but they are growing every year. Zero-hour contracts are most evident in low-paid sectors, such as retailing and hospitality. For example, out of the 23,000 people that Sports Direct employs, 20,000 are on zero-hour contacts. Similarly, 80% of JS Weatherspoon's employees are on zero-hour contracts.

Employees on zero-hour contracts do not have the same of amount of employment rights as contracted employees, principally because they are classified as self-employed. Also, because they do not have secure, guaranteed work hours, their income can be lower than other employees, and can vary from week to week.

These changes mean that the nature of work has shifted since 1948 from being secure, dominated by full-time male manufacturing employment, to low-paid and insecure service sector employment which is increasingly self-employment and part-time, and also more female than before.

Family changes

The Beveridge Report designed the welfare state around a particular type of family. This was a small family type of married mother and father and children, in which the father went out to work as the main 'breadwinner' for the family, and the mother stayed at home to look after the children. This family type is known as the 'nuclear family', as the nucleus of the family is the man as the main breadwinner with the rest of the family built around this main male nucleus. The post-war welfare state constructed social policy around this nuclear family type, for the simple reason that it was the main family type that existed, and Beveridge thought that it would remain the main family type in the future. For example, it was assumed that women would give up work when they became married to have children, and become dependent on the earnings and/or benefits of their husband, regardless of the type of work that either did. This is despite the fact that during the war, many married women worked and contributed to the household.

Graph 9.2 shows that there have been some significant changes in family types in the UK over the last 50 years.

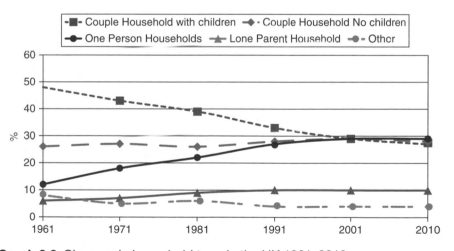

Graph 9.2 Changes in household type in the UK 1961–2010
Source: ONS, 2011, Table 2

Graph 9.2 shows that 'couple households with children', that is the nuclear family, was by far the main type of household in the aftermath of the Second World War. However, there has been a great decline in this nuclear family type and consequent great increase in other family types, to the extent that the nuclear family is no longer the most dominant type of family that exists. In fact, there are both more 'one person households' *and* 'couple household with no children' than the nuclear family type. There has also been an increase in lone parent households during this period. There are various reasons for this, such as fewer people getting married, people getting married later, more people co-habiting, and the increase in divorce. All these changes mean that the nuclear family type that post-war welfare social policy has been constructed around has declined significantly, and other family types are more dominant than this type.

Question

Do you live in a nuclear family, or another family type?

Technological changes

If Beveridge was able to experience life as we do now, he would no doubt be very surprised at the technological changes that have occurred between then and now. Things that we take for granted have transformed the way we live and work. Just looking around your house you can see some of the significant changes that have occurred. For example, things like microwaves, washing machines and dishwashers have become essential components of households over the last 50 years. There are also things outside the house that have changed significantly, such as the number of cars and the possibility of travelling from one side of the world to the next so quickly.

More recently, there has been the huge growth of computing, as evidenced by the fact that we nearly all have mobile phones and access to the internet. This is something that makes our lives more interconnected than previously. In addition, technological changes have also been important in making the world seem smaller. For example, we can instantly be in contact with someone on the other side of the world through the internet in a way that was unthinkable even 20 years ago. We are also influenced by many other different cultures than previously, as we come into contact with them through technology. This is known as the process of *globalization*, that is where the world becomes smaller and we are more interconnected with other parts of the world than previously.

Real Life Box 9.2 **Globalization**

The term globalization refers to the fact that international factors, more than local and national factors, are affecting the way we live and are becoming increasingly important. For example, in the 1940s and for several decades afterwards, most of the goods that people bought would have been British made by British owned companies. But now this is far from the case. The likelihood is that the car you drive, the clothes you wear, the furniture in your house, the TV that you watch, the computer that you use and the smart phone that you surf on are non-British made and non-British owned. Even the TV programmes that you watch could also be non-British made. In addition, international companies that didn't exist 10 or 20 years ago that are now very important companies such as Amazon, Google, Apple, Facebook and Starbucks, the majority of which are service sector companies.

This also highlights the fact that manufacturing in the UK, the act of actually making things, has been in decline over the last 30 years, and most of our manufactured goods are imported from a variety of other countries. Instead, we have become more focussed on service sector jobs, particularly banking and finance.

The significance of these technological changes is that they are changing the way we live, the way we work and the way we socialize with each other, and this can have important consequences. For example, technological changes have been one very important reason for the changes in work detailed above, as technological developments in the workplace have seen more machines used, meaning less need for so many employees in the manufacturing sector, hence the decline in manufacturing employment.

Demographic changes

Demography is the study of the way that the population of a country changes, and why these changes occur. This can be for a number of reasons as detailed below.

When the post-war welfare state was constructed in 1946, the population of the UK was just under 49 million people. Today it is just under 64 million people, which is an increase of 15 million people, or nearly 33%. Table 9.1 shows how the population has increased since then, and also an estimate of how the population will increase by 2031.

Table 9.1 UK population increase since 1946

	Population Millions	% increase since 1946
1946	48.9	-------------
1971	55.9	14%
1981	56.4	15%
1991	57.4	17%
2001	59.1	21%
2011	62.6	28%
2021	67	37%
2031	70.9	45%

Source: ONS, 2012b

As Table 9.1 shows, since 1946 the population has been increasing steadily and significantly, so that by the year 2031, the Office for National Statistics estimates that the population will reach 71 million (ONS, 2012b), which is an increase of 45% since 1946.

There are a number of reasons why the population has increased and continues to increase. One reason is because of increasing *net migration*, meaning that there are more people entering the UK to live than there are people leaving the country to live elsewhere. Migration has been an important aspect of UK society since the Second World War, especially in the immediate post-war period when the government invited immigrants from Caribbean countries like Jamaica and Barbados to fill labour shortages in hospitals, transport and the railways. More recently, there has been an increase in migration from EU countries such Poland, Bulgaria and Romania, and this has led to both present and future increases in the population. For example, between 2003 and 2010, the Polish-born population of the UK increased by nearly half a million people (ONS, 2011a).

However, according to the ONS (2013), increasing net migration is not the main reason for the increases in the population. Instead, the main reason for increases in the population is because of *natural changes*, that is changes that occur due to the nature of the population itself. These natural changes include:

> changes in the birth rate (i.e. the number of people being born)

> changes in the death rate (i.e. the number of people dying)

Most people might think that the most important of these changes is an increase in the birth rate, that is the number of people being born. But in fact, the number of births in the UK has declined throughout the last century, and there have only been two periods when the birth rate has increased for a significant period of time (Hicks and Allene, 1999). The first was the period immediately after the Second World War when a post-war 'baby boom' saw the birth rate increase to 2.6 children per woman. The second was in the 1960s when the birth rate reached 2.8 children per woman. Since then, the birth rate has been falling and now stands at 1.9 children per woman (World Bank, 2014). This means that at present there are less children being born than there has been historically, and less than two children per woman.

This means that the main reason for the increasing population is due to the second natural change that is occurring, that is changes in the death rate, and specifically the fact that there has been a fall in death rate. In other words, more people are living longer. This is relevant to both when people are born and when people become older.

In relation to when people are born, in 1950 the infant mortality rate in the UK, or the number of children who died before the age of 1, was approximately 30 children per 1,000 born. In 2010 the infant mortality rate was just under five children per 1,000 born. This means that you are six times less likely to die as a child today than you were just after the development of the welfare state.

In relation to when people die, in 1950 life expectancy in the UK, that is the age at which people are predicted to die, was 63 for men and 66 for women (Harper *et al.*, 2011). Today, life expectancy is 78 years for men and 83 years for women (ONS, 2014d). This shows that people are living considerably longer that they did in the past, and this trend of living longer will continue into the future. For example, a child born in 2012 has a nearly one in three chance of living until they are 100 years old (ONS, 2014d). This means that the ratio of older people to younger people is higher than it has ever been, and will increase in the future as both the birth rate and the death rate continue to fall.

Table 9.2 summarizes these major natural changes in the population that have been outlined above.

What Table 9.2 shows is that the main reason why the population is increasing is due to falls in the death rate. In particular, the increasing life expectancy for both men and women means that the population increase is being driven by people not dying so early and also living longer. The effect of this is also magnified by the fact that the post-war 'baby-boomers' born during the first increase in the birth rate outlined above are now becoming pensioners, and so there are more older people living at a time that less older people are dying.

Table 9.2 Summary of main natural changes in the UK population, present and future

	Post-war period	Present	Future	Summary
Population (millions)	48.9	62.6	70.9 in year 2031	Population has increased by 45% since 1946, and will continue to increase
Birth rate (number of children born per women)	2.6 children per women	1.9 children per women	1.89 children per women (ONS, 2013)	The birth rate has fallen since 1946, and continues to fall
Infant mortality (number of deaths before age one per 1,000 birth)	30 children per 1,000	5 children per 1,000	Not known	Infant mortality has fallen since 1946, and continues to fall
Life expectancy (number of years expected to live)	66 years for women	83 years for women	87 years for women in year 2035	Life expectancy has risen since 1946, and will continue to rise
	63 years for men	78 years for men	83.5 years for men in year 2035	

Real Life Box 9.3 **A demographic time-bomb?**

The changes outlined above mean that the population of the UK will look very different in 20 years time to what it does today. In particular there will be four main population changes:

➤ an increase in the over 65 population;

➤ an increase in the over 85 population;

➤ a fall in the number of those aged under 16 years old in the population;

➤ a fall in the number of people who are of working age.

In effect, these changes mean that there will be more old people not working in the population at the same time as there are less people working in the population. This has been described as a 'demographic time-bomb', as it suggests a significant change to the make-up of the population which will mean proportionately fewer people of working age to pay for the pensions and care and support that the increased ageing population will require.

In addition to these population changes, there are also changes in relation to the make-up of the population. For example, the number of disabled people has increased from 21% in 1972 to 30% in 2009, which is a large increase (ONS, 2011). More specifically, the chances of being disabled significantly rises with age. While only 6% of children are disabled, 45% of adults over the state pension age are disabled (DWP, 2012b). This is important in the context of the increasing ageing population.

So we can outline four major social and economic changes that are occurring in the UK, and these are family changes, work changes, technological changes and demographic changes. These changes mean that the UK is very different place from that imagined by Beveridge for the post-war period and the post-war welfare state, and this has important effects on the future of social policy.

How are these social and economic changes specifically affecting social policy?

These social and economic changes are having important effects on both social policy income (the amount of money that is received through taxation to spend on social policy) and expenditure (the amount of money that social policy needs to spend), as detailed below. The changes can affect the income of social policy in two ways, both increasing and decreasing income.

Increasing social policy income

On the one hand, the fact that there are more people in the UK means that there is the potential for more people to be employed, and therefore an increase in income tax and other tax revenues. Additionally, as people live longer they can work longer, and so contribute more in taxation to social policy. For example, the number of working pensioners is increasing year by year, with more than one in ten people working beyond the state pension age, a doubling from 20 years ago (King, 2012). The increase in women in the workforce also increases the number of people who could contribute to social policy income. This also means that there are more people available to buy things, and this increased expenditure means that more jobs are created. Overall, as there are more people paying taxation, so there could be the potential for more income from taxation in various forms, not just income tax but also VAT as more people buy more things.

The increased migration that is occurring is also something which could increase social policy income. This is because most people who migrate to the UK are more likely to be in work than their equivalent in the UK (CEBR, 2013). This means that they are able to contribute to social policy income through paying taxation. The simple reason for this is that the kind of people who migrate tend to be the more educated of the country that they are leaving (Rolfe *et al.*, 2013), so these migrants are more successful in securing jobs as a consequence of their relatively high level of education, and so have higher earnings (CEBR, 2013). Moreover, the majority of migrants tend to be young and healthy, that is under 35 and so of working age, and this means that they are more likely to come to seek employment. This could be significant in terms of the *'demographic time-bomb'* outlined above, wherein the fact that the majority of migrants are of working age and do work will mean that this demographic time-bomb has less effect than described.

Real Life Box 9.4 **Benefit tourism**

The idea of benefit tourism has come to prominence over the last couple of years as a reason why expenditure on social policy is increasing. It suggests that the vast majority of migrants come to the UK simply to claim benefits without having made any contribution to the system. Benefit tourism is described as occurring especially in the NHS, but also for benefits such as Jobseeker's Allowance, Housing Benefit and Child Benefit.

Evidence for the existence and extent of benefit tourism is not clear. This is because it is not something that is easy to prove. Also, research suggests that benefit tourism is not a priority for those who migrate to the UK. Rather, it suggests that the majority of migrants who come to the UK come to work and do find employment, as migrants are more likely to be in work than UK-born citizens (CEBR, 2013). More specifically, migrants are also less likely than those living in the UK to receive state benefits or tax credits, and similarly less likely to live in social housing than people in the same region (Dustman and Frattini, 2013). Overall, between 2001 and 2011, it is estimated that migrants contributed £25 billion more in taxation than they received in benefits (Dustman and Frattini, 2013). These data suggest that benefit tourism is not as problematic as has been described recently.

Reducing social policy income

On the other hand, the relatively high unemployment that has occurred over the last 30 years or so has reduced the income available to social policy. In particular, the high unemployment rate for young people aged 18–25 has meant that this is a group that is less likely to be contributing to social policy income than in the past. Additionally, the shift from manufacturing to service sector jobs has meant that the nature of work has changed to increasingly insecure and low-paid, part-time work with more periods of unemployment than before, as evident in the growth of zero-hour contract jobs. All of these reduce the income that is available to social policy through contributions paid by individuals. This is very significant as it was around the tax revenues provided by work that the post-war welfare state as we know it was constructed, and remains the most significant way that social policy is funded, as detailed in Chapter 4.

In terms of demographic changes, the large number of older people who are retiring means that they are also less likely to be contributing as much income through work to social policy than in the past. In addition, globalization changes can also affect the income of social policy, as detailed in the box below.

Real Life Box 9.5 **Tax avoidance**

International companies like Google, Amazon, Apple, Facebook and Starbucks have come to dominate the way we shop. For example, it is probable that you are reading this book having physically brought it on Amazon or as an e-book on Amazon. These companies are good example of the way that the world we live in has become more globalized over the last 30 years.

The international nature of these companies makes it harder to receive tax revenues from them than in the past with home based companies. For example, corporation tax is the main tax that companies pay. In 2012 Amazon had sales of £3.3 billion, but paid no corporation tax during this period (Griffiths, 2012). Similarly, over the 14-year period 1998–2012, Starbucks paid only £8.3 *million* in all taxes, despite making billions in sales. It is a similar case for all the other companies shown above.

This is known as tax avoidance, which is where companies use a variety of legal ways to avoid paying tax. According to HMRC, legal tax avoidance means that £35 billion pounds of tax revenues is not collected each year. This is a significant amount of money, equivalent to the budget for either 'Housing and the Environment' or 'Personal Social Services' as shown in Graph 1.1 in Chapter 1.

Increasing social policy expenditure

An obvious increase in expenditure occurs from the increasing population. The fact that there are more people means that all social policy areas are affected. For example, in terms of housing there is a need for more houses to be built, and this is something which is compounded by changes in other areas, such as the change from the nuclear type family to other family types. So Graph 9.1 above shows that the largest type of household increase is in single households, and this means an increasing need for housing to accommodate the greater number of people living single as opposed to living in a couple or a family. The increases in single parent households during this period will also increase as the total number of households required. Moreover, the fact that more people are living longer and healthier will mean that less houses will be available to those who are younger to buy at an early age, and so a need for more houses for these young people.

Real Life Box 9.6 **Rising house prices: a problem of lack of supply or increasing demand?**

Since 1960, house prices in the UK have risen an average of 400%, and have risen even higher in some places such as London. These price increases have made buying a house too expensive for many people, particularly young people.

There are two main schools of thought as to why house prices have risen so much. The first is that there is a lack of supply of houses, meaning not enough houses have been built over the last 30 years. This means that there is a shortage of houses for people to buy, which is why the price has increased and continues to increase. This suggests that increasing the amount of houses being built would reduce the large increases in house prices.

The other school of thought is that rising house prices has been caused by increasing demand for housing, as a consequence of home ownership being the primary form of housing that is promoted in policy. For example, around 70% of people in the UK own their home or are paying for it with a mortgage. This means that while changes described above like the increasing population and familial changes have some impact, their effect is not as important as the demand caused by the emphasis on home ownership, such as through the Right to Buy policy and more recently the Help to Buy policy. This suggests that reducing the emphasis in policy on home ownership and providing more of different types of housing (i.e. houses for rent) would reduce the large increase in house prices.

The increasing population has also meant a need to increase education provision for all, such as primary schooling, and further and higher education. One particular significant change has been the huge increase in the number of people going to university. In the early 1960s, only about 5% of young people went to university, but this has increased to nearly 50% of young people going to university in 2012 (Department for Business Innovation and Skills, 2013). This large increase in student numbers has meant a huge increase in expenditure on higher education, and this was one of the reasons given for the need to stop providing student maintenance grants to all students and instead introduce maintenance loans and tuition fees.

In terms of income maintenance, there are two main ways in which the changes lead to increased expenditure. The first is due to the way that the nature of work has changed. This has meant an increase in the number of people reliant on out of work income maintenance benefits such as Jobseeker's Allowance and Income Support. It has also meant an increase in the number of people reliant on in-work income maintenance benefits such as Tax Credits to maintain their in-work income as shown in Graph 3.2 in Chapter 3. This is very relevant in the context of the emphasis given towards work as the route out of poverty, and the limitation of this approach as detailed in Chapter 5.

The second way that the changes have led to increases in income maintenance is in relation to the increased ageing population, meaning the need to pay out much more in pensioner benefits both in terms of the number of pensions and in terms of the length of time for which the benefits are paid out. More specifically, not only is there a need for more benefits like pensions, but also for pensions that last longer. This point emphasizes why the State Pension has the highest expenditure of all income maintenance benefits, as detailed in Chapter 2.

In terms of health, the increasing population will also have an important impact on the NHS resources, in the sense that more people using the services will mean more expenditure required. In particular, as more people are living longer, so there will be more people with specific age related health needs, such as dementia. This will increase the expenditure on health in important ways.

Real Life Box 9.7 **Dementia: 'one of the greatest enemies of humanity'**

The 2010 Coalition government Prime Minister David Cameron described dementia as 'one of the greatest enemies of humanity'.

Dementia is the name for a group of diseases that lead to a gradual decline of how the brain functions. Perhaps the best known type of dementia is Alzheimer's disease. It is incurable, and slowly interferes with a person's ability to carry out the normal tasks of daily living. There are many different types of dementia, but all tend to cause problems with memory, language skills, information processing, mental agility, understanding and judgement. In some advanced forms of dementia, the person is unable to get up and move, or has no interest in eating or drinking.

Although it is possible to get dementia as young as 40, dementia is mainly a disease that affects people as they get older. Approximately one in twenty people over the age

▶

of 65 has dementia. However, by the age of 80 about one in six are affected, and one in three people in the UK will have dementia by the time they die.

There are 800,000 people who have been diagnosed with the dementia in the UK so far, which costs an estimated £23 billion. However, the Alzheimer's Society predicts this number will increase to 1 million by 2021 and 1.7 million by 2051, which will mean that this cost will significantly increase.

The ageing population is also increasing the need for personal social services expenditure, particularly in social care. This is because as people live longer, so their need for social care increases, either in their home or in a care home. There is also care provided for other groups, such as for disabled people and those who are sick. But it is care for the elderly which has become the most prominent type of social care needs.

Real Life Box 9.8 **What is social care?**

Social care describes a range of services and workers who work with both adults and children in a variety of circumstances where there is a specific vulnerability, such as children at risk of abuse, frail older people, people with mental health problems, people with learning disabilities and disabled people. By the early 21st century there were some 1.6 million people using social care services, with some 1.4 million people working in the social care workforce, which is more than the entire NHS workforce (Glasby, 2009: 352), and this is predicted to rise as the population gets older (Carers UK, 2014).

Most expenditure on social care is on the elderly in the form of residential care and nursing care, and nursing care is the most expensive as it requires specialist medical attention. This is the type of care that could increase as people live longer and so get conditions that require more intensive care.

There can be different levels of social care need, from extensive and ongoing care required to treat chronic conditions such as dementia, respite care to relieve those who provide ongoing care, for example to those with a disability, and also care which is infrequent, such as providing meals on wheels.

In the past, such social care needs were seen as a family concern, and this was possible when potential carers, usually women, were available. However, with the changing economic nature of society, such as the need for two household employment to avoid poverty as we saw in Chapter 5, such carers are not as numerous as in the past. This means that there is much more requirement for health care needs to be met by social policy in some form.

A rapidly ageing population and longer life expectancy means that there is an ever increasing need for care and support, but this need is quickly outstripping the number of family members able to provide it. This problem will very likely become even more critical over the coming years, as while the *demand* for such social care is expected to increase by over 50% between 2007 and 2032, the *expenditure* required for social care provided to adults is expected to rise by only 20% (Carers UK, 2014: 3).

Reducing social policy expenditure

There are several ways in which these social and economic changes can reduce the expenditure on social policy. The technological changes outlined above mean that we are able to do things more quickly and also in a more efficient manner. So for example in relation to health, the NHS can now provide things like operations in a quicker and more efficient manner, meaning that more operations can be carried more cheaply and cost-effectively, and in a speedier manner. Also, this may mean that there is not such a need for labour intensive places like hospitals. Instead individuals can be diagnosed and treated in the community for minor health problems using technological advances such as the phone or on the internet. This was the rationale behind *NHS Direct*, which is now *NHS 111*, where people phone in and speak to a nurse about their problems, and suggestions for treatments may be given over the phone, therefore avoiding a visit to the GP or to the A&E department of their hospital. Technological changes such as mobility scooters have already made an impact for disabled people, and this could mean that there is less need to employ carers for tasks such as getting out and about.

In terms of social care, the fact that so many people are living healthier for longer may mean that they are able to take care of each other for longer, and this reduces the need for social care. For example, 'older people provide a range of formal and informal volunteering services to their communities worth over £10 billion per annum to the national economy, plus a number of benefits which cannot readily be quantified' (Blood, 2013: 4). There is the potential for this contribution to increase as more old people live longer.

In addition, there could also be an increase in familial care such as grandparents able to look after their grandchildren instead of the children requiring nursery care, and this could mean less expenditure for social policy on childcare, which is the second most expensive item of expenditure for families with children, after the mortgage. More childcare might also be possible by parents themselves due to the more flexible types of working that technology enables. So for example, rather than having to go into the office everyday, it is possible for individuals to work from home and to fit their working day around their lifestyles, as a consequence of high speed internet and computing.

Which of these social and economic changes will have the most significant effect on social policy?

So far this chapter has presented the social and economic changes and their effects on social policy in a way which would seem to indicate that they are separate and not related in any way. However, a close reading of the changes makes it obvious that these changes are related in very specific ways.

So for instance, the main work changes have been increasing unemployment, increasing part-time working and increasing lower paid service sector jobs. These changes have occurred just as there has been a move away from the single male breadwinner nuclear family to other family types. The combination of these changes has meant that these other family types are less likely to be able to support each other through work, and so be more reliant on social policy benefits.

Additionally, the rise in self-employment has been driven by the increasing population who see self-employment as a way to gain work at a time of relatively high unemployment. These changes in work are also being driven by technological changes, as more hi-tech machinery is used to replace humans in manufacturing, meaning less lower skilled manufacturing jobs available.

Technological changes are also affecting the demographics of the country, in terms of both enabling more people to stay alive once born, and keeping people healthier and alive for longer. The resulting increasing population is in turn driving the increasing demand for service sector employment such as social care, as older people need more people to look after them, and is also driving the demand for more technology to support this. And globalization has also been important in the migration that we have detailed above, in terms of enabling people to move more quickly and easily between countries.

This means that these social and economic changes are interrelated and dependent on each other, and this can intensify their effects. The Office for Budget Responsibility (OBR) (2013) (which advises the government on income and expenditure issues) has identified demographic changes in general and the ageing population specifically as the change which will affect social policy expenditure the most out of all future changes identified above. This is because of the possibility that the government could end up having to spend more money on age-related items such as pensions and health care on an ongoing basis.

What specific social policies have been put in place to deal with the future effects of these social and economic changes?

There have been a number of specific policies put in place to deal with these social and economic changes in all social policy areas. The social and economic change which the government has identified as having the most significant effect in the future is the ageing population. So this section mainly focuses on policies concerned with personal social services, as this is the social policy area which will very likely be most affected by the ageing population. These policy changes will be used as a way to generalize the social policy changes in other areas, and will be summarized briefly at the end of the section.

The most obvious effect of ageing population on personal social services is a need for more extensive social care and nursing care provision to deal with the increase in the number of older people. Already, over 50% of personal social services expenditure is on older people (those aged 65 years and older), and the likelihood is that this will increase as the ageing population increases (Health and Social Care Information Centre, 2013). One of the main reasons for this is the cost of social care. For example, in 2012 the average cost per week of living in a care home was £528 per week, which works out at £27,144 per year. This is more than the average earnings of £26,075 shown in Table 4.1 in Chapter 4. This amount spent on care will very likely increase with the ageing population, and with the increases in diseases such as dementia detailed above.

Over the last 20 years or so, there has been an emphasis in personal social services policy on the *'personalization'* of care. The main aim of personalization is 'involving and putting people at the centre of the process of identifying their needs and making choices about how and when they are supported to live their lives ... so that all systems, processes, staff and services are geared up to put people first' (Carr, 2010: 3). In practice, this means tailoring care towards individual needs, rather than a having a one size fits all approach for everyone.

An important aspect of this personalization emphasis has been the individual having some responsibility for deciding their care needs and also for meeting their care needs. A good example of this is the policy of *direct payments* as a way for individuals to directly meet their care needs. Direct payments are where individuals are assessed by social workers as needing a specific *personal budget* to meet their social care needs. This budget is then given to the individual directly (hence the name direct payments) to meet their care needs how they wish. They can then choose from state, private, voluntary or individual care providers. So direct payments are also a good example of the mixed economy of welfare discussed in Chapter 8.

Real Life Box 9.9 **Personalization, direct payments and personal budgets**

These three terms have been very important in the development of Personal Social Services over the last 20 years.

➢ Personalization refers to an emphasis in social care on actively involving services users in the care that they receive.

➢ Direct Payments refers to giving individuals the financial resources to meet their own care needs.

➢ Personal Budgets refers to the amount given to individuals to meet their own care needs.

All of these three processes are possible for those who receive personal social services benefits, such as those needing care either in their home or in an institution. In 2010, the coalition government made it a requirement that all users of social services in England were given a personal budget to buy their own care and support, but this requirement has since been dropped (Brindle, 2012).

Over the last ten years, expenditure on direct payments for adults has more than doubled, from £450 million in 2007–2008 to £1.2 billion in 2012–2013 (Health and Social Care Information Centre, 2013). One of the main reasons why there has been such an emphasis on direct payments is because it is significantly cheaper to give the individuals a direct payment to meet their own care than it is for their care to be arranged by the state. This has meant the trend over the last 20 years or so has been towards greater individual responsibility for social care.

Table 9.3 summarizes the main changes that have occurred in all social policy areas to deal with these social and economic changes.

Table 9.3 shows that there have been significant policy changes in all social policy areas. It also highlights that the general emphasis on individuals taking more individual responsibility for their social care, which is evident in the personalization of personal social services, is also evident in other social policy areas. For example, for education the cost of higher education has been passed on to the student through tuition fees and maintenance loans, and for income maintenance the raising of the retirement age and the auto-enrolment of employees into pensions both emphasize the individual either working longer or the individual saving more for their retirement.

Table 9.3 Summary of main policy changes to deal with the social and economic changes

	Main overall aims	Main policies
Health	➤ Reduce overall expenditure on the NHS by making it more efficient and ➤ Have more health services provided by other providers, such as private providers	➤ Changed the structure of NHS to give GPS more responsibility ➤ Increased patient choice in healthcare services
Education	➤ Increase the educational attainment of young people to compete in the globalized world ➤ Reduce state expenditure on higher education by shifting cost to the student	➤ Increased School Leaving Age ➤ Increased Tuition Fees and Maintenance Grants for higher education
Housing	➤ Increase the amount of home-owners ➤ Match housing size to family size more appropriately in the social rented sector	➤ Increased private house buying through Help to Buy ➤ introduced the 'Bedroom Tax'
Income maintenance	➤ Increase the amount of the state pension ➤ Increase the amount of pension that an individual receives at retirement ➤ Increase the amount of years an individual works before that can receive the State pension	➤ New State Pension of £148 per week ➤ Auto-enrolment of employees into a pension ➤ Raised the retirement age for the State Pension to age 68 by 2046
Personal social services	➤ Increase individual responsibility for providing social care	➤ Social care costs capped at £75,000 per person ➤ Personalization of social care needs

Real Life Box 9.10 **Auto-enrolment of pensions**

To deal with the fact that people are living longer, but many are not saving enough for their retirement, the government has introduced the auto-enrolment of all employees into a pension scheme. This means that rather than having to choose to join a pension scheme, your employer automatically puts you into one from the first day of your employment. The only way that a person cannot be part of auto-enrolment is to actively say they do not want to be part of it, or to earn below a certain amount. Paying into an auto-enrolment pension scheme will be in addition to paying National Insurance contributions to gain entitlement to the State Pension when you retire. This means that

▶

◀

you get two pensions on retirement, the State Pension and an additional auto enrol-
ment pension, and so this increases the income that you receive when you retire.

Auto-enrolment started in stages in October 2012 and will be completed by 2017. This
will mean that by 1 April 2017, if you are at least 22 years old, work for someone else
and you earn above a certain amount your employer will automatically enrol you into a
pension, unless you actively choose not to be enrolled.

Question

Should the state be more generous in what it provides in terms of benefits for older
people as we are all living longer with a higher demand for long-term care needs?

The New Labour government in the period 1997–2010 introduced some of
the changes in Table 9.3, while the 2010 Coalition government introduced
some others. The key point is that in general, there is not much disagreement between the main political parties about the need for policy changes
and the types of policy changes that should occur. A good example of this
is in relation to increasing the State Pension Age. This was something that
was started by the New Labour government and continued by the 2010
Coalition government. Where there is disagreement is generally in terms
of how fast and how far the changes should go, with the 2010 Coalition
government, as part of its austerity social policy focus, implementing
changes much faster than set out by the New Labour government. This
highlights that there is a general consensus not only on the need for social
policy changes to deal with these social and economic changes, but also
the direction that future social policy changes should take.

Summary

This chapter has outlined some of the important social and economic
changes that have occurred and are occurring in the UK. These include
changes in the family, work, technology and demography. The chapter has
shown that these changes are having important effects on the nature of
our society to the extent that the world we now live in is very much different from that in which Beveridge constructed the post-war welfare state.

Not surprisingly, these changes are also having important effects on the income and expenditure of all social policy areas. In some instances these changes are beneficial for social policy, but in other instances they are very unfavourable to the functioning of social policy as we know it today, and therefore to the future functioning of social policy. It is also important to note that these changes are linked together and feed off each other, which can work to intensify their effects.

The government has identified demographic changes in general and the ageing population specifically as the change that will affect social policy the most in the future. Personal social services is the area that will be most affected by the ageing population and this chapter has outlined important policies that have been put in place to deal with the effect of the ageing population. The emphasis in policy has been on personalization, and particularly the individual taking more responsibility for meeting their welfare now and in the future. This increased emphasis on individual responsibility for meeting welfare is also evident if we analyse the policies put in place in other social policy areas to deal with the social and economic changes. This is the case regardless of which government has been in power for the last 20 years, and this suggests a consensus that will dominate social policy in the future.

Key Point

Social, work, demographic and technological changes have a huge impact on social policy in ways that mean its future looks very different from the cradle to grave welfare state that Beveridge outlined.

10

HOW CAN YOUR IDEOLOGICAL BELIEFS MAKE AND CHANGE SOCIAL POLICY?

The aims of this chapter are to:

1. **Provide a basic understanding of the two main ideological beliefs of social policies past, present and future**

2. **Enable you to locate and understand your own ideological beliefs about key aspects of social policies**

3. **Detail how your ideological beliefs can make and change social policy**

The previous chapters have outlined significant events that have marked the development of social policy from the past to the present, and also possibly for the future. We have seen that social policy has changed significantly over time, and is almost unrecognizable from that which was provided during the middle of the 19th century, and will probably be unrecognizable in the future. What hopefully has become most apparent is the way that different governments can disagree significantly in their approach to social policy, in terms of how and why social policies are provided, as is evident from the different policies which they put in place. What should have become evident throughout the book is that such differences can have a significant impact on the outcomes and effectiveness of the policy, and so understanding the reasons for these differences is very important.

This chapter presents a simplified account of the notion of ideology as a way to account for these differences in social policies. In its simplest meaning, ideology refers to the beliefs that individuals and groups have about society in general, and so in defining ideology as important to the development of social policy, this chapter explores the beliefs that individuals have about society in general.

An important part of the process of understanding ideologies relevant to social policy is locating and understanding your own key ideological beliefs about social policy, and this chapter provides the opportunity for you to do this in relation to five key aspects of social policy.

By the end of this chapter, you should understand the notion of ideology and the importance of ideology to the development of social policies, and also be able to articulate and explain how your own ideological beliefs can make and change social policy.

What is ideology?

While you may not be aware of the term ideology itself, you most likely have come across some different types of ideologies. Terms like socialism, capitalism, Marxism, totalitarianism, Thatcherism, communism, feudalism, liberalism, feminism, racism and environmentalism all refer to a specific type of ideology. And you have definitely heard of the three main political parties, the Conservative Party, the Labour Party, and the Liberal Democrats.

You may have strong agreement or disagreement with some of these ideologies, and this is because, apart from the *–ism* suffix, what they all have in common is that they all describe the belief system for a particular way of life. For example, capitalism describes a system of living in which the ownership of money is very important, while environmentalism describes a system of living in which the concern for the environment is very important. This means that they provide an explanation for living life a certain way, which includes a specific rationale for doing things in a certain way, as opposed to another way.

Thinking about it, whatever decision we make has an underlying reason behind it, even though it may not be readily apparent. Otherwise, without an underlying logic to the decisions we make, we would very quickly go crazy. As a simple example, think about the reason(s) you chose to study at university. It is very unlikely that you simply woke up one day and decided that you wanted to go the university. This is because choosing to go to university was not the only option open to you, it is very likely that you could have chosen to do other things, for example go into work, take a gap year, continue in work, do an apprenticeship, or even do nothing. Most probably, it was a decision that was reached over a period of time, with a specific goal in mind, such as to pursue an interest in a particular subject, as a way into a particular job, to progress in your current career, or as the most interesting thing to do at this point of your life, and there might be numerous other reasons not mentioned here. The key point is that you made your decision with an ultimate *goal* in mind (such as employment, further knowledge, training or career progression), having decided that university was the best *method* for achieving that goal.

Why is ideology important to social policy?

We can apply this essence of our everyday decision-making to the development of social policies. As we have seen so far in previous chapters, governments always have a choice of which type of social policy they put in place, and there have been various different types of policies enacted by different governments at different times. To take health as an example, governments over time have chosen to provide health benefits that are paid for exclusively by the individual (e.g. the Poor Law period before the Liberal government at the beginning of the 20th century), health benefits that are dependent on the employment status of an individual (e.g. the health insurance schemes of the Lloyd George government) or health benefits that are free at the point of use for all (e.g. the creation of the NHS by the Attlee government). More recently, the 2010 Coalition government has reorganized the NHS so that doctors take more responsibility for its finance and day-to-day decision-making. Similar variations apply to other social policy areas.

Various factors can be used to explain these different developments in policy. For example, on the one hand, events in society can impact on the development of social policy, such as the impact the Second World War had on the Beveridge Report and thus the post-war 'welfare state' of Clement Attlee's government. On the other hand, a lack of money can also be detailed as an important factor, as evident from the austerity social policies of the 2010 Coalition government, so it is possible that such developments are driven by financial considerations.

Such factors have been and undoubtedly remain important to the development of social policies. However, the problem with such accounts of social policy development is that they do not really take into account the underlying theories and beliefs of individuals that can lead to specific policy change. If all social policies were driven by such issues and events, how do we explain the fact that there are often vast disagreements between individuals and governments about the types of policies that should be put in place even from the same event? There are very rarely periods of consensus about the nature of social policies, as evident from the disagreements you see today about social policies. Additionally, while certain types of policy are sometimes presented as inevitable, history shows us that this is not necessarily the case.

The prime example of this is the huge contrast between the social policies at times of *austerity* of the Attlee government in the post-war period and the 2010 Coalition government. On the one hand, the austerity social policies of the Attlee government saw the creation of the modern welfare state, built around Beveridge's notion of cradle to grave welfare, and epitomized by the creation of the NHS in 1948. In contrast, the austerity social policies of the 2010 Coalition government have been characterized by the notion that welfare is the cause of austerity, leading to huge cuts in welfare. The fact that there are such disagreements should highlight to us that the choice of social policy is very often an individual preference for a specific type of policy, and this is where the importance of ideological beliefs about the best way to achieve a specific outcome becomes significant.

What ideological beliefs do you have about social policy?

An important part of the process of understanding ideologies relevant to social policy is being aware of your own ideological beliefs, and this section provides the opportunity for you to locate and understand your own ideological positions about key aspects of social policy. It also aims to highlight the huge contrast in approaches to social policy that are possible.

In the five boxes below are descriptions of five key ideological aspects of social policy. These descriptions are followed by two contrasting belief statements about the ideological aspect of social policy. Read the belief statements and chose the statement that most closely matches your belief about the aspect of social policy. You need to be as honest as possible when choosing your belief statements, as this will aid your understanding of the topic and belief being discussed. After each box, there is a description of the significance of this ideological aspect to social policy benefits.

Ideological aspect 1: the cause of social problems for social policy

One of the most important contrasting beliefs in social policy is whether social problems are caused by the *individual* or by *society*. This contrast is most evident in an issue like unemployment, as shown in the choice of the two statements below.

A) I believe that social problems such as unemployment are *individual* problems, and so believe that *individuals* should be primarily responsible for dealing with them.

B) I believe that social problems such as unemployment are *societal* problems, and so believe that *society* should be primarily responsible for dealing with them.

Agreement with the first statement implies that you believe that unemployment is caused by the failings of the individual, such as through an individual's lack of employment qualifications, an individual's lack of willingness to work or an individual's lack of appropriate employment skills, such as attitude or aptitude.

On the other hand, agreement with the second statement implies you believe that unemployment is caused by the nature of society, such as the lack of available jobs in a society, the lack of good quality jobs in a society or the lack of jobs that match the skills of individuals.

These different beliefs are important because they will shape the type of unemployment policies that you put in place to deal with them. So for instance, if you believe that unemployment is caused by the individual, you will put in place policies that are meant to deal with these individual failings, such as reducing unemployment benefit levels to encourage the unemployed to take any available work, which occurred under the Thatcher government in the 1980s as shown in Chapter 3, and under the 2010 Coalition government.

On the other hand, if you believe that unemployment is caused by the nature of society, you will put in place policies that are meant to deal with these societal failings, as shown occurring in the Chapter 3 under the Attlee government in the late 1940s, where an emphasis on 'full employment' in policy meant the government nationalized industries to provide more jobs for individuals.

We can see that these differences in belief about whether it is individuals or society that are the cause of social problems extend to other social policy areas, such as ill health, low educational attainment, low income, and poor neighbourhoods and housing.

Ideological aspect 2: the extent of social policy responsibility

Beliefs about the extent of social policy responsibility centres on whether social policy should only deal with problems in a *narrow* way, or should deal with problems in a *broad* way.

A) I believe that social policy responsibility for issues such as housing should be narrow, dealing only with essential issues such as the lack of housing.

B) I believe that the social policy responsibility for issues such as housing should be broad, dealing with non-essential issues such as the quality of housing.

Taking housing as an example, you might believe that the key issue for housing policy is a narrow focus on ensuring only that there are enough houses for individuals to live in. This would mean that the focus of social policy would be on the provision of land and the availability of finance for those wishing to build and buy houses.

On the other hand, you might believe that housing policy should go beyond a simple emphasis on the number of houses to include the wider focus on the quality of housing that is available. This might include attention to additional issues such as the size of houses, minimum quality standards and ensuring that there are enough different types of housing tenure, such as to buy, to rent or for social housing.

If you believe in a narrow focus on housing, your policies will reflect this. The period of Industrialization is an example when government concern was encouraging the building of housing to deal with urbanization and population growth, not with the quality of housing. More recently, the *'Help to Buy'* policy of the 2010 Coalition government has provided financial incentives for house buyers to encourage them to buy more houses.

On the other hand, if you believe in a broad focus on housing, this will be evident in policies during the Liberal Reforms at the turn of the 20th century with the 1909 Housing and Town Planning Act, which required houses to be built to a certain standard and required a planned approach to urban growth, such as in relation to sanitation.

We can see that these differences in belief about the extent of social policy extends to other social policy areas, in relation to quality of life, types of jobs, levels of social security income, and neighbourhood quality.

Ideological aspect 3: entitlement to social policy benefits

Beliefs about who should be entitled to social policy benefits reflects a contrast between beliefs that benefits should be based on *contributions* or on *need*, thereby limiting or extending who receives social policy.

A) I believe that entitlement to social policy benefits such as social security should be based on *contributions*, and given only to those who have paid tax and national insurance.

B) I believe that entitlement to social policy benefits such as social security should be based on *need*, and given even to those who have not paid tax and national insurance.

Taking social security as an example, you might believe that only those who have contributed into the system through tax or national insurance should be entitled to benefits. This is evident in benefits such as contribution-based Jobseeker's Allowance, Maternity Allowance and Incapacity Benefit. These are called *contributory benefits*, and mean that some people are not entitled to such benefits because they have not contributed, even though they might have a need for it.

On the other hand, you might believe that need should be the most important factor that determines whether a person is entitled to benefits. Having free and universal access to the NHS is a good example of where need is the deciding criterion for entitlement. Need can be also be related to having an additional responsibility, such as looking after a child as related to Child Benefit, or having a low level of income, such as related to Income Support. Within social policy, some needs based benefits can be means-tested, meaning that they can only be claimed if your income is below a certain level, such as Income Support, non-contributory Jobseeker's Allowance or Housing Benefit. Or some needs based benefits can be non means-tested, meaning that is does not matter how much money you already have, such as Disability Living Allowance and Carer's Allowance.

In policy, these differences become readily apparent. If you believe that entitlement should be based on contributions then policies such as the introduction of contribution-based Jobseeker's Allowance by the Conservative government in 1995 reflect this, as it made the benefit more generous in terms of the amount paid to those who had made National Insurance contributions against those who had not made National Insurance contributions.

On the other hand, if you believe that entitlement to social security should be needs based then policies such as the Tax Credits introduced by the 1997 New Labour government reflect this. Non-contributory and non means-tested benefits such as the Winter Fuel Allowance, also introduced under the New Labour government, reflect the way in which needs based beliefs become apparent in policy.

We can see that these differences in belief about the criteria for entitlement social policy extends to other social policy areas, such as in relation to entitlement to social care for the elderly, entitlement to student loans and grants, and entitlement to dentistry benefits.

Ideological aspect 4: paying for social policy

Beliefs about how social policy should be paid for reflect contrasting positions about whether social policy should be paid for by each *individual*, or through general *taxation*.

A) I believe that social policy benefits such as education should be paid for by the *individual*.

▶

◀

> B) I believe that social policy benefits such as education should be paid for through general *taxation*.

Taking education as an example, the claim that the individual should pay for it is reflective of a belief that education is an individual benefit, so the individual should pay for it. This would be in the form of direct payment by the individual, such as through private schools rather than through comprehensive schooling paid for by general taxation, as it would be unfair to compel people to pay for something like education that they either do not use or do not benefit from. Furthermore, this stance believes that if the individual pays for education, it is a more efficient method of providing social policy as only those who need it will pay for it, meaning that only education which is required will be provided. The debates around the need for university tuition fees is the best example of this argument.

On the other hand, the argument that taxation should pay for education rests on two contrasting beliefs. Firstly, that education actually benefits the wider society, not just the individual. This means that the contribution that society makes is repaid by the fact that educated individuals make it a richer society through the jobs they create, and this collective gain means that the contribution of society is justified. On the other hand, if individuals have to pay for their education, most people would find it too expensive, and so would not be able to afford to send their child to school. This would be detrimental to the development of society in the longer run, as exemplified by the high cost of childcare and its impact on limiting mothers' ability to work.

In policy, these differences are apparent. If you believe that paying for education should be the responsibility of the individual, policies such as the introduction of means-tested tuition fees in September 1998 and the abolishment of student maintenance grants and their replacement with student loans by the New Labour government reflect this. The 2010 Coalition government increased the maximum amount of Higher Education Tuition Fees for students to £9,000, meaning that students have had to take on more higher education loans to pay for these fees and for maintenance costs.

On the other hand, a belief in the payment of education through taxation is reflected in policies such as the implementation of the Butler Education Act by the post-war Labour government of Clement Attlee, which provided secondary education as a free and universal right for all.

We can see that these differences in belief about how social policy should be paid for extends to other social policy areas, such as to health care benefits through the NHS, social care benefits like care homes and housing benefits like house buying subsidy schemes.

Ideological aspect 5: the principal objective of social policy

Beliefs about the objectives of social policy encompass all of the above beliefs, but differ in terms of whether *freedom* of individual action or *fairness* should be the principal
objective of social policy.

A) I believe that the principal objective of social policy benefits such as health should
be to ensure equal access to provision for all, as *freedom of individual action* is very
important to society.

B) I believe that the principal objective of social policy benefits such as health should
be to enable equal outcomes from provision for all, as *fairness* is very important to
society.

A belief that equal access to social policy should be its principle objective reflects a view that social policy should be minimalist in scope. This
is linked to the notion that giving individuals the freedom to make their
own choices about welfare is very important, as individuals are seen as
best able to make decisions about their welfare. So by making benefits
such as health available through equal access, you are providing individuals with the freedom to act in ways that are beneficial to their welfare.
Equal access can relate to the type of provision made, such as all having
access to a GP, or the number of hospitals. The provision of such equal
access does not require any additional action to ensure or enable people
to use such services, as it should be left to the free choice of individuals
whether they use such services.

A belief that the principal objective of social policy should be equal
outcomes reflects the belief that social policy should be extensive in
scope. This is linked to the notion that ensuring there is a fair division of
resources in society means that there are better outcomes for society overall, as people are able to make better choices when they have a guaranteed
minimum standard of living. So, benefits such as health should serve to
equalize the outcomes for those who are less advantaged with those who
are more advantaged, as it ensures that they are all able to pursue their
welfare in a more meaningful and effective way. Ensuring equal outcomes
can relate to policies such as providing more health funding per individual, and providing more health benefits in one area compared to another.
As is apparent, such policies for equal outcomes can mean less equal provision for some, but this is justified as it leads to more equal outcomes and
thus a fairer society.

In policy, a belief that equal access is relevant to freedom of choice
is reflected in policies such as the incentives provided to private health

insurance during the period of Thatcherism, when individuals were encouraged to use their freedom to provide additional welfare services for themselves. The 2010 Coalition government increased the freedom of choice for services available to individuals in the NHS by enabling services to be provided by the private sector and charities.

However, Beveridge's call for a comprehensive system of welfare to overcome inequalities in health, as set out in the previous chapter, is reflective of an emphasis on equal outcomes in health.

We can see that these differences in belief regarding the underlying objective of social policy extends to other social policy areas, such as debates surrounding the construction of social housing or private housing, comprehensive and private schooling, and high or low levels of social security benefits.

What are the major similarities and differences in social policy ideological beliefs?

We can explore in more detail these ideological belief statements in terms of their similarities and differences. It should have become apparent that these beliefs are interrelated and complementary of each other, and Table 10.1 highlights this by collating the belief statements together.

Questions

1. Read the list of 'A' statements. Do you notice any underlying themes or trends in terms of the beliefs that they outline?

2. Read the list of 'B' statements. Do you notice any underlying themes or trends in terms of the beliefs that they outline?

'A' statements – individualism

From reading the list of 'A' statements, it should have become apparent that there is an emphasis in these statements on the individual taking responsibility for their own welfare, and that social policy should be focussed on enabling individuals to provide for their own welfare needs as much as possible. This is because underlying such statements is belief that the goal of social policy should be ensuring maximum freedom of

Table 10.1 Ideological beliefs summarized

	A	B
The cause of social problems for social policy	I believe that social policy problems such as unemployment are *individual problems*, and so believe that *individuals* should be primarily responsibility for dealing with them	I believe that social policy problems such as unemployment are *societal problems*, and so believe that *society* should be primarily responsibility for dealing with them
The extent of social policy responsibility	I believe that the extent of social policy responsibility for issues such as housing should be *narrow*, dealing only with essential issues such as the lack of housing	I believe that the extent of social policy responsibility such as housing should be *broad*, dealing additionally with non-essential issues such as the quality of housing
Entitlement to social policy benefits	I believe that entitlement to social policy benefits such as Jobseeker's Allowance should be *based on contributions*, only to those who have paid tax and national insurance	I believe that entitlement to social policy benefits such as Jobseeker's Allowance should be *based on need*, even to those who have not paid tax and national insurance
Paying for social policy	I believe that paying for social policy such as education should be the responsibility of the *individual*	I believe that paying for social policy such as education should be through general *taxation*
The objective of social policy	I believe that the objective of social policy such as health should be to ensure equal access to provision for all, as *freedom* of individual action is very important to society	I believe that the objective of social policy such as health should be to enable that there are equal outcomes from provision for all, as *fairness* is very important to society

individual action and individual responsibility for social policy. For this reason, this type of ideology belief is termed *Individualism*, as its emphasis is on the individual as having primary responsibility for meeting their own welfare needs. In the statements above, the emphasis on the individual as at the core of the ideology of individualism makes itself apparent in relation to the cause of social problems, the extent of social policy, entitlement to social policy benefits, paying for social policy, and the overall objective of social policy. Specific ideological perspectives which this term refers to that you might have heard of are capitalism, neo-liberalism, conservatism and classical liberalism.

Real Life Box 10.1 **Individualism exemplified**

Ex-Prime Minister Margaret Thatcher, talking to Women's Own magazine, 31 October 1987

"I think we've been through a period where too many people have been given to understand that if they have a problem, it's the government's job to cope with it. 'I have a problem, I'll get a grant.' 'I'm homeless, the government must house me.' They're casting their problem on society. And, you know, there is no such thing as society. There are individual men and women, and there are families. And no government can do anything except through people, and people must look to themselves first. It's our duty to look after ourselves and then, also to look after our neighbour. People have got the entitlements too much in mind, without the obligations. There's no such thing as entitlement, unless someone has first met an obligation."

'B' statements – collectivism

The nature of the B statements are in contrast to those of A. Rather the emphasis is on society taking responsibility collectively for individuals' welfare. This means that social policy should be focussed on identifying ways in which society can enable individuals to meet their welfare needs. This means that social policy is required to enable society to provide for individuals' welfare as much as possible. This is because underlying the statements is the belief that the goal of social policy should be ensuring that society is as fair as possible, and a belief that ensuring fairness in society means that resources need to be shared out more equally among members of society. For this reason, this type of ideological belief is referred to as a *Collectivism*, as its emphasis is on society collectively having a responsibility for meeting the welfare needs of individuals. In the statements above, the emphasis on society as having a collective responsibility that is at the core of the ideology of collectivism makes itself apparent in relation to the cause of social problems, the extent of social policy, entitlement to social policy benefits, paying for social policy, and the overall objective of social policy. Specific ideological perspectives which this term refers to and which you might have heard of are socialism, communism and feminism.

Real Life Box 10.2 **Collectivism exemplified**

The Labour Party Manifesto, 1945

"There are certain so-called freedoms that Labour will not tolerate: freedom to exploit other people; freedom to pay poor wages and to push up prices for selfish

▶

profit; freedom to deprive the people of the means of living full, happy, healthy lives ... the Labour Party is prepared to achieve it by drastic policies and keeping a firm constructive hand on our whole productive machinery; the Labour Party will put the community first and the sectional interests of private business after. Labour will plan from the ground up – giving an appropriate place to constructive enterprise and private endeavour in the national plan, but dealing decisively with those interests which would use high-sounding talk about economic freedom to cloak their determination to put themselves and their wishes above those of the whole nation."

Question

Looking back at the historical periods outlined in Chapter 3, which type of ideology can be said to refer to which periods?

How do these ideological beliefs become specific social policies?

So far we have established that all individuals have underlying beliefs about the things that they do. These beliefs reflect themselves in both the way we choose to do things and the outcomes we are trying to achieve. The activity above has exemplified this by specifically outlining how your position on important aspects of social policy is underpinned by your ideological beliefs about the nature of social policy. Furthermore, we have seen that these ideological beliefs have important implications for the direction of social policies, as there is always more than one way in which social policies can be made to deal with an issue.

From analysing how these ideological beliefs make themselves evident in social policies, we can see that when social policies are made, they reflect two important related features of ideology:

➤ beliefs about what individuals think the world should be like (*ideological goals*);

➤ beliefs about how individuals think these goals could be achieved (*ideological methods*).

These are discussed in detail below.

Ideological goals

Ideological goals refer to beliefs about how we think the world should be like. This refers to the ultimate reason for the action taken. In previous chapters, we saw specific policies having specific goals, such as:

➤ punishing those in poverty (the New Poor Law);

➤ improving the conditions of those in old age (the introduction of Old Age Pensions by the 1906 Liberal Government);

➤ reducing 'want' (The 1946 Attlee government's full employment policy);

➤ increasing the amount of people who owned their housing rather than renting (the Right to Buy policy of the 1979 Thatcher government);

➤ increasing the income of those in work (the introduction of the National Minimum Wage by the 1997 New Labour government); and

➤ reducing government expenditure overall on social policy (the austerity policies of the 2010 Coalition government).

Ideological methods

Ideological methods refer to beliefs about how we think our ideological goal would be best met. This refers to the actual course of action taken. Again, we saw in previous chapters that social policies can be provided in a variety of methods, such as:

➤ the individual themselves can be expected to provide for their own welfare (the New Poor Law);

➤ the state can accept some limited responsibility for provided certain social policies (The 1906 Liberal Government);

➤ the state can accept extensive responsibility for providing social policies (the setting of the NHS by the 1948 Attlee post-war government);

➤ private companies can be incentivized to provide social policies (the incentives provided for more private health care and private pension by the 1979 Thatcher government);

➤ there can be collaboration between the public and private providers (the PFI initiative of the 1997 New Labour Government);

➤ the family, community groups and voluntary services can be encouraged to provide social policies (the emphasis given to the Big Society by the 2010 Coalition government).

Linking goals to methods

Ideological linkage between goals and methods is an important aspect of the development of social policies over time, as without it the ideology of individuals would not make sense. This can be seen from the beliefs, goals and methods outlined above. Talking about policies in terms of their ideological consistency allows us to see the bigger picture about policies, rather than seeing them as incremental developments of society. They also enable us to generalize about the direction of policy in the present and the future, and we can outline wider aims and rationales of policy, beyond those that are stated by policy makers.

Ideological differences

However it is apparent that the goals of different governments differ, with the goal of one particular government being totally rejected by another government, even in relation to the same issue. The contrast between the Attlee government's emphasis on full employment and the Thatcher government's subsequent rejection of this is a good example. Similarly, the methods of different governments also differ, with the contrast between the New Poor Law period and Attlee's post-war government being prime examples. This reinforces the point made earlier that there is very often ideological disagreement between different governments about what the goal of social policies should be.

Real Life Box 10.3 **Unemployment policy at a time of austerity**

As we saw in Chapter 3, periods of austerity can lead to very different types of social policies. This is most evident in relation to unemployment policies, where ideological beliefs about the cause of unemployment lead to very different policies. This difference is shown in Figure 10.1 and Figure 10.2 below.

Figure 10.1 shows the Individualist approach to unemployment, often termed the 'supply side approach'. In this approach, the emphasis is on increasing employment through increasing the 'supply' of those available for work. This is done through, for example, the government increasing the skills of those not in work, and reducing the levels of out of work social policy benefits, such as unemployment benefit. This is from the ideological belief that unemployment is caused by lack of individuals willing or able to take available work.

Figure 10.2 shows the Collectivist approach to unemployment, often termed the 'demand side approach' (or sometimes the 'Keynesian' approach, after John Maynard Keynes, the economist who pioneered this approach). In this approach, the emphasis is on increasing employment through increasing the 'demand' for work. This is done by increasing the amount of work available for individuals to take by, for example, the government building more roads, houses or schools. This is from the ideological belief that unemployment is caused by the lack of available jobs in society.

▶

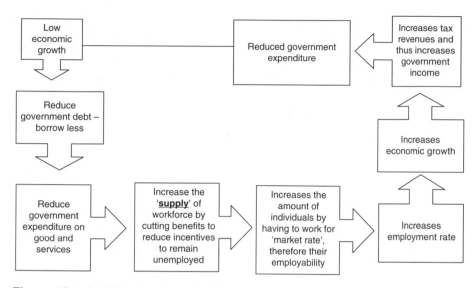

Figure 10.1 Individualist 'supply side' employment policies

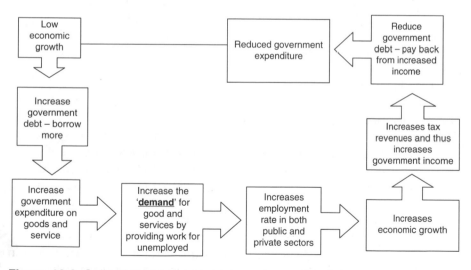

Figure 10.2 Collectivist 'demand side' employment policies

An interesting point to note from both Figure 10.1 and Figure 10.2 is that they both start and finish at the same points – it is the middle bits that are different for both. This emphasizes how Individualist and Collectivist ideological beliefs can result in divergent social policies in very important ways.

These ideological beliefs that underpin unemployment policies can be related to other social policy areas, such as health, education, housing, personal social care and income maintenance.

Questions

1. Looking at the two approaches, which approach do you think the current government is taking?
2. Is this consistent with its ideology?

What is the ideological basis of Labour, Conservative and Liberal Democrat social policies?

This makes understanding the ideological basis of political parties very important. At the time of writing, the three main political parties in the UK are the Conservative Party, the Labour Party and the Liberal Democrats. The Conservative Party has an individualist ideology, as evident in policies outlined particularly during the period of Margaret Thatcher. The Labour Party is a collectivist party, as evident in policies outlined particularly during the period of Clement Attlee.

The Liberal Democrats is a party which is in between these two ideologies, as evident in policies during the Liberal government of Lloyd George. These differences can be shown in Table 10.2.

If we look at an exemplar policy for the Conservative Party, such as the introduction of free schools, we can readily observe the ideology of freedom within them. Their policies require individuals to provide for their own welfare as much as possible, rather than welfare being provided collectively, and they arise from the belief that the goal of social policy should be maximum freedom of individual action.

On the other hand, an exemplar policy for the Labour Party, such as the introduction of the NHS, emphasizes the ideology of fairness within them. The emphasis of their policies is on society taking responsibility for individuals' welfare from the belief that that ensuring fairness in society means that resources need to be shared out more equally among members of society.

An exemplar social policy of the Liberal Democrats, such as the introduction of the £10,000 income tax threshold, emphasizes elements of both freedom and fairness. Their policies take some limited collective responsibility for meeting welfare needs, but also focus on the importance of individual responsibility for meeting welfare.

Table 10.2 Political parties, ideology and social policies

Political party	Ideology	Goals	Methods	Exemplar social policies
Conservative Party	Individualism	Freedom is the most important aim in society	Ensuring freedom of individual action means that we should take individual responsibility for our own welfare as much as possible	– Reductions in social policy expenditure in general – Reductions in specific social policy benefits e.g. unemployment benefits – Privatization of key nationalized utilities e.g. gas, electric etc. – Reductions in personal taxation e.g. income tax – Less universal access to benefits, more selective access e.g. housing benefit – Incentives for more private and less state welfare benefits e.g. private pensions and private healthcare
Liberal Democrats	Individualism/ Collectivism	Freedom and fairness as interrelated goals within society	Ensuring freedom AND fairness through entitlement to equal legal and political rights for all, and qualified endorsement for social and economic intervention as a means of promoting personal development	– A more redistributive tax system e.g. an increased income tax threshold – Contributory based social policy benefits e.g. the Basic State Pension – Increase in the relative value of some welfare benefits e.g. pensions – Insurance based schemes of social policy e.g. health and unemployment – Extensive state involvement in education provision e.g. financing of education – A basic minimum level of income e.g. the minimum wage
Labour Party	Collectivism	Fairness is the most important aim in society	Ensuring fairness by the collective action of sharing out resources more equally among members of society	– Increases in social policy expenditure in general – Increases in specific social policy benefits e.g. state pension – A more redistributive tax system e.g. increases in income tax – Less selective access to benefits, more universal access e.g. NHS – More state and less private welfare provision e.g. council housing – Non-contributory welfare benefits e.g. Tax Credits

Real Life Box 10.4 **The Protection of Freedoms Act 2012**

When the Conservative and Liberal Democrat Coalition government came into power in 2010, one of the first pieces of legislation they put in place was the Protection of Freedoms Act 2012. The main aims of the Act were:

> ➤ stop councils snooping;

> ➤ end the storage of DNA of innocent people;

> ➤ reduce the bureaucracy of CRB checks;

> ➤ end 28-day detention;

> ➤ stop schools deciding on their own to take fingerprints of children;

> ➤ make stalking a criminal offence;

> ➤ end wheel clamping on private land;

> ➤ delete historical convictions for men who have had consensual gay sex with someone who was over 16.

The measures above are concerned with a broader definition of freedom beyond established specific social policy areas, more focussed on freedom in relation to civil liberties. This reflects that the notion of freedom within both Conservative and Liberal Democrat ideology extends beyond social policy issues, to include beliefs about the importance of freedom in all aspects of life.

Can you describe other UK political parties as being individualist or collectivist?

You most likely have heard of, or maybe even voted for, other political parties such as UKIP (UK Independence Party), the Green Party, the Respect Party, the BNP (British National Party), Plaid Cymru and the SNP (Scottish National Party). We can still describe these parties in terms of being either individualist or collectivist, with subtle differences of emphasis. To make this easier to understand, we can place all these political parties on a scale in terms of their emphasis on individualism or collectivism. When this is done, political parties are generally referred to in terms of being either *left wing, right wing* or *centre*, and this is shown below in Figure 10.3.

In Figure 10.3 below, the terms individualist/collectivist and left wing/ right wing are interchangeable, which means that they are terms which can be used instead of each other with the meaning staying the same. So the Labour Party can be described as a being both collectivist and left wing, and the Conservative Party can be described as being both individu-alist and right wing. And to refer to someone as right wing is the same as saying they are individualist; and to refer to someone as left wing is the same as saying they are collectivist.

Using a *continuum* scale like that in Figure 10.3 below enables us to see at a glance how different political parties differ subtly in terms of their emphasis on either individualism or collectivism. This subtlety is enhanced by the use of the terms left wing/right wing/centre, as it means that the ideological beliefs of parties can be more accurately described. So, for example, we can describe the Liberal Democrats as a centrist/centre party, because of their combination of individualist and collectivist ideo-logical beliefs, and Liberal Democrats can also be described as moderate, as their ideological beliefs are close to the centre. On the other hand, where a party's ideological beliefs are far from the centre, they are categorized as being extreme left or right wing, such as the BNP or Respect.

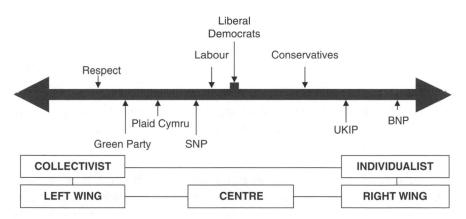

Figure 10.3 Major political parties' ideologies

What is the significance of your ideological beliefs to the development of social policies?

As discussed above ideologies consist of both goals and methods. In a democratic society like the UK, it is through political parties like the Conservatives, Labour, the Liberal Democrats and others that ideologi-cal beliefs are translated into practical social policies when those parties are elected into government. It is here that ideologies become important because, as should be evident by now, the way we vote is influenced by our ideological belief. Even not voting is significant, because a political party gains power in the absence of our vote. So our ideological belief shapes the way we vote, and this is turn shapes the nature of society, and thus social policy, because 'ideologies of welfare are linked to the politics of welfare, and different political allegiances and practices are based in different ideological perspectives' (Alcock, 2008: 182).

A note of caution

Hopefully, what has become apparent is that ideology represents the beliefs of an individual or group. It is important to distinguish the notion of belief from the notion of fact when talking about ideologies. Ideologies are not facts, for the simple reason that the claims made by ideologies are very hard to prove as facts. For example, can we really say for definite that freedom of individual action is more important than fairness in the allocation of society's resources? We may believe it, but we cannot state it as fact. This highlights two important features about ideologies:

1. Ideological beliefs claim to be *the* truth, but actually represent *a* truth (or what someone thinks is true)

2. Ideological beliefs only offer a partial and self-interested view of social reality

This means that as students of social policy, we should take note and apply the following observation of Leach (2009: 7) when analysing the ideological basis of social policies:

> A one-sided or inadequate view of an ideology may not reflect prior prejudice, but simply weaknesses or bias in the source material. The best safeguard against falling for a partial, narrow or eccentric interpretation of an ideology is to read widely, but always critically. Contrasting interpretations, including both hostile and sympathetic treatments, should be deliberately sought out. Such an approach will help to identify both points of agreement and controversy. In all reading a questioning, sceptical approach should be adopted. Nothing should be taken on trust. It is often useful to attempt to discern the author's perspective. To know that a particular writer is Marxist, a conservative or a neo-liberal may assist in the interpretation, and also suggest critical questions.

Summary

This chapter has presented a simplified account of the notion of ideology in order to highlight its importance to the development of social policies past, present and future. It has defined ideology as our underpinning beliefs which rationalize what we do and why we do things. The past and the present of social policies has shown us that there is always more than one way to deal with social problems, and this is where the importance of ideological beliefs becomes evident in social policies. This is the essence of the notion of ideology, the belief that the specific way we do things (our methods) are the best way to achieve our specific objectives (our goals).

We can summarize ideological beliefs relevant to social policy in terms of their emphasis on individualism or collectivism, and we have seen how a focus on each can hugely change the way that policies are constructed. This chapter has enabled you to locate and understand your own ideological positions about key aspects of social policy in terms of individualism or collectivism. We have also seen that all political parties have ideological beliefs which differ subtly in terms of their emphasis on either individualism or collectivism, and therefore their social policies. This is important to understand in a democratic society like the UK, as your ideological beliefs are translated into practical social policies when you elect political parties into government.

Key Point

Social policies are not simply made but are greatly influenced by the ideological beliefs which we all have about the nature of society and social problems.

11

IS RELYING ON SOCIAL POLICY BENEFITS OVER A LONG TIME AN EASY LIFE?

Simon Heng

The aims of this chapter are to:

1. **Provide a detailed everyday account of the reality of being reliant on social policy benefits**

2. **Compare and contrast the negative and beneficial outcomes of being reliant on social policy benefits**

This chapter aims to bring together the main themes and issues explored in all the previous chapters to provide a real life experience of what it is like to be reliant on social policy. It is written by someone who for the last 20 years has been reliant on social policy benefits. This provides a first-hand account of the real life relevance of the key themes and issues that this book has discussed in previous chapters, such as:

➢ the significance of cradle to grave social policy benefits;

➢ the amount of benefits that specific groups receive;

➢ the pooling of risks through taxation;

➢ the causes of poverty;

➢ levels of entitlement to social policy;

➢ the relevance of different type of needs;

➢ the emphasis on the mixed economy of welfare;

➢ the future trend towards individualization and personalization;

> the importance of ideology to social policy;

> social policy at a time of austerity.

It also explores new themes of service user perspective and participation in social policy. Throughout the chapter, there will be a focus on contrasting some of the harsh realities of social policy with some of its beneficial outcomes. This should enable you to reflect on some of the terms which are often applied to benefits recipients, such as dependency/independence and deserving/undeserving and to consider whether living on benefits is an easy option.

By the end of this chapter, you will understand in detail the real life experience of living on social policy benefits, and be able to articulate whether reliance on social policy provision is an easy option.

Who am I?

My name is Simon Heng. I am 55 years old, and I live in Worcestershire, England. I am tetraplegic, which means that I am virtually paralysed from my shoulders downwards, and have little sense of feeling throughout most of my body. I have lived with this condition for 20 years, and I have needed 24 hour care with all physical aspects of my life during this time. I currently live independently, and employ a team of people to assist and enable me to live in and participate in family and community life. My care is funded through financial support from my local authority, the Independent Living Fund and welfare payments, in particular, aspects of the Disability Living Allowance (DLA). I receive a mixture of social policy benefits – DLA and Employment Support Allowance (ESA).

In this chapter, I will describe how the welfare system in the UK has both assisted and hindered my ability to live with my disability. Over a period of years, the different parts of the system have enabled me to regain much of my capacity to be an active, self-directed part of my community, rather than just a passive recipient of services; to be an effective parent, able to enjoy many of life's experiences; and to survive in reasonable mental health. This chapter will also touch on the growth and shrinkage of the service user movement, and consider the effects of the austerity social policies of the 2010 Coalition government on my life.

How did I become reliant on social policy to meet my needs?

Before my illness, I worked for a voluntary agency which offered counselling services to people with drink problems and their families. I trained as a counsellor, and I was managing a service of a team of counsellors, and developing my skills as a trainer of counsellors and primary care workers. I was looking to develop my career in senior management in the voluntary sector; I would estimate that I was earning the national average wage when I had to stop working.

Nineteen years ago, as I recovered from an operation which removed a tumour from my spinal cord, I discovered that I was paralysed from the neck downwards. I had known that there was a chance that the operation would leave me unable to walk, but I hadn't realized what this would really mean. I didn't realize that I wouldn't be able to use my arms and hands, or even sit unaided. It felt as if I had been bound in a straitjacket. For the rest of my life. That was just the beginning.

What has been the impact on my quality of life?

In terms of subsistence needs, I had become doubly incontinent, which was distressing. Just as bad, I had lost my sense of proprioception – the sense of where the body is in space. The wiring for my sense of touch had either been disconnected or, in some places, badly rewired. If I was moved, or touched in particular places, my body went into uncontrollable spasms. But I could still feel some parts of my body, in an odd sort of way. I was in a state of panic for days. Longer, perhaps. I can't remember.

Through this terror, I realized the worst: I had lost my freedom. My freedom to go where I wanted, when I wanted. My freedom to scratch an itch, or brush away a fly. My freedom to hug my children, to pick up a book, to brush my teeth, to clean my backside. I was going to need other people to do these things for me. I couldn't even choose who that person was going to be.

We assume that we have the right to choose when, where and who will touch us: without consent, physical contact is assault. Now, to survive, I had to trust anyone who was sent to me to perform the most intimate actions, for the rest of my life. For the foreseeable future, I would have to tolerate personal care from the next stranger walking through my door. The freedom to choose who helped me to wash, dress and toilet became the most important freedom of all.

Through rehabilitation in a specialist spinal unit, I became used to people washing, clothing, toileting and manipulating my body. I was given and learned to use a powered wheelchair, controlled with my chin. I had some mobility, at least. With their help, I learned to direct my physical care. But, after six months, I was still in hospital, detached from, and afraid of, the outside world.

As I had become ill, my participatory needs also became affected. My relationship had broken down; my previous home would have been inaccessible anyway. So I moved into a hostel for people with physical disabilities in a town near friends and relatives. With my mother's and my friends' help, my two young children came to visit me on a regular basis, but I wanted more than that. I still wanted to be part of their lives, to play my part in their development, to enjoy their childhood and their company.

What has been the effect on my income and standard of living?

I had also lost my financial independence. With my limited energy and mobility, unpredictable toileting needs and fluctuating health (wheelchair users are prone to frequent chest and bladder infections) I could not earn enough to support myself, as I had previously done. This meant that my standard of living fell dramatically, and I was effectively living in poverty.

I had to move into a hostel called Freda Eddy Court to get used to being disabled, before moving on to more independent living. I soon discovered that some people had lived there for five years or more: there just weren't enough properties suitably adapted for people with disabilities in the locality – certainly not enough if one had to rely on social housing – for everyone to be accommodated within the county.

Care and support was provided by a team of local authority care workers, supplemented by agencies and volunteers, through the Community Service Volunteer scheme – young people, mainly from Europe and the UK, who were willing to give up a few months of their time for accommodation and living expenses. Although we residents had individual bedrooms, this was my first experience of group living since I had shared a house when I was a student.

Many of the residents went to the local day centres. Sometimes we went into the nearby town. There were occasional group excursions organized by the staff team. Many residents, like me, needed individual escorts, to help with moving around safely or with shopping. Due to staffing levels, time for escorting was, of course, rationed. As a result of this, so was our access to the community. Although we had a budget for food, after deductions for rent there was little more than pocket money left out of our benefits, and this meant that my standard of living fell significantly during this time. I couldn't provide, in the way that I wanted to, and was used to, for my children. I couldn't socialize as easily as before, because I couldn't afford meals in restaurants or even cafes, or to go to the pub. I certainly couldn't afford the transport – I would need specially adapted taxis to accommodate my wheelchair – to join in social events with my friends and relatives.

How easy has it been to gain entitlement to benefits to enable me to lead a normal life?

Even though it seemed like an enormous step down from being a property owning private individual, what I learned at Freda Eddy Court was how to survive as someone with a disability in this society. I learned how to navigate through the labyrinthine benefit system and how my fellow residents had learned to cope with prejudice and ignorance. We discussed which injustices angered people, and politicized them, and which were just accepted as unchangeable. Group homes like these, as well as the day centres, I began to realize, had become the seedbeds for informal trades unions of the disabled. Not only were they safe environments where people could develop companionships with those of similar outlooks, disadvantages, experiences and predicaments, where they could share their thoughts and feelings knowing that they would be understood, but they were also places where that shared consciousness could become politicized, and from where action could be organized. In some ways, the officially organized activities, such as arts and crafts, shopping trips or visits to the cinema often seemed of secondary importance.

It was in these circumstances that I learned about the debates around the medical and social *models of disability*, and the difference between having an impairment and being disabled by circumstances in the society I lived in. For example, my mobility is *impaired*, but I am *disabled* if a building doesn't have wheelchair access.

Real Life Box 11.1 **The medical model of disability v. the social model of disability**

When talking about the disability that a person has, there are two main ways in which we tend to define and describe the disability.

The *medical model of disability* is a way of talking about disability that emphasizes the effect of the disabilities that the person has on what they can do. This means that there is a focus on the way that the disabilities of the person limits what they can do. For example, if we consider why a person in a wheelchair cannot access a building with steps, from a medical model perspective, we would say that the reason why this person cannot access the building is because they have an impairment that means they cannot use the steps. So the only way that the person would be able to access the building is if they did not have the disability in the first place. This is why it is called the medical model of disability, because it focuses on a medical solution to disability, in this case eliminating the disability of the person.

▶

The *social model of disability* is a way of talking about disability that emphasizes the effect that society has on what a disabled person has. This means that the focus is on the way that society limits what a disabled person can do. For example, if we consider the same example of why a person in a wheelchair cannot access a building with steps, from a social model perspective, we would say that the reason why the person cannot access the building is because the steps limit their access. So it would be possible for the person to access the building if changes were made to the design and construction of the building, for example putting a ramp or a lift in place. This is why it is called the social model of disability, because it focuses on the way that society can both limit and enhance the lives of disabled people, in this case eliminating specific barriers that restrict what disabled people can do.

This level of consciousness and solidarity was very important for the times I have had to fight really hard to gain entitlement to benefits which would improve my quality of life. For example, I had applied to the local authority for social housing, but, after three years, I had had no offers. I had asked for somewhere with an extra bedroom, and a small garden, because I wanted my two small children to be able to stay with me and to have somewhere to play in safety.

Eventually, I was offered a series of one-bedroom flats. When I complained about this, I was told that these were the only properties available which were suitable for someone with my level of disability. Apparently, the very few adapted houses large enough for families had been let, and I would either have to take a one-bedroom place or wait until something became available. Unofficially, I was told that there was no provision for people with my level of disability to be active parents. I was also told that I could only refuse so many offers before my name would be removed from the housing list.

It seemed like a classic example of a lack of joined up thinking, and integrated working. I discovered later that some of the team – including the manager – at Freda Eddy Court had begun to think that I was becoming institutionalized. They thought that my refusal of small apartments was because I was afraid of moving out. They didn't appreciate how much I wanted to live with my family, to share responsibility for my children's upbringing.

After I appealed to my local MP for help to fight my corner, I was referred to a housing association, which was in the process of having new homes built in the town. They were keen to work with me: although they had previously adapted their properties for tenants with disabilities, they wanted to experience collaboration with a disabled person to build a property specific to their needs. I was invited to meet with the architect and project manager at crucial points in the planning and the build. And so a three-bedroom house was built to my family's needs. With some changes to their basic house plan, my new home was to be accessible and, at the same time, still look like a family home. All this was funded by government grants to the housing association.

Another example: in the mid-1990s, when the local authority was threatening to reduce the adult social care budget, we service users, with all forms of impairment, from all parts of the county, besieged County Hall on the day of the crucial meeting about our services. We made every attempt to get local media coverage, including television and radio. As a result, we were invited to speak at the meeting. At the time, it was an unprecedented move by both council officials and politicians. And this had mainly been organized through the day centres, hostels and group homes.

These examples show that unless I and others had persisted with fighting to gain entitlement to things to improve our lives, then we would not have received such benefits, and this would have impacted very negatively on my life and those around me.

What are the different ways that my needs have been met?

After 18 months of planning and building, I moved into my new home. I could start building an independent life again and start taking responsibility for looking after my children, again, after five years. I needed 24 hour care, but I also wanted the freedom to be flexible about my routine. But Homecare service, run by the local authority, could only offer visits, run to a strict timetable, so I would have to get up, eat and go to bed at set times. What was on offer wouldn't take account of the flexibility needed within a family, so this wasn't a viable option for me. Standard care provision, the in-house Homecare service, wouldn't give me the independence I wanted for me, because it would just be institutionalizing me in my own home.

So, for a few years, I used a team of young volunteers, through the European Volunteer Service (EVS) and Community Service Volunteers (CSV), backed up by agency staff to help with the more intimate personal care. I could at least express a preference about which agency staff were sent to me, but I still didn't have real freedom of choice. The voluntary personnel changed rapidly, as each was with me for just a few months. I had to induct every new person myself into my daily routine, my risks and preferences. In many cases, I was language tutor and cookery teacher to many of them. On the whole, it was a good arrangement. I met many bright, enthusiastic young people from around the world: some became friends, and I'm still in touch with many of them. My children got to meet people from a wide variety of cultures, people to play with physically, as I couldn't, and some positive role models. If house cleaning wasn't as good as I would have liked, then it was a small price to pay. In reality, this was 24 hours a day care, on the cheap. Even so, it worked for me.

Eventually, the volunteer scheme came to an end: the coordinators of the voluntary services had decided that using volunteers for personal care was exploitation. Apparently, digging ditches for environmental conservation schemes was less exploitative.

Luckily for me, the closure of the volunteer scheme coincided with the introduction of Direct Payments; when I was told that I could control my own budgets, meaning that I could employ my own care team, I was both happy and apprehensive. It pleased me, because I could now choose who was going to perform my personal care and who would be involved in my life. I did wonder if I could manage everything successfully.

For example, how was I going to cope with the complexity of employ-ment law, payroll, tax and national insurance? To tell the truth, I was actu-ally scared of dealing with Inland Revenue. Additionally, could I rely on the Independent Living Fund, and the local authority, who would, between them, be supplying the money for my care, to pay up on time? Did I want the responsibility for people's livelihoods? If I couldn't run things efficiently, it wouldn't just affect me – people's mortgages, rents and bills would rely on my ability to consistently organise.

I was lucky enough to have had experience as an employer, in a sizeable voluntary organization. I had training in recruitment and selection; I knew how to advertise appropriately, conduct fair, legal selection procedures, and I knew the importance of clear contracts of employment. A friend with accountancy experience helped me write a spreadsheet which would help me run the payroll. I knew I would be audited, so I would have to keep accurate records. I wondered how other people would cope without these advantages if they took on Direct Payments.

I didn't expect my social workers or anybody in the local authority to help me out with any of this: I didn't think that they would have the necessary knowledge or skills – after all, this was new territory for them as well as me. What I didn't expect was that my budget would be calculated in the same way that the authority calculated the costs of its internal posts. I quickly discovered that this meant that there was no allowance for 'on-costs', that is the cost of employing someone that is in addition to the wages that they receive, such as Employers' National Insurance contri-butions or pensions, which, for internal posts, were absorbed in huge local authority budgets. So initially, my budget didn't cover holiday and bank holiday payments, or the costs of covering those staff holidays, or even employer's National Insurance payments, employers' liability insur-ance, sick pay … I didn't even have a budget for advertising for new members of staff.

It took a great deal of discussion, a few months – while my allowance was running short – and agreement from the authority's accountants before my payments were adjusted to take account of the true expense of an independent care package.

I was one of the first in the area to take on Direct Payments; it was to be a steep learning curve for both myself and my funders. The local authority quickly learned that they would need to support people to do this, and contracted a voluntary organization to offer training, support and financial services, like payroll for example, to service users. Even so, a number of other early adopters fell into difficulties; one close colleague even became bankrupt. It is hard to imagine what kind of effect that had on his self-confidence or his ability to cope financially after that experience.

This could have been foreseen. Many service users and their families had little recent experience of managing anything more than their benefits payments, so it was unreasonable to expect them to cope with budgets of many thousands of pounds, with a number of responsibilities, without appropriate training and support. It is hardly surprising that some people used funds allocated for their care to pay daily living expenses when, as is all too frequent, the money ran out. I was lucky. I had acquired the necessary awareness and skills before my disability. Without acquiring these skills, I would not have been able to meet my needs as required in the new mixed economy of welfare for care.

What have been the advantages of having to take responsibility for my welfare?

After six years, which had felt like an eternity, I had some independence. With the help of my family, my children could stay with me on a regular basis. I could support my football team, and visit friends and relatives without weeks of planning and negotiation; I made new friends, and organized a film club, which showed independent and foreign films every week. I was invited to speak of my experiences to Health and Social Care students at the local higher education institutions. I hadn't got my life back, but I had as much physical independence as I could hope for.

At the same time as Direct Payments were being introduced, the service user movement was developing stronger voices. Social Work departments were encouraging the development of service user involvement, not only at an individual level, but also collectively. What started out as residents meetings and day centre users meetings, discussing issues specific to a particular institution, began to address wider concerns about levels of service delivery, standards of service, and even how they would like to see services change. My local social services department firmly committed itself to this, firstly by organizing and funding meetings – in our rural area, paying for and organizing for people to attend meetings was a key factor – encouraging discussion around developing user led organizations (ULOs), and following this with financial support for these ULOs to become independent.

Service users were invited to become involved at many levels in adult social care, from feedback and monitoring about existing services through to strategic planning. We were well supported, in terms of help with preparing for meetings, the provision of advocates for those who had difficulty in expressing their opinions, and physical help for those of us who needed it. The emergent groups were invited to send representatives to consult with officers and members about existing and future services and their developments; we were invited to participate in the selection of managers in the social work department, and even given opportunities to speak at full council meetings when adult social care was on the agenda.

I became heavily involved in the service user movement. As chair of one of the groups, I found myself attending meetings perhaps four days a week. I was grateful for the opportunity to be active, to feel that I was contributing in a positive way. I felt that I was becoming more confident, increasingly sure of my abilities; the self-confidence and assurance that I had lost over the years that I had become ill and disabled had begun to return. For the first time as a disabled person, I had a positive self-image.

All of this also gave me chances to meet many other people with impairments of various kinds. I had to address my own prejudices about people with disabilities (don't assume that just because someone is disabled they can't have prejudices about other people who are disabled!), and I learned to appreciate and admire my colleagues' spirit, resilience and optimism. By listening to their stories, complaints, ambitions and resentments, I began to realize the full extent of deprivation, discrimination and lack of opportunity experienced by many. Also, I began to realize how many people with disabilities have been not just excluded, but historically hidden from mainstream society, whether in the huge, old institutions and asylums, in the group homes and hostels, or just in their family homes, trapped by lack of appropriate transport, support or finances.

Just as my eyes were opening, the wider disability movement were becoming increasingly successful in getting disability issues onto the mainstream agenda: the Disability Discrimination Acts were passed and the Disability Rights Commission was formed, although this was soon amalgamated into the Equality and Human Rights Commission. Big retailers began to make their checkouts wider, and buses started to kneel.

To me, it seemed that disabled people were on the way to becoming fully included in mainstream life. As far as the organization of our services were concerned, 'Nothing about us without us' was the new mantra: the government was encouraging employers to think more positively about taking on people with impairments, reasoning that if someone can manage the complexities of living with a disability, they could well have acquired organizational and management skills which could be useful in the workplace.

Then, within what seemed like a few short months, the economy collapsed, there was a change of government, and everything that supported my independent lifestyle seemed under threat.

What effect has the austerity social policies of the 2010 Coalition government had on my ability to meet my needs?

Under the twin objectives of reducing public expenditure and reforming the welfare system, the austerity policies of the 2010 Coalition government targeted each part of the structure that allowed me not only to organize my own life, but also to aspire to fuller equality for myself and my disabled colleagues.

As part of the drive to reduce expenditure, the new government ordered several departments to close, and the Independent Living Fund (ILF) was to be one. The ILF was providing a third of the funding for my care. We were told that this money would be transferred to the local authorities; we also found out that these transferred funds would not be ring-fenced, which meant that my local authority could choose to use this 'extra' money for any purpose, not just my social care.

When we questioned the local authority, we were reassured that our current care arrangements would continue. When we asked them how long this ILF-related funding was promised for, it seemed that nobody knew.

Soon afterwards, in anticipation of soaring adult care costs and reducing funding, the local authority proposed a Minimum Expenditure Policy. This would mean that the budget for an individual's care package could not normally exceed the cost of keeping that person in a care home. We realized that many of our individual budgets could easily exceed this; I was told that the new policy wouldn't affect existing arrangements, unless I had to be reassessed, if my circumstances changed.

So, would the demise of the ILF, and the transfer of the funding, count as a change of circumstances? If this supplementary funding dried up after a few years, would *that* count as a change of circumstances? At the time of writing, no one I asked could answer these questions. This is one of the reasons I feel insecure about my future.

Over the last few years, disabled colleagues and their families, unpaid carers of and advocates for the disabled relatives have reported that reassessments of their care needs have often led to a reduction in their funding, each reassessment causing disruption, hardship and misery in its wake.

Each time, the person telling their story has said the same sort of thing: the disappearance of day services has put increased pressure on informal carers. Without a change of circumstance, reduction in funding has meant less paid care, which means that people are becoming more isolated and less well looked after, or, again increased pressure on their relatives.

We recently discovered that central government had ordered a 25% cut in each local authority spending an adult social care, so even more savings have to be made. Each time I have an assessment, I worry that my funding will be reduced, even though I have no informal carers, and that less than 24 hour care would quickly compromise my health, let alone my independence.

Then, my home was under threat. The government's initiative to use social housing more effectively, the so-called Bedroom Tax, came into effect in April 2013. The intention of this measure is to encourage people in under occupied properties to move to smaller accommodation, freeing up larger properties for larger families. As my house has three bedrooms, and my youngest child is at university, I was assessed as having two extra bedrooms, and so my housing benefit was reduced by 25%. When I appealed, on the basis that my 24 hour care included the need for carers to use a bedroom, this was altered to a 14% reduction.

Real Life Box 11.2 **The Bedroom Tax**

The Bedroom Tax was implemented by the 2010 Coalition government in 2013. Its main aim is to increase the amount of larger houses available to larger families in the social rented sector. This is done by applying a charge for every un-occupied spare bedroom that a house has, if the person is claiming housing benefit to pay some or all of their rent.

So, for example, if a single person lives in a two-bedroom social rented house, they have to pay a surcharge for the extra room. The charge is 14% of your rent for one room and 25% of your rent for two bedrooms. So, someone with a one 'spare bedroom' whose rent is £100 per week has to pay at least £14 of the rent themselves to their landlord. Someone who has two or more 'spare bedrooms' whose rent is £100 per week has to pay at least £25 of the rent themselves to their landlord.

The alternative to paying the surcharge is to move out into a smaller house, which is the main intention of the policy, so that a larger family can move in. There are exemptions from the bedroom tax, such as pensioners and people living in some types of supported accommodation, but generally it applies to most people.

Even though I explained my house was designed and adapted to my needs, and that there were no suitable properties for me to move to (I'd waited for over five years for my present house), even though I pointed out that my daughter would have nowhere to stay out of term time, and so this would increase my social isolation, I would still be liable for the charge – with no additional income.

After a few months, I discovered that I was entitled to the Discretionary Housing Payment, a central fund, administered by the district council, which would make up the shortfall. The district council didn't inform me or anyone else I knew who had been subject to the Bedroom Tax that we could apply for this. I'd had to find hundreds of pounds to pay the shortfall in my rent, which I could ill afford. At the time of writing, I'm still trying to claim this back from my landlord.

My daily living expenses have been covered by a variety of welfare benefits: Disability Living Allowance, Incapacity Benefit and Income Support. The government is claiming that many of those claiming Incapacity Benefit are actually capable of work, so, even though the Department for Work and Pensions is aware that I am severely disabled, I was required to fill out a 20 page form which seemed to consist of the following two questions: 'Are you fit for work?' and 'Do you have a lot of money in savings?' The next 19 pages were effectively filled with variations on the questions 'Are you *sure* you're not fit for work?' and 'Are you *sure* you don't have a large amount of savings?'

I felt my spirit being crushed as I completed this form. I do not need to be reminded, over and over again, that I am severely disabled, to the point where I cannot take on regular employment and so be financially independent. I do not need to be reminded that I only have a small amount of savings, so, again, I am not financially independent. I was thoroughly miserable for the rest of that day and angry at the insensitivity of the process.

Once again, I was also anxious about what decision would be made. This time, I was judged to be entitled to the benefits I was claiming. But going through this process has made me wonder what the introduction of Universal Credit is going to bring for me.

Real Life Box 11.3 **Universal Credit**

Universal Credit (UC) is a new benefit which the 2010 Coalition government planned to introduce between 2013 and 2017. The 2010 Coalition government says that its main aim is to increase the incentives for working to make it much more attractive to work than to be on benefits, and to simplify the benefit system to make it easier to claim and receive benefits.

Universal Credit will replace the following six benefits:

➢ Jobseeker's Allowance;

➢ Housing Benefit;

> Working Tax Credit;

> Child Tax Credit;

> Employment and Support Allowance;

> Income Support.

This means that rather than receiving separate payments for each of these benefits, those on Universal Credit will receive one single payment. The government estimates that this will make claimants about £16 a month better off than with the previous separate benefits.

It is important to note that Universal Credit is not universal, but is means tested, meaning that it changes with circumstances. This means that some people will be worse off under the Universal Credit than under the previous system, such as those with complex needs and disabilities.

Also, having a bank account and internet access are necessary to receive Universal Credit.

Along with the threats to my personal circumstances, the effectiveness of the service user movement has been severely eroded. Funding for user led organizations has been withdrawn completely, or cut back severely. In some cases, grants have been replaced by service level agreements with local authorities: rather than being the independent voice of service users, these organizations are now contractors, operating service user involvement on the local authority's terms. Otherwise, they have simply collapsed and disappeared, leaving service users without a collective voice.

Nationally, the Disability Rights Commission has been absorbed within the Equalities and Human Rights Commission, which, arguably, dilutes effectiveness of the work towards equality for people with disabilities. Even within this new organization, the Disability Committee is due to have its powers removed, becoming merely advisory to the main commission.

All of this, alongside the government's assertion that many Disability Living Allowance claimants are not actually disabled (although official DWP estimates are that less than 1% of claims are fraudulent), disabled people, and service users in particular, are being demonized as scroungers, undeserving of their benefits and, by implication, the allowances made for them. It is no coincidence that reported hate crime against people with disabilities has risen dramatically in the last few years. Not only are we more visible, our own government is now making us pariahs.

Summary

Over the past 15 years, I feel that those of us with disabilities have been climbing towards the summit of integration into society, where consideration – institutional, psychological, physical and financial – for our differences has been well-established. It seems that the story of the last five years has been one of a rapid slide away from that summit.

Although my situation has some security, and although legally, various bodies have a duty of care for severely disabled people, I wonder what will happen to those who will come after me, born with or acquiring their disabilities. Will this duty of care only extend to keeping people alive, whether in their own homes or in the new institutions? Will the next generation have to fight the same battles as we had to? Will we or they get enough support from politicians and professionals, administrators and policymakers, to win this battle for our independence again?

For me, claiming state benefits has not been a lifestyle choice, but a necessity. I could not have had an independent life without these sources of funding. The process involved in claiming, and in many cases, needing to constantly reapply for the same benefits is time-consuming and fraught with difficulties. Claiming benefits calls for constant resilience, assertiveness and perseverance to press my case, with the continuing need to appeal against decisions denying me the benefits I am legally entitled to.

The level of income I get from benefits, when taken as a whole, might look generous, but given that it funds all of my needs, these payments cost the state less than it would to keep me in residential care and afford me the chance of independence and reasonable mental health – something I wouldn't have if I were forced to live in an institution. My disposable income (what I have to spend on food, utilities, travel, Internet access and, if possible, entertainment) leaves me below the official poverty line. I don't take holidays and I can't afford a coffee at Starbucks or to pay full price for food; I shop for bargains. Even if I wanted to, I couldn't afford to drink alcohol.

For me, the benefits I claim are enough to live on – but only barely, and with good budgeting skills. If I hadn't been blessed with a quick mind and mathematical ability, I doubt that I would be able to stay out of debt. Most people I know with disabilities are living in, or on the edge of, inescapable debt.

I can only hope, for myself personally and for all of those who are or who will become disabled, that we can start to reverse the tide, soon. Many of us won't be able to do that without the assistance and understanding of the kind we have had up to now, but refined with the wisdom of our lived experience.

Key Point

Having to rely on social policy over a long time is far from an easy life, but is a constant struggle to try to have an existence that is as close to normal as possible, and the austerity policies of the 2010 Coalition government have made this struggle harder.

12

WHY IS STUDYING SOCIAL POLICY RELEVANT TO YOU?

The main aim of this book has been to outline the real life significance of social policy to you, your family, friends and the community you live in. It has attempted to do this principally by continually detailing how the study of social policy is relevant to your everyday real life. If you have read the book throughout, this real life relevance of studying social policy is hopefully the one thing that has become the most apparent and interesting aspect of finding out what is social policy.

This makes studying social policy both exciting and important to a better understanding of you as an individual and the society you live in, and the focus of this concluding chapter is to summarize ten key reasons for the excitement, importance and relevance of studying social policy.

Reason 1: Social policy is relevant to you because of the important benefits you, your family, friends and community are receiving

The most important fact that should have become most apparent to you from reading this book is that social policy is of ongoing practical relevance to you because you are either receiving social policy benefits now as we speak, or have received social policy benefits in the recent past, whether cash or in-kind. For example, if you are university student reading this book, you will be receiving an in-kind benefit in the form of higher education. And it is very likely that whoever you are, you, your family, your friends and people in your community have visited a GP, or received some form of cash benefits such as either Child Benefit, Housing Benefit, Jobseeker's Allowance or Income Support, all are which are forms of social policy benefits. In the future, you will very likely receive health or social care in some form, or the State Pension. This means that the social policy benefits you receive are way more extensive than you might think, and so it is the case for other people you know, such as your family, friends and community.

Reason 2: Social policy is relevant to you because it impacts on your life from cradle to grave

This book has also used the term 'benefits' in a broader sense than simply referring to cash benefits. It has used it to include any social policy provision that someone receives. So for example, we can also define the NHS as an in-kind benefit as it is something that you receive, and the same for education. Defining benefits in this way shows that your entitlement to social policy provision covers the spectrum of your life throughout the years, from birth to old age. We can define this as Cradle to Grave social policy entitlement, which means that you have entitlement to provision from the moment you are born until you die. For example, the moment you were born you were entitled to free NHS treatment, you had to undertake compulsory schooling from early childhood to late adolescence, you are probably studying at University as you read this and so receiving higher education maintenance loans, and if you are working you are entitled to at least the National Minimum Wage. Entitlement to health and income benefits will continue throughout your life, and when you retire you will very likely be entitled to some kind of State Pension. Social policy also regulates things that you can and can't do, such as the age at which you can drink or smoke. Defining social policy in this way enables us to see that you receive benefits at many points throughout your life, meaning that you are more reliant on social policy benefits than you might think.

Reason 3: Social policy is relevant to you because you pay for it constantly

Social policy is also relevant to you because you pay for it, mainly through taxes. These can be taxes from working or taxes from what we spend. Everyone pays taxation of some type, regardless of whether they are working or reliant on income benefits such as Jobseeker's Allowance, which effectively means that everyone is entitled to social policy provision. So unless you do not work, do not buy anything at all, do not smoke, drink or drive, you will be making some contribution to government receipts, and therefore to the payment of social policy. This also means that social policy would only be irrelevant to you in terms of not paying for it only if you have never worked or bought anything in your life, which is highly unlikely. This book has also shown that taxation funded social policy ensures a level of welfare and health that most individuals would not be able to afford if they had to pay for it themselves. This is because most people receive more in social policy benefits than they pay in taxation. This gives us all an interest in the nature and the direction of social policies, and this is what makes studying social policy so interesting.

Reason 4: Social policy is relevant to you as it enables you to meet your welfare needs

The importance of social policy to improving your health and well-being is apparent when considering the welfare needs that we have. If we accept that we all have universal welfare needs such as the need for food, water, shelter, warmth and good health, meaning that everyone has these needs regardless of who they are or where they live, this places an obligation on society to ensure that such needs are met through social policies. This book has shown that the historical development of social policy in the UK has led to significant improvements in the health and well-being of the society, and has the potential to continue to do so. For example, the development of the free healthcare provided by the NHS has meant that the health of the population now is vastly improved to what it was before the NHS existed before the Second World War when there was the need to individually pay for health treatments. Education is another example where social policy has effected real changes, if we compare the literacy of the population now to what it was before education became a legal right and responsibility at the turn of the 20th century. This point is reinforced if we compare the extensive nature of social policy in the UK with the less extensive nature of social policy in other countries. This highlights that social policy can enable you to meet your health and well-being needs in important ways.

Reason 5: Social policy benefits is not just about Jobseeker's Allowance for the poor

When people think about the most expensive social policy benefits, they tend to think about income benefits that the poorest sections of society receive, such as Jobseeker's Allowance, Income Support and Housing Benefit. An important reason for this is that the notion of benefits has become deliberately associated only with the poor, from the media and also from government. What this book has shown is that if this was the case, then the amount spent on social policy would be much smaller than it is, as expenditure on Jobseeker's Allowance is £3.4 billion and for Income

Support it is £2.6 billion, which represents a small percentage of total expenditure on social policy. In fact, it is the State Pension which is the cash benefit that has the highest expenditure by a long way, at £87 billion. There is also more money is spent on providing Maintenance Loans and Grants to students, housing support through Housing Benefit, Child Benefit, Tax Credits and Disability Benefits than on Jobseeker's Allowance. If we additionally take into account expenditure in-kind benefits such as health, primary and secondary education, Free School Meals, free 15 hours childcare and Right to Buy, we can see that expenditure on these benefits are also higher than expenditure on unemployment benefits.

This is because of the cradle to grave nature of social policy, and the way it covers the spectrum of the lifecycle means that it is not just poor people who receive the benefits, but a range of people who you might know. They are also likely to be reliant on other benefits such as the NHS and education. Additionally, it is better off people rather than poor people who are more likely to access benefits such as higher education and housing subsidies such as Right to Buy and Help to Buy. They are also more likely to receive higher quality social policy, such as access to the best schooling through being able to afford to buy houses near good schools, or having the knowledge to access high quality healthcare. They are also more likely to live longer, and so receive benefits for longer, such as pensions and social care.

Together, this shows that it is not just the poorest in society who receive social policy benefits. If it was just the poorest who received social policy benefits, then the amount spent on social policy would be considerably less than it is. In fact, everyone you know is likely to be receiving some form of social policy benefit, and most people receive more in social policy benefits than they pay in. This means that you, your friends, family, neighbours and community are likely to be more reliant on social policy benefits than you or they might think.

Reason 6: Studying social policy is important because it provides an understanding of how 'austerity' social policies are affecting you

A key theme of this book has been to contrast the way that social policy has changed over the last 30 years. This book is being written at a time of 'austerity' social policies, that is the claim that cuts in social policies are necessary due to a lack of money. This is something that has been specifically emphasized by both the 2010 Coalition government and the 2015 Conservative government, arising from the claim that the need for austerity has been caused by excessive spending of the welfare state. This emphasis on austerity is having a huge impact on social policies in all areas. For example, it is the reason given for the huge increase in Student Tuition Fees in 2012, the cuts to income benefits such as Child Benefit, the lack of finance to build new houses, the changes to the NHS to make it more business-like, and the limited expenditure available for social care.

This means that the austerity social policies that have been put in place are often outlined as inevitable and the only rational way in which social policy could or should be made. This emphasis on austerity has intensified the general trend in social policies over the last 30 years, which means that the welfare state is now qualitatively different from the Beveridge welfare state that was created in the aftermath of the Second World War. An obvious contrast is evident from the fact that if you were going to university 30 years ago, you would not have paid tuition fees, and it is very likely that you would have received maintenance grants, not maintenance loans. This means that leaving university without having incurred significant debt from tuition fees and maintenance loans would have been the norm for you, not the exception that it is now. There are many other examples of how social policy has changed. This has changed the nature of your entitlement to specific social policies, and will continue to do so if austerity remains an important aspect of social policy over the next couple of years. Studying social policy is a good way to understand the context, rationale and reasons for these changes.

Reason 7: Studying social policy is important to you because it gives you an understanding of how social and economic changes will directly affect your welfare in the future

Social and economic changes that are occurring in the family, work, technology and demography are having important effects on the nature of our society to the extent that it is inevitable that the future of social policy will look very much different from that which Beveridge constructed the postwar welfare state. In particular, these changes are having important effects on the income and expenditure of all social policy areas. In some instances these changes are beneficial for social policy, but in other instances they are also very unfavourable to the functioning of social policy as we know it today, and therefore to the future functioning of social policy. These changes will have a direct impact on your social policy in the future.

Reason 8: Studying social policy is relevant because it provides an understanding of how you can make and change social policy

What we believe heavily influences what we do in everyday life, and this is also the case for social policy. A recurring theme within this book is that there is always an alternative way to provide social policies, as evident in the differences shown in the chapters between: absolute/ relative poverty, universal/selective benefits, progressive/regressive taxation, participatory/ subsistence needs, and the mixed economy of welfare. What this shows is that social policies do not simply happen, but occur from the active choices that governments make, and we saw that all political parties have ideological beliefs which differ in terms of their emphasis on either indi-vidualism or collectivism, and therefore their social policies.

We can see from looking at the historical development of social policy that the social policy of 150 years ago is vastly different from the social policy of today, both in terms of the scope and the way it is provided. To re-visit the example of the Second World War, there is no doubt that the Second World War did have an important effect on the development of the post-war welfare state, in terms of providing an impetus for change. But it is also evident that such change only occurred because there was an ideological belief from those in power that such a change was needed, and a need for collectivist social policies to deal with social problems. This reinforces the fact that social policy does not just happen simply as a consequence of events, but that it is people who make social policy, as a consequence of the ideological beliefs that they have. This is important to understand in a democratic society like the UK, as your ideological beliefs are translated into practical social policies when you elect political parties into government. This is why an important focus of studying social policy is understanding and analysing the ideological beliefs that you have, so that you can make an informed and reasoned decision about which social policies you choose to support when voting.

Reason 9: Studying social policy is important to give you a better understanding of the everyday reality of reliance on the welfare state

Over the last 30 years or so, there has been a growing belief within society that social policy benefits are overgenerous, and that those who receive social policy benefits are generally undeserving, as a consequence of them being unwilling to work. This has led to a state where stigmatizing those who receive certain benefits has become the norm both from politicians and the public. And TV programmes such as 'Benefits Street' in 2014 have reinforced this belief that almost all welfare recipients are lazy and living in a 'something for nothing' society, which encourages dependency. This has had important implications on the outcomes for service users. It is built out of an assumption that problems like unemployment, homelessness and ill health are mainly caused by the individual, in terms of the choices that they make in life and how individuals live their lives. It is in this context that the cradle to grave welfare state that we know has reduced in scope: by the reduction of benefits to some groups; by making it harder to receive benefits, such as Jobseeker's Allowance; or by passing responsibility for providing welfare state to the individual, such as in relation to public health and housing.

This book has shown that being reliant on income benefits such as Jobseeker's Allowance or Income Support is an important contributory factor to the high poverty rate in the UK, but not in the way that people think. Rather, such benefits provide an income which is significantly below the poverty line which means that should you become reliant on such benefits, the small amount of money you receive will very likely mean that you live in poverty. This is something that is evident from the chapter written by Simon Heng on the long-term effects of living on benefits. Rather, the level of income he receives from benefits is enough to live on – but only barely, and only with good budgeting skills. Like most people reliant on benefits, his disposable income (what he has to spend on food, utilities, travel, internet access and, if possible, entertainment) leaves him below the official poverty line. This means that he is unable to take holidays, to have a coffee at Starbucks, or to pay full price for food. And he is only able to stay out of debt due to his mathematical ability.

Additionally, the process involved in claiming and needing to constantly reapply for the same benefits is time-consuming and fraught with difficulties. This means that claiming for benefits calls for constant resilience, assertiveness and perseverance – just to claim benefits that you are legally entitled to. Just think about the process of claiming for your Student Maintenance Grants, and you begin to get some idea of why being reliant on benefits is not an easy lifestyle choice.

Reason 10: Studying social policy is a relevant way to make a real difference to many peoples' lives

The history of social policy reminds us that the welfare state emerged from real problems within society. In particular, it was the levels of poverty and disease that led to the creation of the welfare state in the first place. Moreover, the majority of principles that to greater or lesser extent underpin social policies today, such as social insurance, means testing, redistributive taxation and full employment, all have their origins in the historical development of social policy.

This means that a study of the past of social policy is very much relevant to understanding why social policy exists as it does in its present form today. It also highlights that social policy in the past has made a real difference to the lives of many people, and contributed significantly to the development of society, and continues to do so today. However, what we tend to see today is that often governments choose to ignore the lessons of the past, which is often to the detriment of the effectiveness of the social policy and those who the social policy is aimed at.

The major social and economic changes that are occurring in society suggest that there will be a real need for different social policies which can ameliorate the worst effects of these changes. Making policies that may solve such problems is the essence of social policy. For instance, rising poverty and inequality are arguably the most serious problems within society, and this is one area where it is evident that social policy is failing, as shown by the fact that most people in poverty are actually in work. Studying social policy provides you with the possibility of deep and meaningful engagement with the reality of poverty and inequality. This is something that could make a real difference to many people in many ways, including friends and family, through the action that follows from this deep and meaningful engagement grounded in reality. This means that the study of social policy is the study of real life, which goes a long way to answering the question of what is social policy, and this has hopefully stimulated you towards further more detailed study into other aspects of social policy.

REFERENCES

Chapter 1

HM Treasury (2014) *Budget 2014*, London: HC1104

Chapter 2

Browne, J. and Hood, A. (2012) *A Survey of the UK Benefit System*, London: Institute for Fiscal Studies

DCLOG (2014) *Right to Buy Sales: April to June 2014*, England, London: Department for Communities and Local Government

DCLOG (2014a) *Help to buy (equity loan) scheme monthly statistics*, Online: https://www.gov.uk/government/statistical-data-sets/help-to-buy-equity-loan-scheme-monthly-statistics, accessed 22 August 2014

DWP (2014) *Long term projections of pensioner benefits: Tables*, Online: https://www.gov.uk/government/uploads/system/uploads/attachment_data/file/328432/long-term-projections-pensioner-benefits-tables-2014.xlsx, accessed 5 August 2014

DWP (2014a) *Benefit expenditure and caseload tables 2014*, Online: https://www.gov.uk/government/uploads/system/uploads/attachment_data/file/310483/outturn-and-forecast-budget-2014.xls, accessed 10 August 2014

HM Treasury (2014a) Public Expenditure Statistical Analyses 2014, *Cm 8902*, London: The Stationery Office

Independent Commission on Fees (2014) *Analysis of trends in higher education applications, admissions and enrolments*, Online: http://www.independentcommissionfees.org.uk/wordpress/wp-content/uploads/2014/08/ICoF-Report-Aug-2014.pdf, accessed 10 June 2015

McInnes, R. and Rutherford, T. (2013) Social security benefits and expenditure, *Commons Library Standard Note SN/SG/2656*, Online: http://www.parliament.uk/briefing-papers/SN02656.pdf, accessed 14 August 2014

The Observer (2013) *Benefits in Britain: Separating the facts from the fiction*, Online: http://www.theguardian.com/politics/2013/apr/06/welfare-britain-facts-myths, accessed 12 August 2014

ONS (2013a) *Annual Survey of House and Earnings*, London: Office for National Statistics

ONS (2014) *The Effects of Taxes and Benefits on Household Income, 2012/13*, London: Office for National Statistics

Tudor Hart, J. (1971) The Inverse Care Law, *Lancet*, 1: 405–412

Chapter 3

Beveridge, W. (1942) Social Insurance and Allied Services, *Cmd 6404*, London: HMSO

Denman, J. and McDonald, P. (1996) Unemployment statistics from 1881 to the present day, *Labour Market Trends*, January 1996: 5–18

DWP (2013) *Tax Credit Expenditure in Great Britain*, London: Department for Work and Pensions, Online: https://www.gov.uk/government/uploads/system/uploads/attachment_data/file/223090/gb_tax_credit_estimates.pdf, accessed 1 March 2015

Englander, D. (1998) *Poverty and Poor Law Reform in Nineteenth-Century Britain, 1834–1914: From Chadwick to Booth*, Harlow: Longman

Ferriman, A. (2007) BMJ readers choose sanitation as the greatest medical advance since 1840, *British Medical Journal*, 334: 111

Fraser, D. (2009) *The Evolution of the British Welfare State 4th Edition*, Basingstoke: Palgrave Macmillan

Gazeley, I. (2003) *Poverty in Britain, 1900–1965*, Basingstoke: Palgrave Macmillan

Gladstone, D. (1999) *The Twentieth Century Welfare State*, Basingstoke: Palgrave Macmillan

Gladstone, D. (2003) History and Social Policy, in P. Alcock, A. Ersking and M. May (eds), *The Student's Companion to Social Policy*, Oxford: Wiley Blackwell, pp. 25–30

Hamlin, C. (1995) Could you starve to death in England in 1839? The Chadwick-Farr Controversy and the loss of the 'Social' in public health, *American Journal of Public Health*, 85(6): 859–866

Hamlin, C. and Sheard, S. (1998) Revolutions in public health: 1848, and 1998?, *British Medical Journal*, 317(7158): 587–591

Harris, B. (2004) *The Origins of the British Welfare State*, Basingstoke: Palgrave Macmillan

Lister, R. (2006) Children (but not women) first: New labour, child welfare and Gender, *Critical Social Policy*, 26(2): 315–335

ONS (2013) *Labour Market Statistics – Integrated FR – Unemployment by Age & Duration*, Online: http://www.ons.gov.uk/ons/datasets-and-tables/data-selector.html?cdid=LF2Q&dataset=lms&table-id=09, accessed 20 December 2013

Robins, J. (ed.) (2011) Unequal before the law? The future of legal aid, *Solicitors Journal*, Online: http://www.younglegalaidlawyers.org/files/Releases_Responses/Unequal_before_the_law_legal_aid_report_june_2011.pdf, accessed 29 November 2013

Rowntree, S. (1901) Poverty: *A Study of Town Life*, London: Macmillan and Co

Taylor-Gooby, P. (1988) The future of the British welfare state, *European Sociological Review*, 4(1): 1–19

Titmuss, R. (1958) *Essays on the Welfare State*, London: Unwin Books

Woodward, D. (1981) Wage rates and living standards in pre-industrial England, *Past and Present*, 91(1): 28–46

Chapter 4

Barr, N. (2001) *The Welfare State as Piggy Bank: Information, Risk, Uncertainty, and the Role of the State*, Oxford: Oxford Scholarship Online

Broughton, N., Ezeye, O., Hupkau, C., Keohane, N. and Shorthouse, R. (2014) *Open Access An Independent Evaluation*, London: The Social Market Foundation

Crossley, T., Philliphs, D, and Wakefield, M. (2009) *Value added tax*, Online: http://www.ifs.org.uk/budgets/gb2009/09chap10.pdf, accessed 10 March 2014

HM Treasury (2014) *Budget 2014*, London: HC1104

ONS (2014a) *Annual Survey of House and Earnings*, London: Office for National Statistics

ONS (2014b) *The Effects of Taxes and Benefits on Household Income, 2012/13*, London: Office for National Statistics

Osbourne, H. (2014) Renting in London 'costs twice as much as elsewhere', *The Guardian*, 27 January, Online: http://www.theguardian.com/money/2014/jan/27/renting-london-costs-twice-elsewhere, accessed 15 March 2014

Redmond, J. *et al.* (2014) What do graduates do? 2014, *HECSU/AGCAS*, Online: http://www.hecsu.ac.uk/assets/assets/documents/wdgd_september_2014.pdf, accessed 9 January 2015

Rutter, J. and Stocker, K. (2014) *Childcare Costs Survey 2014*, London: The Family and Childcare Trusts

Useful websites

http://www.taxguideforstudents.org.uk/

Chapter 5

Boffey, D. (2011) Children with internet access at home gain exam advantage, charity says, *The Guardian*, 21 May, Online: http://www.theguardian.com/education/2011/may/21/children-internet-access-exam-advantage, accessed 2 April 2014

Bolton, P. (2012) *Fuel Poverty. House of Common Library Note SN/SG/5115*, London: House of Commons

Brewer, M., Browne, J. and Joyce, R. (2011) *Child and Working-Age Poverty from 2010–2020*, London: Institute for Fiscal Studies

Davis, A., Hirsch, D., Smith, N., Beckhelling, J. and Padley, M. (2012) *A Minimum Income Standard for UK in 2012*, New York: Joseph Rowntree Foundation

DWP (2014b) *Household Below Average Income An Analysis of the Income Distribution 1994/95–2012/13*, London: Office for National Statistics

HomeOwners Alliance (2012) *The Death of a Dream: The Crisis in Homeownership in the UK*, London: HomeOwners Alliance

Jin, W., Joyce, R., Philiphs, D. and Sibiets, L. (2011) *Poverty and Inequality in the UK: 2011*, London: The Institute for Fiscal Studies

KPMG (2013) *Structural Analysis of Hourly Wages and Current trends in Household Finances*, Henley on Thames: Markit Group Limited

Lambie-Mumford, H., Crossley, D., Jensen, E., Verbeke, M. and Dowler, E. (2014) *Household Food Security in the UK: A Review of Food Aid. Final Report,* London: Defra

Low Pay Commission (2012) *National Minimum Wage Low Pay Commission Report 2012*, CM 8302

Low Pay Commission (2014) *National Minimum Wage Low Pay Commission Report 2014*, CM 8816

MacInnes, T., Aldridge, H., Bushe, S., Kenway, P. and Tinson, A. (2013) *Monitoring Poverty and Social Exclusion 2013*, New York: Joseph Rowntree Foundation

McKay, S. and Rowlingson, K. (2009) Income Maintenance and Social Security, in P. Alcock, M. May and S. Wright (eds), T*he Student's Companion to Social Policy 4e*, Chichester: Wiley Blackwell, pp. 317–323

McVeigh, K. (2010) Most children living in poverty are not from workless households, report finds, *The Guardian*, 6 December, Online: http://www.theguardian.com/society/2010/dec/06/children-poverty-working-parents, accessed 2 April 2014

ONS (2012a) *Family Spending 2011*, London: Stationery Office

Pennycock, M. and Whittaker, M. (2012) *Low Pay Britain 2012*, London: Resolution Foundation

Ramesh, R. (2013) How private care firms have got away with breaking the law on pay, *The Guardian*, 13 June, Online: http://www.theguardian.com/society/2013/jun/13/care-firms-law-on-pay, accessed 4 April 2014

Smithers, T. (2014) Millions of people without the internet pay £440 more each year for utility bills, *The Guardian*, 2 July, Online: http://www.theguardian.com/money/2014/jul/02/millions-without-internet-pay-440-pounds-more-on-bills, accessed 2 April 2015

Townsend, P. (1979) *Poverty in the United Kingdom: A Survey of Household Resources and Standards of Living*, Harmondsworth: Penguin Books

Westlake, A. (2011) *The UK Poverty Rip-Off. The Poverty Premium 2010*, London: Save the Children

Chapter 6

British Future (2013) *State of the Nation*, London: British Future

Citizens Advice Scotland (2012) *Myth-busting: The real figures on benefit fraud*, Online: http://www.cas.org.uk/features/myth-busting-real-figures-benefit-fraud, accessed 17 April 2014

DWP (2010) *Tackling Fraud and Error in the Benefit and Tax Credit Systems*, London: Department for Work and Pensions

DWP (2012a) *Income Related Benefits: Estimates of Take-up in 2009–10*, London: Department for Work and Pensions

DWP (2014c) *Fraud and Error in the Benefit System: Preliminary 2013/14 Estimates (Great Britain)*, London: Department for Work and Pensions

Full Fact (2011) *Welfare reform bill*, Online: https://fullfact.org/files/2011/03/Welfare_Reform_Bill_2R_Briefing.pdf, accessed 14 April 2014

Glennerster, H. (2009) *Understanding the Finance of Welfare 2nd Edition*, Bristol: The Policy Press

HMRC (HM Revenue and Customs) (2012) *Child Benefit, Child Tax Credit and Working Tax Credit Take-up Rates 2010–11*, London: HM Revenue and Customs

HomeOwners Alliance (2012) *The Death of a Dream: The Crisis in Homeownership in the UK*, London: HomeOwners Alliance

Kennedy, S. (2010) *Child Benefit for Higher Rate Taxpayers, House of Commons Library Standard Note SN/SP/5732*, London: House of Commons

Kitchen, S. *et al.* (2012) *Free School Meals Pilot Evaluation, Research Brief DFE-RB22*, London: Department for Education

Lawson, N. (2013) Why Britain will suffer if the welfare state pays out only to poor people, *The Guardian*, 5 June, Online: http://www.theguardian.com/commentisfree/2013/jun/05/britain-welfare-state-labour, accessed 10 April 2014

Morelli, C. and Seaman, P. (2005) Universal versus targeted benefits: The distributional effects of free school meals, *Environment and Planning C: Government and Policy*, 23: 583–598

National Audit Office (2011) *Means Testing HC 1464 Session 2010–2012*, London: National Audit Office

Titmuss, R.M. (1968) *Commitment to Welfare*, New York: Pantheon

Walker, C. (2011) For universalism and against the means test, in A. Walker, A. Sinfield and C. Walker (eds), *Fighting poverty, inequality and injustice A manifesto inspired by Peter Townsend*, Bristol: Policy Press, pp. 133–152

Wyness, G. (2010) Policy changes in UK higher education funding, 1963–2009, *DoQSS Working Paper No. 10–15*, London: Institute of Education

Chapter 7

Aziz, Z. (2013) NHS rationing should not be driven by cost, *The Guardian*, 12 February, Online: http://www.theguardian.com/society/2013/feb/12/nhs-rationing-not-driven-cost, accessed 5 May 2014

Bosanquet, N., Cawston, T., Haldenby, T., Nolan, P. and Seddon, N. (2010) *Fewer Hospitals, More Competition*, London: Reform

Campbell, D. (2014) NHS group considers charges for crutches and neck braces, *The Guardian*, 16 April, Online: http://www.theguardian.com/society/2014/apr/16/nhs-charges-crutches-neck-braces-proposa, accessed 5 May 2014

Cawston, T. and Corrie, C. (2013) *The Cost of Our Health: The Role of Charging in Healthcare, Reform Ideas No 9*, London: Reform

Crisis (2014) *About homelessness*, Online: http://www.crisis.org.uk/data/files/publications/1406%20Crisis%20Homelessness%20briefing.pdf, accessed 5 June 2014

DCLOG (2014b) *English Housing Survey. Headline Report*, London: Department for Communities and Local Government

Doyal, L. and Gough, I. (1991) *A Theory of Human Need*, New York: The Guildford Press

Duffy, S. (2013) A fair society? How the cuts target disabled people, *Centre for Welfare Reform*, Online: http://www.centreforwelfarereform.org/uploads/attachment/354/a-fair-society.pdf, accessed 3 June 2014

Independent Commission on Fees (2013) *Analysis of University Application 2013/2014 Admissions*, London: The Sutton Trust

Maslow, A.H. (1943) A theory of human motivation, *Psychological Review*, 50(4): 370–396

McVeigh, T. (2014) Nathan was born at 23 weeks. If I'd known then what I do now, I'd have wanted him to die in my arms, *The Guardian*, 20 March, Online: http://www.theguardian.com/society/2011/mar/20/nathan-born-premature-life-death, accessed 4 June 2014

National Obesity Forum (2014) State of the nation's waistline, Online: www.noaw2014.org.uk, accessed 16 May 2014

Prescription Charges Coalition (2014) *Paying the price. Prescription charges and employment*, Online: http://www.prescriptionchargescoalition.org.uk/uploads/1/2/7/5/12754304/prescription_charges_and_employment_report_feb_2014.pdf, accessed 5 June 2014

Ramesh, R. (2011) Andrew Lansley trumpets his market-led patient voucher scheme, *The Guardian*, 4 October, Online: http://www.theguardian.com/politics/2011/oct/04/lansley-trumpets-patient-voucher-scheme, accessed 10 May 2014

Rolnik, R. (2013) Press statement by the United Nations special rapporteur on adequate housing as a component of the right to an adequate standard of living and to non-discrimination in this context, *Mission to the United Kingdom of Great Britain and Northern Ireland 29 August to 11 September 2013*, London, 11 September 2013

Wheater, R., Burge, R., Sewell, J., Sizmur, J., Worth and Williams. J. (2013) The international survey of adult skills 2012: Adult literacy, numeracy and problem solving skills in England, *Research Paper Number 139*, London: Department for Business, Innovation and Skills

WHO (1946) *Preamble to the Constitution of the World Health Organization*, New York: WHO, USA.

Chapter 8

Botti, S. and Iyengar, S. (2006) The dark side of choice: When choice impairs social welfare, *Journal of Public Policy & Marketing*, 23(1): 24–38

Burn, K., Henderson, V.W., Ames, D., Dennerstein, L. and Szoeke, C. (2014) Role of grandparenting in postmenopausal women's cognitive health:

Results from the Women's Healthy Aging Project, *Menopause*, 21(10): 1067–1074

Carers UK (2011) *Unpaid carers save £119 billion a year*, Online: http://www. carersuk.org/news-and-campaigns/press-releases/unpaid-carers-save-119-billion-a-year, accessed 11 June 2015

Fotaki, M., Ruane, S. and Leys, C. (2013) *The future of the NHS? Lessons from the market in social care in England*, Centre for Health and Public Interest, Online: http://chpi.org.uk/wp-content/uploads/2013/10/CHPI-Lessons-from-the-social-care-market-October-2013.pdf, accessed 29 May 2014

Heywood, F. and Turner, L. (2007) *Better Outcomes, Lower Costs Implications for Health and Social Care Budgets of Investment in Housing Adaptations, Improvements and Equipment: A Review of the Evidence*, London: Department for Work and Pensions

Hine, R., Peacock, J. and Pretty, J. (2008) *Care Farming in the UK: Evidence and Opportunities*, University of Essex, Colchester: Department of Biological Sciences

Murray, J. (2011) Are the public paying the price for freeschools?, *The Guardian*, 10 October, Online: http://www.theguardian.com/education/2011/oct/10/fee-paying-versus-free-schools, accessed, 26 May 2014

National Audit Office (2013) *The Role of Major Contractors in the Delivery of Public Services', HC 810*, London: Stationery Office

Stanley, J. and Rome, S. (2013) Residential child care: Costs and other information requirements', in C. Lesley (ed.), *Unit Cost of Health and Social Care 2013*, University of Kent Canterbury: Personal Social Services Research Unit

Whitby, K. (2011) Why are school governors so old and white?, *The Guardian*, 19 October, Online: http://www.theguardian.com/education/mortarboard/2011/oct/19/school-governors-old-and-white, accessed 25 May 2014

Chapter 9

Blood, I. (2013) *A Better Life: Valuing Our Later Years*, New York: Joseph Rowntree Foundation

Brindle, D. (2012) Councils no longer required to give all social services users a personal budget, *The Guardian*, 26 October, Online: http://www.theguardian.com/society/2012/oct/26/councils-social-services-personal-budget, accessed 2 April 2015

Carers UK (2014) *State of Caring 2014*, London: Carers UK

Carr, S. (2010) *Personalisation: A Rough Guide*, London: Social Care Institute for Excellence

CEBR (2013) *Impact of EU labour on the UK*, Online: http://www.cebr.com/reports/migration-benefits-to-the-uk/, accessed 5 June 2014

Chakrabortty, A. (2011) Why doesn't Britain make things anymore?, *The Guardian*, 16 November, Online: http://www.theguardian.com/business/2011/nov/16/why-britain-doesnt-make-things-manufacturing, accessed 6 June 2014

Department for Business Innovation and Skills, (2013) *Participation Rates in Higher Education: Academic Years 2006/2007–2011/12 (Provisional)*,

Online: https://www.gov.uk/government/uploads/system/uploads/
attachment_data/file/306138/13-p140-HEIPR_PUBLICATION_2011-12_2_.
pdf, accessed 11 June 2015

Dustman, C. and Frattini, T. (2013) *The Fiscal Effects of Immigration to the UK,
Discussion Paper Series CPD No 22/13*, London: Centre for Research and
Analysis of Migration, University College London

DWP (2012b) *Family Resources Survey*, London: Department for Work and
Pensions

Glasby, J. (2009) Social Care, in P. Alcock, M. May and S. Wright (eds),
The Student's Companion to Social Policy 4e, Chichester: Wiley Blackwell

Griffiths, I. (2012) Amazon: £7bn sales, no UK corporation tax, *The Guardian*,
4 April, Online: http://www.theguardian.com/technology/2012/apr/04/
amazon-british-operation-corporation-tax, accessed 10 June 2014

Harper, S., Howse, K. and Baxter, S. (2011) *Living longer and prospering?*, Oxford:
Oxford Institute of Ageing

Health and Social Care Information Centre (2013) *Personal social services:
Expenditure and unit costs, England 2012–13, Final release*, Online http://www.
hscic.gov.uk/catalogue/PUB13085/pss-exp-eng-12-13-fin-rpt.pdf, accessed
6 June 2014

Hicks, J. and Allene G. (1999) *A Century of Change: Trends in UK Statistics Since
1900, Research Paper 99/111*, House of Commons Library Research Paper:
House of Commons

Kennedy, J., Moore, T. and Fiddes, A. (2013) *Living Wage Research for KPMG
Structural Analysis of Hourly Wages and Current Trends in Household Finances*,
Oxon: Markit

King, M. (2012) Number of Working Pensioners up 85%, *The Guardian*, 13 June,
Online: http://www.theguardian.com/money/2012/jun/13/number-working-
pensioners-up-ons, accessed 10 June 2014

OBR (2013) *Fiscal Sustainability Report*, London: Stationery Office

OECD (2001), *OECD Employment Outlook 2001: June*, OECD Publishing,
doi: 10.1787/empl_outlook-2001-en

ONS (2011) *Social Trends 41*, London: Office for National Statistics

ONS (2011a) *Statistical Bulletin: Polish People in the UK – Half a Million Polish
Residents*, London: Office for National Statistics

ONS (2012b) *Statistical Bulletin: 2011 Census – Population and Household
Estimates for England and Wales*, March 2011, London: Office for National
Statistics

ONS (2013) *Statistical Bulletin: Annual Mid-year Population Estimates, 2011 and
2012*, London: Office for national Statistics

ONS (2013a) *Industries in the UK economy 1948–2012*, Online: https://twitter.
com/ONS/status/370849371115372544 accessed 6 June 2014

ONS (2014c) *Labour Market Statistics, May 2014*, London: Office for National
Statistics

ONS (2014d) *Statistical Bulletin National Life Tables, United Kingdom, 2010–2012*,
London: Office for National Statistics

Rolfe, H., Fic, T., Lalani, M., Roman, M., Prohaska, M. and Doudeva, L. (2013) *Potential impacts on the UK of future migration from Bulgaria and Romania*, London: National Institute of Economic and Social Research

World Bank (2014) Fertility rate, total (births per woman), Online: http://data.worldbank.org/indicator/SP.DYN.TFRT.IN, accessed 14 June 2014

Chapter 10

Alcock, P. (2008) *Social Policy in Britain*, Basingstoke: Palgrave Macmillan

Leach, R. (2009) *Political Ideology in Britain 2nd edition,* Basingstoke: Palgrave Macmillan

INDEX

Note: specific social policies are *italicised* e.g. *Child Benefit*

1